Behind Her
Wedding Veil

Behind Her Wedding Veil

Struggles of
My Rebellious Mother

Kk. Panday

VAJRA
BOOKS

Published & Distributed by
Vajra Books
Jyatha, Thamel, P.O. Box 21779, Kathmandu, Nepal
Tel.: 977-1-4220562, Fax: 977-1-4246536
e-mail: bidur_la@mos.com.np
www.vajrabooks.com.np

First Published 2015

ISBN 978-9937-623-37-7

Printed in Nepal

*To all who are
part of this Story*

*'Conspicuously Missing' is my Grandmother
Occasion: Dasain Tika Day – October 1934 AD*

Contents

Foreword: Dr. Rudolf Hoegger   xiii

Editor's Impressions: Mr. Scott Berry   xix

First Reader's Impressions: Dr. Arjun Karki   xxi

Prologue   xxiii

Acknowledgements   xxix

Part ONE

**Father's *Janma Kundali* –
Rescued from the Funeral Pyre**   3

An Astrologer's Dilemma   6

Grandmother's Misery – Destiny Unfair   10

Repaid with a Jacket – Debt Paid   17

Life with Father and Grandmother   19

Uprooting of the Family   21

Father Joins the Army   23

Moving Hither and Thither   26

The Red House   30

A Change in Fortune   34

Foes Disguised as Friends   35

Life unlike His Love of Flower - Father in Life   42

Father's Habits and Hobbies 45

His Failing Health 48

Rescuing a Fellow Creature at Pashupati 49

The Family Priest Violated the Rituals 58

A Dream of My Father 59

Long Way to Graduation 63

Growing up at Jawalakhel 66

Jyapu Heritage my Destiny 67

Immersed in Spirituality 73

'Amusing' Moments 74

'Not so Amusing' Moments 86

The Awe, the Pain and the Fear 95

Sports and Games 98

Educating Life and Life in Education 101

The Terror of Yakthumba 106

Revolt against Tyranny 108

From Failure to Success 111

No more a Vegetarian 117

Long Way to Graduation 121

Dreaming of an University Education 134

Janma Kundali Recreated 140

Struggles of My Rebellious Mother 145

My Mother, the Maicha 145

My Sisters and My Mother's own Sister 148

Understanding Mother's Time in Rebellion 152

Her Principles and Struggles against Social Taboos 156

Damned the Class and Caste Consciousness 161

Educating Daughters! 167

One Day the Priest returned with Vengeance 168

Defiant Acts 170

Chronicling of Mother's Last Days 176

Living Memories of my Mother 183

Torturing the Loving Heart 187

Mother on Treks 188

In Gratitude to my Mother 192

Part TWO

Kin, Kith, Neighbours and Strangers 197

Loss that could hardly be made up 198

Shadow in Captivity 199

Grandfather Misunderstood 202

Obligation Forgotten 203

Ungrateful, Wicked and Worthless 204

Missing Gratitude 207

Loyalty, Par Excellence 208

A Day in the Life of Vataspati Vaidya 215

A Gift for Life 219

A Visit from the Pitri 221

Somebody to Turn to – New Era 225

Prestige Pinned 231

A Turn in the New Millennium 237

Eluding Give and Take 239

A Day for Pandays at Singha Durbar 242

Para-Normal Death – early 1950s 245

Greed Unquenched 249

Land and Luck 250

Moments with Friends 257

A Single Deed that made someone Unforgettable 263

Did He or Didn't He? 266

Associated for Friendship 268

Photo Making a Big Difference 271

In all Respects a Nepali 274

The Loss of a Nepali Legacy 277

What was he to us! 281

Tenzing, Hillary and Hagen 297

Tenzing Norge and Jamling Sherpa 298

'*The Sun rises in the North*' 300

Struggling and Revolting Character 303

A Tribute to a Buddhist Scholar 310

A single letter of the Alphabet making a Difference 313

Truanting with a warm Heart 315

Hate and Love with Computer 320

A Democrat Through and Through 325

The Cost of Believing in Democracy 333

A Highest Intellectual Mind 335

Unsolicited Friendship 338

A Day at Osho Restaurant 345

'*Ahead by Four Days*' 348

After all, it was the Palace! 353

Forbidden to Smile 353

A Royal Intellectual 357

Annoyed by Truth 362

Did he or did he not deserve Congratulation? 372

The Scary Pencil 374

Singing for the Palace 377

The Path to the Palace 378

The Henchmen at Large 381

The cursed Royal Handshakes 386

The Nepali Royals in Zurich 390

Pride Prevails 393

Men of Integrity – The Sardars 395

Royal Wrath 406

Royal Intimidation 409

Dipendra in Environmental Activity – Uninterested 410

Part THREE

A Tryst with Gods 415

Muktinath for me alone 416

Baraha Avatar 422

Surya Binayak – the Ganesh facing the Rising Sun 423

Pawankali, the Elephant God 425

Spirituality of my Parents and Grandmother 426

A Shocking Revelation at Dandapakhar 430

Temple of the Sacred Tooth Relic of Lord Buddha 431

Solacing Dreams 435

The Rays from my Right Palm – ca. 1950 435

Mother Continued assuring me – 1975 436

Dreaming of a Fish Pond – 2001 438

The Decorated Elephants my Savior – 2004 439

What Averts what enables things we do! 442

Centenary Celebration 444

A Reflection 445

Foreword

Development is a Struggle within – All over the World

In the fall of 2014, Kk. Panday asked me to read the draft of the present book and to comment on it spontaneously from the point of view of a Western friend.

Krishnakumar and I have been colleagues and partners in international development cooperation for almost forty years. In my eyes, Kk. has always been a good example of a credible development worker. I have been looking up to him and to his enduring, but gentle determination to overcome gender prejudice and caste barriers in whatever leadership he had assumed. Also, I have been a student and follower of his continuous efforts to turn the prevalent development paradigm upside down: change – according to him – must not only start at the top, but at the bottom as well: new ideas are not only created in intellectual circles, but also in village homes or in slums.

In the course of the years, I have often wondered about Krishnakumar's convictions and capacities. In which human, social or institutional conditions did they have their roots? What have been the supporting conditions for them to grow?

In the present book, Kk. himself provides an answer: according to him, the one decisive force and <u>influence</u> shaping his life and personality came from his mother who – although of rural origin and illiterate – clearly set his standards. She must have been a personality of extraordinary mental and social independence, who did not care too much about the rigid rules by which the various Hindu castes used to be separated from each other. Kk. takes pleasure in telling various stories about his mother, who, for example, spontaneously invited people from other castes and localities for a meal in the inner sanctuary of her Chhetry kitchen. He recalls how, against all established principles, she did not wait to have her dinner until her husband would return late from his regular evening-long *tete-a-tete* with his friends, but would eat with the children, keep his food near the fire and go to bed.

Again and again, throughout the chapters of this book, we learn how decisive this model role of the mother has been in shaping Krishnakumar's character and in building his strength to tackle serious challenges on his inner and outer path.

I was – and still am – deeply moved, when I read Krishnakumar's various passages about his mother, her struggles, her convictions, her teachings and – above all – her sufferings. Much of all this was hidden 'behind her wedding veil', as the title of the present book suggests. It seems to me that the image of the veil is a confirmation of the old wisdom, that human development in its true sense does not take place on the public stage nor according to mainstream criteria, but in personal struggles, often in suffering. Development has its roots not primarily in the outer world, but in inner realities. This holds true for many of us!

The special quality of Krishnakumar's present writing becomes apparent in the unobtrusive way the author bears testimony to this timeless truth.

Towards the end of his account, Kk. refers to a dream he had as a boy of about seven: In the Dream he was standing at the window on the first floor of his parental house gazing at the landscape outside. His right hand was raised high. He saw the hills brightly lit in orange and red. Most amazingly, however, the source of the light was a beam that oozed out from the center of the boy's right palm.

Applying my Western understanding of development psychology, I am tempted to say that this dream might well reflect an important aspect of the life task lying ahead of the boy. In Nepalese art, both Buddhist and Hindu, the center of the palm (*karamadhya*) of Gods or Saints or Buddhas often appears as a source of energy or even as an eye throwing a special light and deeper understanding onto the outer world. The conjunction of hand and eye, as e.g. in the case of *Avalokitesvara*, may be understood as a symbol of conscious activity, as a blend of action and comprehension.

Dreams, even when seen by ordinary people, often speak in a solemn language which sharply contrasts with our day-to-day conversational habits. This should not mislead us, however, to identify the dreamer – of course – is no God, not a Saint nor a Buddha. On the other hand, the dream's symbolism may well apply to an inner task imposed on the dreamer. In Krishnakumar's case, as I understand it, such a task could have been to throw new light upon (to develop a fresh understanding) of the '*Nepali Hills*'. They would stand as a metaphor of the culture and creativeness found in the rural areas all over Nepal. The fact that this new light (fresh understanding) is originating in the dreamer's hand may underline his inner obligation for active commitments; theoretical concepts and political slogans would not suffice.

Having been a companion of Kk. Panday over decades, I have become a witness of many such illuminating practical commitments in the service of Nepal. All these commitments have taught me to better understand the nature of human and social development. Today, I am gratified at reading Krishnakumar's text about his personal development process taking place (like the one of his mother) 'behind the veil', in the depth of his heart and in the solitude of individual struggles or dreams. I believe that the most important struggles we all have to go through take place within ourselves –'behind the veil'. My friend, I believe, has lived up to the dream of his childhood and was not shying away from difficulties, failure and guilt implied in the task.

When reading Krishnakumar's account, I deeply feel that the human realities of Nepal and Switzerland, of East and West, of tradition and modernity are very close to each other. Often, they might be identical. I am grateful for this insight!

Dr. Rudolf Hoegger
Switzerland

Editor's Impressions

Those of us from afar who think we know a bit about Nepal often find we have a lot to learn. It was a pleasure editing the present memoirs because the author lived through times I can only imagine. It is incredible, for example, to be told of a time when Kumari Pati—now that busy road between Jawalakhel and Lagankhel—was a long grassy field where children could safely play because there was only one vehicle a day; or on a more somber note, a time 'government' was so oppressive that a Rana strongman could confiscate anyone's property at will. And then just try to imagine the days when a Prime Minister would make an official visit wearing his under vest; or when Newar and non-Newar alike in Patan spoke the Newar tongue, and there were primary schools in that language.

Through the history of one family, the author gives us a unique glimpse of the evolution of Nepal over the past century. The personal journeys of his grandmother, mother and father and not least of the author himself have a great deal to tell us about where Nepal has come from and where it is going.

Though this book ranges far and wide, it is always to the greatest single influence in his life—his mother—that the author returns. His insights into the problems faced by his mother, as well as his grandmother, tell us a great deal about how far some (though unfortunately not all) women in this society have progressed. Today women all over Nepal are demanding their rights, but his mother's struggle was a lonely and courageous one which was to have a profound impact on her son, and was to take him all over the world and back again. The book is a fitting tribute to a remarkable woman on the centenary of her birth.

Scott Berry

First Reader's Impressions

My Two Words

I believe it was in 1974 when I first met Dr. Krishnakumar Panday during Integrated Hill Development Project days in Dandapakhar near my home village Petku in Sindhupalchok district. Subsequently, I had the opportunity to interact with him on many occasions and became familiar with his passion for innovative community development work and his extraordinary skills to engage with the local village farmers to bring positive changes in their own lives and that of their communities. That had made a distinct and positive imprint in my young mind. However, I was not aware of his literary talent until recently when he asked me to read and also to write a reflection on the book he has written in memory of his beloved mother. I was not sure if I was the right person for that task. Nevertheless, I did not dare to refuse his request, primarily because of my respect for him.

Upon reading this book, I got a better understanding about the way he was brought up as a child and the way he grew up as a young man shaping his values, his world outlook and his basic character. The description contained in the book shows that Dr. Panday was a bold, inquisitive and determined person right from his young days. At the same time, he is also a man of compassion and courage to go against the tide when things do not make sense. Both his grandmother and particularly his beloved mother – a woman of strong conviction, deep compassion, resilience and keen sense of justice – had played an instrumental role in making what he is today. And this book clearly is a great tribute for her 100th Anniversary.

This book eloquently describes the typical feudalistic culture governing the social norms of our low middle class families about a century ago. Reading the description about the enormous burden (physical, mental and social) that the women in those days had to bear without having access to even the most basic necessities of human life makes one cannot help but become resentful. Though poverty may also have contributed to that situation, I believe, it mainly resulted from the prevailing social values which were largely selfish and both exploitative and discriminatory against the poor and the powerless. It was not only his mother and grandmother who were the victims of those values, but his own father who became orphan at an early age had also to bear the brunt of those unfair practices. Despite their continuing personal suffering, the amount of love and generosity these women have demonstrated to the fellow human beings is absolutely extraordinary.

Having witnessed the pain and suffering brought upon by such unjust feudal practices, Dr. Panday not only chose to refrain from such practices but refused to bow down before the powers of the day both within and outside Nepal. At the same time his admiration and respect for people who worked hard and stood for truth and principles is greatly appreciable.

Above all, Dr. Panday did not feel any inhibition to describe the truths as they were and whether it relates to his own family members or otherwise. I admire his moral courage for that and wish to congratulate him for his integrity. As a matter of fact that further enhances the authenticity of this book. Though the focus of the book revolves around his family and friends, I believe it is going to be a great resource for those, especially our younger generation, who wish to get an insight as to what our society was like about a century ago.

Dr. Arjun Karki

23rd January 2015   Physician – Internist

Prologue

Writing about my family

When I look at the immediate hills in front of me from the valley where I live, I see further away high hills, and more beyond, and behind them the Himalaya; mist or haze that rises and veils the beauty or the dirt underneath and between them. The horizon offers wonders for me to behold, something to relate to others. Such was the recounting, recapturing and the digging out the story of my past and of my parents.

It began with digging into my family history, opening unknown sites for objects that could highlight its past – almost like an archeologist. I had stashed and archived papers, letters from my parents, from kith and kin, my siblings and friends relating events that took place while I had been away. There were letters from my illiterate mother, dictated to my sister.

I needed to look at friends and neighbors as well, as much as into the history of my family, clan and events that shaped the personalities of my parents that eventually produced my character. I refreshed my memory of what

Grandmother told me as bedtime history telling, and what my mother told me during our numerous short and long walks.

My family history is for me a hidden treasure of its struggles while in misery, pride in its success, or of its screaming when in pain. Stories of pain and struggles of my family may not be much different, from those of other families, but the context, color and time-line of ups and downs might differ.

Just as the flares of fire, memories shoot up in our coronas changing in color and intensity, in seconds. They turned up in fragments of events from within the family or from its contacts, kith and kin. I collected and collaged, otherwise they might have ended up scattered and become myths tomorrow to be told either in an exaggerated way or in rudimentary details. I was surprised by confirmation of impressions from my childhood experience even late in life when I started writing about it.

My parents did not give away many details of their lives, although they didn't hide their feelings either. Discussions with my father didn't reveal much: his secrets remained untold, even to me. But I pieced together their real life, taking into consideration changes in their life style, happenings at home and consequences of their deeds. Their behavior more than anything else betrayed secrets.

Some life aspects were as banal as they appeared, and even banal aspects I valued and gave a place in my writing, that filled the gaps. In the end they could not escape my peeking and nailing them in the context of relevance with life they lived and mine. They were apt to talk about or assume feelings they would have had or that went through them. But I wrote them listening to my heart. I do not know whether this is morally justifiable. The path I took may look a zigzag, but so is one's life, at least mine, not excluding some hiatus.

I have written of what happened to me personally or described events either of which I was a subject myself, a witness to the happenings or confidant of the closest persons. I also wrote to let you know about my society through my eyes and through the contacts of my family, through the circle of my friends in Nepal and in other countries.

At many an occasion family stories were complemented with bits and pieces of what other senior relatives had to tell. They were interesting anecdotes. That and other pieces enabled me to put together a history of a simple Nepali family such as ours, whose ancestry had 500 years of written history, fiercely defended family honor, a chain of contributions to Nepali nation building and a pride showing hard work, too proud to give in under adversity.

The whole thing started with the *janma kundali* of my father. In fact we never came to see Father's *janma kundali* during his lifetime which he too might have kept out of his own sight after the death of his mother and never ventured to look into the Pandora's Box of Disclosures of his Fates and Elements. Did he fear truth hidden in the *janma kundali*?

For the first time, fifty years or more after my birth, it came to me, the *janma kundali* of my father. But it was at the very sad moment of my life, at the cremation of my Father.

Early, in January 2013, we rolled open our father's *janma-kundali*, that I had rescued it from the funeral pyre of my father. We examined it from top to bottom, just out of curiosity. We found my father's date of birth: it was Saturday, 7th Baisakh 1970 Bikram Sambat (19th April 1913 AD), and not Baisakh 6th (18th April 1913) as he had always assumed it to be.

He had performed *Satyanarayan Puja* on his birthday, the sixth day of the Nepali year's first month, Baisakh. It was a big surprise; we all had erred! We realized Father's birth centenary day was approaching: Saturday, 20th April, 2013 – just 12 weeks ahead of us.

And so the mission of this book was borne: to present my parents in 3-dimensions, on the occasion of their respective centenary birthdays: Father's on Saturday, 7th Baisakh 2070 BS (April 20, 1913 AD) and Mother's on Tuesday, 24th Falgun 2071 BS (February 24, 2015 AD).

'*A Day in a Century*', as the lyricist Gopal Prasad Rimal wrote. I felt this celebration should inspire me to dig up the histories of my parents, to see where we – particularly I--stood. It could happen to me, only once in my lifetime, once in this century. My thought was wandering to the time when Father, Grandmother and Mother were alive and six of us siblings were together. The events encouraged me to share all this and more with a wider readership, precursor or the pretext that resulted in this write-up. I shall try to focus on two magnificent persons in my life, my mother and father; their legacy and imprints in me in particular. This is also an account of personal journey in the family, homeland and around the world.

Family photo of Dasain, autumn 1934, old photographs, memorabilia and what not, all these materials were there. Then there were objects of family heirlooms in the possession of my family: old family weapons from my grandfather which my father handed over to me for keeps, something valuable like my mother's wedding veil, and common and cultural utensils inherited. They all had a say. They were the start up to arouse memories and recollections.

I want my readers to walk along with me to experience my narration. I do not expect responses in the physical sense if you feel touched in anyway of what I wrote, sentimentally poetic or pathetic.

I would say,

You will feel that I lived much like many of you did.

2015   Kk. Panday

Acknowledgements

I wanted to make a 'gift' to my mother *pitri*, a book on her life with us. I have also to tell the next generation her story on her behalf. It should take into consideration the context around her positive rebellious nature, her silent sufferings and personal struggles.

The launching of this book was going to be part of the celebration of my mother's centenary birthday on 24th of February 2015.

With so much distraction around and disruption of utilities, in the country, to bring out a book of this size and context was a big deal for me. It was Sharada, my wife who foresaw the potential of the materials from family history I had put together.

She inspired me to take up the writing seriously. Whenever a thing looked detached and lost its direction it was the interaction with her which helped me to find my way back. It gave me immense pleasure while *Writing about my family*.

Although I had eighteen months' time for writing the book, starting after Father's centenary birth anniversary on 20th of April 2013 and October 2014, to meet January

2015 printing dead line, I was hard pressed to work relentlessly. In fact I have used the time to write also in Nepali, for the Nepali audience.

It was very intense and energy consuming. In view of the looming February 24th of 2015, I could hardly afford to devote enough time on my children, in-laws, grandchildren, and cousins, my plants and animals. I thank them all for their patience.

Anyone editing the draft of my book needed sufficient knowledge and understanding of Nepali society and culture and skill of making something out of a Nepali's writing in English palatable to Western readers. Scott had it all.

In fact I met him for the first time with the draft of the book in a pen-drive at Vajra Books, Thamel. I am grateful to Mr. Scott Berry and Mrs. Naoko Berry. For all his efforts my grateful thanks go to my friend Scott, who edited this book, without whose keen and questioning mind this book could not have taken the shape that lies in your hands now. It snatched much time from Scott, and Naoko was punished for it. I pray for her forgiveness and I thank her equally for her support.

With the same breath I would like to thank two of my valued longtime friends, Dr. Rudolf Hoegger from Switzerland and Dr. Arjun Karki (Physician-Internist), who were the first ones to read my final draft of this book and took it in their heart to contribute the complementary write ups on their first impressions.

I have taken the liberty of writing about my kin and kith. To enliven my points I have also quoted matters from our dialogues over the years. I am grateful to those who are no more and thank you all who are around for the friendship I cherish.

Last, but not least, I need to thank Mr. Bidur Dongol, Proprietor of Vajra Books and Publications, Thamel, Kathmandu and Mr. Ram Krishna Dongol of Dongol Printers for all their timely support. I would like to thank Mr. Rabindra Dongol for page-layout for the press and thank Mr. Nabindra Dongol for helping me to give shape to my designs for the book's jacket.

Part ONE

Rescued from the Funeral Pyre

Long Way to Graduation

My Rebellious Mother

Father's *Janma Kundali* -
Rescued from the Funeral Pyre

We had time to plan for a small celebration to share the life and struggles of my mother, grandmother and here particularly of Father, with a wider circle of friends and families. We believed such should reach out beyond the home and hearth. We decided to honour him, for who he was and appreciate him for what he meant to us all

We organized a gathering of close relatives and of friends at our home at Kitini, Godavari. The moment was the 100th Birthday Centenary Celebration of my father, 83 years of which he lived.

The facts and findings about him and his family were presented to the gathering. It gave us the feeling that it was the right thing to do, its meanings not kept confined within narrow circle of the family. My parents in heaven (*Pitri*) have surely valued the especially dedicated celebration for them. We should have our *Pitri*'s blessing to make life worthwhile to live.

I was unaware of the tradition of destroying the historic family document or evidence, *janma kundali*, during the cremation ritual of the owner. Only when I was going through the last rites of my father was I surprised by the malpractice.

In Nepal the ritual of placing the *janma kundali* on the chest of a dead body lying on its back on the funeral pyre and burning it is justified unquestionably by many people, saying, '*It is our tradition.*' Whose tradition they were thinking of? When it came to my father, I departed from the traditional last rite of passage.

If it were forbidden by tradition to keep it safe, why could King Prithwi Narayan Shah's twelve feet long *janma kundali* be displayed at Gorkha Durbar Museum? Was that a fake one, a copy, or was the real one not allowed to go into flame with the King?

Was it an exception? Or was it written anew centuries later, to show to the people more than what he was in life? It was perhaps the intrigues of the rulers to delete the life history of commoners, no matter how much a person contributed to the society and the nation, and even to the rulers themselves. They became simply non-entities, ghosts after death.

The *janma kundali* of the common folk are required to be destroyed by placing them on the pyre, and that deletes the history. My immediate reaction was that I should retrieve it. I asked the officiating priest,

Will it be against or in conformity with the Shastra if I do it?

Is there any mention of it being prohibited in the holy books at all?

I did it what I wanted and made sure that the *chinha* (*janma kundali*) was not lost while I went through mourning, ruffled fire and shuffled wood on the burning pyre by the holy but dirty Bagmati River.

At least Father's *Janma-Kundali* came home. This time it was in my possession but I had yet to see it. When relatives learnt about it they were shocked and scorned me.

It scares us knowing you keep the janma kundali of a dead person at home.
Even if that belongs to your Father, it is scary!

They did not feel comfortable to see the *janma kundali* of a dead person at my home, not even Father's. We kept it confidential, preventing access of strangers. But it meant much to me.

I don't care. Why should I? I am not scared. In fact I feel more secure now. We did not have any authentic document of our family history, but now we have this janma kundali. I did not want it to commit '*sati*'. That is all.

Over time they, the perpetrators of so called tradition, would not sustain their protest. We are raised to accept that the *janma kundali* contains the astrological secrets of the person. The best trained astrologers could read it, to tell about the past, relate to the present to avert immediate misfortunes and predict the future events and happenings of the person concerned. It also contains the names of father and the records of astronomical momentum of birth, the first letter of the secret name and other details. With that we can directly relate it to our ancestors. We become part of the past and part of the future generations. But that is true for the living person. We justify its keeping secure during the person's life.

There is a widely followed tradition of consulting an astrologer, either because of an auspicious event or a suspicious situation about the paranormal condition of a living person. Doing the same about the dead person is impossible because the *janma kundali*, as per the tradition, was cremated together with the body.

In our case the *janma kundali* had survived from the burning pyre. Although, it was not done normally, I wanted to have Father's *janma kundali* read as proof of what an astrologer could say about a dead person's past life. It indeed exposed certain feelings and events he had suppressed from letting us know. We came to the conclusion that in some aspects the astrologer could be counted upon.

An Astrologer's Dilemma

There was a surprise in store for us all. From the time of his cremation and onward Father's *janma kundali* was kept confidential, we did not think of un-rolling it. Seventeen years after the death of my father I happened to open it unintentionally and read it when we noticed that his birth-centenary was approaching, in 3 months' time.

Partly out of curiosity and partly out of need to know some hidden aspects of my Father's psycho social history, my wife Sharada and I decided to go to a good but completely unfamiliar astrologer. We heard from a priest of the Sankata temple, that the nearest astrologer in our area was Mr. Joshi at Lagankhel. We showed him the *janma kundali*. He was pleasantly surprised to find a 100 years old *janma kundali*, 'his first.' He must have assumed right in the beginning that my father was alive, otherwise there would not be this *janma kundali* lying before him. The astrologer did not have the courage to ask us about Father, lest we be hurt.

As he started to read it, we could notice him becoming nervous. He felt uneasy and disappeared from the room three times within the half hour we were there, pretending to go to his wash room. He came back and told me,

As a son you should have heard everything from your father, shouldn't you?

Even a son one would not know of his father's childhood ups and downs in life unless somebody told him. He must also be interested in family history, and have a father who is open to his children. I insisted that he tell us about my father's past present and future.

As a son you should have heard everything from your father. He repeated.

In fact there are very few fathers I have met in my locality who would share their history with their sons or for that matter with their wives or daughters. Everybody maintains secrecy of intimate part of one's life, as much as possible.

Our insistence paid off. He started to tell about Father's past but in brief. He avoided to talk about the present and future of my father. Did he know by his skill that my father had already lived out his present, and that his future had been denied a long time ago?

I felt a little shiver on my back. What had he found from the *janma kundali*? Did he assume we were playing hide and seek with him and with my father's *janma kundali*?

Looking at the Janma Kundali first he started to note something down on a piece of paper, perhaps translating astrological figures to relate to the events Father went through! What he told us about his past later astounded us enough.

He invited trouble in 1955-56AD.
In my mind I tried to figure out what that could have been! I was 12 years old. I remembered him telling us he had to leave the Pioneer Work Brigade, an army job.
His close friend and commander of the Pioneer Battalion fell into disgrace and was dismissed from the service. With that, Father too got demobilized. To what degree was he involved in the corruption? I have no clue.
He became spiritual!
This too was expected. It must have been when we fell into deep economic difficulties, Father lost his job. We could only trust in God. We might have survived through loans taken by him. In desperation perhaps, he intensified his gambling habits pouring oil on the fire. We suffered more.
His closest relatives hurt him in the Eighties.
Could it have been his youngest son in Dasain, 1984 AD, who denied Father his right to bless him?

Or the lady who frequently came to see him and in the end tried to get him to sell his house to her and move into a flat at the advanced age of 70?

Early in 1975, he was troubled, sick and sad.

On 20 February 1975, my mother died. He had sent me a telegram on 21st Feb. at 1110 and immediately two days later, he had written a letter,

God's will, you lost your mother, console yourself, you have your father.

Again after the 13 days ritual of mourning, he wrote on 5th March 1975,

She turned us into orphans, God's will!

But that he was so deeply troubled, sick and saddened by the death of my mother was a big surprise for me. Was it the guilty feeling that he carried all along for decades, simply abandoning her without any fault on her side after she had borne him nine children?

In her life, Mother had to experience Father's suppressions and excesses in many ways, womanizing, and gambling, frequent shifting and loosing of house and property; economic downturns of his making, neglecting children's well-being, their education and care.

The astrologer was right in all the four counts. He had to overcome some psychological difficulties, at least, to murmur so much. Did he know the *janma-kundali* belonged to a dead man? Perhaps!

After seeing him nervous and restless we were convinced that he suspected it to be from a dead man. But when a man comes to show a *janma kundali* even when that is a hundred years old, the astrologer cannot gather the courage to suspect it. But he did not tell us to our faces.

It had been impolite on our part to hand it over to him, and we knew it. We thought we had better not reveal the truth.

We did not apologize although he deserved our apology. That the astrologer could also say something about a dead person surprised me!

A *janma kundali* that lay for a while on the dead body is held as unclean, and portends ill omen. It was slightly risky thing we did. But we did come to an important clue of his psycho-social pains that he kept for himself, which we were not aware of while he lived.

I did not care what my relatives said about me keeping a dead person's *janma kundali*. During Father's birth centenary celebration I presented it to friends and close relatives who had come to me. Many relatives had only heard about it as the *prize document for posterity*.

Nobody, not even the ones who were earlier scared to hear about it, found that I had done anything wrong. It was even worth doing, many agreed lamenting and regretted retrospectively that they had missed the chance, and an important family document had gone into the flames to be blown away by the wind.

Grandmother's Misery – Destiny Unfair

My father's story rightly starts with the story of my grandparents. The *janma kundali* confirmed the name of my grandfather, which was Subedar Jagatbahadur Panday

Kaji. We were confused over the years whether it was Jagya or Jagat. It turned out in our clan lineage that Jagya in fact was my father's grandfather.

My grandfather Jagatbahadur Panday Kaji, second son of our great grandfather Jagyabahadur served as an officer in the Jabar Jung Battalion. In 1915 AD he had to leave behind his first and only child, Naran my father at the tender age of only 22 months.

He was one of the 7501 men contingent of the Nepal army deputed by the then Premier Chandra to support the British in neighbouring India solely for garrison duty, so that the British Army could go to the front. Did the British trick us? Did they send the Nepalese contingent to the war zones of British India? My grandfather Subedar Jagatbahadur Panday fought in the war in North-western Frontier Provinces and was killed right in the beginning of the battles around the time of our clan festival in March 1915. Is it a coincidence that Father too was to die around our clan festival, which takes place every 12 years, celebrated under the Full Moon of February in 1996?

All that came home were his blood-stained bedding and belongings. It was devastating to my grandmother who was too young to see the looming legacy of his death. Grandmother soon got over her mourning period but the hardest time was yet to start. Grandmother's life after the death of my grandfather took a different but painful sharp turn. She was treated differently the moment the blood stained bedding (*gunta*) of my Grandfather arrived home. Her life without a husband as a widow commanded no empathy. Treatment by the family members, adults or juvenile, was harsh to bear.

We have treasured the bedding tie (*guntakas*) made of wood with two heads of swans on either side of it and his sword and other armour. Anyone knowing my grandfather would call him 'Sano Panday', the little Panday. I too needed only to say I was the grandson of the little Panday that was sufficient to establish my identity in the locality.

An astrologer named my father *Thaba Jung* when he was 6 days old (on the '*chhainthi*' छैंठी night). He was born on Saturday 19th of April 1913. Father was not old enough to remember anything of his father. He grew up without his guardian father. My grandmother was too busy in her daily chores at home and could not give enough motherly care, love and time to my father. She had no means to give adequate attention to him, and that made her feel very poor.

She knew it was unjust for him, but she had no choice than but to harden her heart and send him over to her brothers in Bihebar, at the tender formative age of five. Grandmother parted from him with a heavy heart hoping that he would get the attention, nutritious food and care that he deserved. Of course that could not replace her role. It must have been around 1919.

Bihebar, a valley of streams, lies on the other side of Phulchoki, to the north east part of the mountains behind Sisneri Hill, Kabre. The house was close to a stream where Mama-uncle had a water mill. There they milled maize to fine flour and grits (*chyankhla*).

Father went to the forested hills of north east part of Phulchoki everyday taking his Mama-uncle's cattle. He was lost among animals, and comrades, playing truant and gambling. He enjoyed the freedom and there was no one to restrain him nor would he refrain from doing what he liked. Grandmother came to know of this much later.

In Bihebar, his diet consisted mainly of maize. The high altitude valley of Bihebar was not suitable for growing rice. The red variety of maize was cooked like red rice and the white variety of maize was suitable also making *khir* (a sweet dish). But there was no alternative, all three times a day he had to eat maize not much differently prepared. He got fed up and began to dislike maize. He even placed maize dishes at the lowest rung of his food hierarchy. This had implications later in our family menu.

Mother had to cook rice, if not for all, at least for Father at almost every meal, and make it very tasty because he said he deserved it as the sole bread earner. Father seldom appreciated my mother's contributions, which were substantial compared to his, made through her work on our sprawling garden land with maize, finger millet, dry land rice (*ghaiya*), beans and soya, potato, cow milk, composts and many other things..

Grandmother and I developed an especially close bond. She would share her stories of her pains and pleasures in life. She would tell me many interesting tales, but mainly stories interspersed with sad events and bad conditions of our family. That aroused my interest more although they made me sad. I wanted to know more.

Sharing time with her infant boy and managing a myriad of tiny to big household chores for the family of the elder (*jetha*) brother of my grandfather were becoming too difficult for her. Streams of guests would come during winter times from far and near. I remember Father's *mit* (religiously bonded friend, and my *mit*-father), coming to visit us with exotic gifts of local food and wooden pots etc. They would stay for days at a time.

I heard from my grandmother that many relatives in the countryside would leave home to be guests of their relatives in relatively affluent areas, in order to save their own food reserves to last longer till the next harvest, which was not always guaranteed. Food shortage in the hills was acute over the winter months. People also needed a lot of foodstuff during the planting times; hence those who could make trips would leave home and make rounds visiting kin and close friends. My *mit*-father was not an exception. We did not let him feel that we too were in a similar situation of scarcity.

Grandmother began to develop asthma from her hard job at home looking after the store, cooking and keeping the kitchen and utensils shiny. An hour or two of freedom over the day she used for smoking *tamakhu* (sweetened tobacco) which became her habit, but that exaggerated her asthma suffering. She even shared *chilim/tamakhu* with her son, my father, when he too started smoking *tamakhu* (paste of sweetened tobacco).

She started suffering in the worst way. She was more tired day by day and her body became feeble, never to recover. In the end it was asthma and tiredness took her life, in 1964.

Her daily chores started at 3 am and the first shift ended at noon. The second shift would begin at 2 pm and last till 10 pm. She suffered from chronic sleep deficit. She had to work 18 hours every day year in year out without a piece of cloth on her back. In the kitchen it was a tradition to cook without wearing a blouse. Even in winter she could not wear a blouse to cover her bare back and her chest that faced the fires. Even if she had had a blouse, she had no occasion to wear it.

Winter or summer, the annual round of seasons turned within the four walls of her kitchen. She was literally confined to those four walls. I do not know whether she ever told me that she could venture out of that house even at special festival times.

She never mentioned of getting a helping hand in her kitchen work. She was cooking for a 25-member huge family, and not all the members would come to eat simultaneously. She had to wait for the last person to come to eat. They all would eat to fill their belly and take many servings and would not guess what was left in the pots.

It would then be her turn to gulp what was left in the pots. Countless times she had either to cook additional food for herself or eat what little leftover was available for her. Most of the days she did not have the will or the energy to cook additional food which also meant washing the pots and starting anew even for cooking a small amount. She would rather forgo extra cooking. She was chronically hungry and suffered from malnutrition.

For over 18 hours of drudgery every day she had to sit on the floor, squatting on a piece of wooden plank, *pirka*, mostly in front of the firewood hearth to cook, to prepare food. Over time she could walk only bent over, crippled for ever!

I never saw her walking upright. In the beginning I thought she was a hunchback, but she was not. I can hardly imagine the kind of abode she must have had as a widow of a fallen soldier, my grandfather, to hide herself for her 5 hours of escape at night from the backbreaking daily chores working for the 25 family members. Every night it must have been a time for her silent weeping. Feeling sapped of energy, feeling lonesome, especially while my father as a boy was away to Bihebar, thrust upon her by her fate.

In the family photograph taken after the festive meal on the Vijaya Dashami of autumn 1935, she is conspicuously missing. All the others, even the tiny tots are to be found in the photographs. Did nobody think of her during the historic photo session of the family? My father, my mother and even my 9 months old sister Sita on mother's arm are there. Or was it because she could not leave the Dasain hearth? Sure enough, as she related to me the story with a sad tone in her voice, she was in the kitchen, blowing the *pungmange dhungro* to keep the fire wood burning.

Or she did not have a new *chaubandi cholo* (a Nepali blouse) and *fariya* (a Nepali farmer lady's sari worn like a frock) for the Dasain photos? Her first photo, was a black and white, I shot in 1961. That I have for my future generations.

Nobody in the house would think of getting her a new dress, although she was the one toiling day and night for the family, like a slave. She wished she could buy a new blouse; that was her dream wish.

She had hardly two hours' time from noon till 2 pm, a kind of break from the kitchen, but not always. It would be too much to expect that she would have time to rest between the kitchen chores in the day time. She had washing to do too, if not for all. One could not sit in the kitchen to cook without a freshly washed dress. That meant she had to wash her dress every day and bathe in the early mornings.

Repaid with a Jacket – Debt Paid

When I was a young boy, Father provided me with the things I needed since he had some earnings from his job. One day he showed me a new coat. I asked him if it was for him, but it wasn't.

Then for whom is it? It is too big for me now.

Of course it wasn't for me either. Then he started to tell me the story of his cousin, with a little bitter tinge in his words.

When I was around 10 years of age, back from Bihebar, I wanted to dress like my other cousins and not look like a pakhe (rural lad) anymore. Your grandmother was working like a slave at home and had no income.

She could not afford to help me at all though I was her only child.

My elder cousin Mahila Dai Tripur was wearing a new tailor-made jacket his father gave him for Dasain. He looked cute in the new jacket. I asked Mahila Dai whether he could ask Uncle to buy a coat for me too.

I did not have the courage to ask him myself. I was the boy with a widowed mother without income. Tripur reacted rather angrily: 'Who do you think you are? You have no father to give you a coat. This coat is from my father.'

I remained quiet and never in that house would I talk about a jacket again. I vowed to repay him one day, but repay him in a positive way.

Father seemed sad about the episode even now and still sounded deeply hurt. The new coat Father bought about 30 years after Tripur's angry words was meant not for anyone else but for Tripur. Father said,

I am now going to pay back Mahila Dai in my own way.

That Father could keep his secret for so long surprised me! Not only was he denied a jacket, unlike his junior cousin, Kanchhabuba, Father did not get the opportunity to go to school.

We never heard how he learned reading and writing simple Nepali. But later he needed to be at least *'simple literate'* for his army job.

Life with Father and Grandmother

Father's concern for appearance was almost like an obsession, with dress, daily meticulous nursing of his fine little moustache, shiny shoes, and the *birketopi*, the Turkish cap, sustained over his life. With his Khas-Mongol heritage he barely had a beard people could notice. He had no side-whiskers and what little hair he had on his chin was often pulled out with tweezers. But he developed a habit of demonstrably shaving his beard with lather of shaving soap, a luxury then, at least for us.

He wore meticulously ironed clothes back when the iron was to be heated with glued charcoal. It gave mother additional regular drudgery. His clothes needed to be washed by traditional laundrymen (*dhobi*). He could hardly afford this sort of lifestyle without slowly depleting the family's household budget.

Grandmother did not have time to indulge in religious rites, temple visits or to celebrate festivities. It was simply a rare luxury for her. Her sun rose in her kitchen and set in the kitchen. Her spirituality had to be kept suppressed. The only thing luxurious she wished for herself was to get some sleep and rest.

The Panday clan, descendants of the Kaji of Gorkha, Ganesh Panday, had a place in the society, an honourable one but still when Father was growing up, Grandmother was worried that he would have difficulty finding a wife. His life without his own father around as guardian was adding to his problem. That was outwardly so. Grandmother would tell me that that was a lame excuse.

We had rich kin in the same big house. Our large family with a large tract of land was living relatively affluently. Outsiders did not see that only I and my son were poor. Many Chhetris rejected your father, because he was from the indigenous Khas community and not of high caste. I wanted a Chhetri, a high caste girl as my daughter in law, for my son, as I am. Richer Pandays were sometimes acceptable to some Chhetris. But your Father could wed your mother without problem from her Silwal Chhetri parents' side. The family of Sano Panday was respectable in the area. Only much later would they know of our dire situation?

To be widowed at the very tender age of around 20 and left with only one child was a curse within the family and in the society. She was taken probably as a harbinger of bad luck. She herself started feeling she was not normal, cursed by her fate. In the Hindu society, particularly among the Chhetri and Brahmins, then, the taboos of prohibition or restrictions of this, prohibitions of that, inflicted on widows were unbearable. But grandmother would not tell me bad things about others in the house. She seemed to have suffered them silently.

In those days, people were dying from banal ailments and epidemics which hit every year like cholera, smallpox, and measles. For grandmother, news of every incident of such disease meant a time of fear, sleepless nights and despair. The constant fear she had was that disease would snatch away her only child, Naran.

The world around and her own destiny were treating her unfairly. That might have been the reason she developed a grudge against '*god.*' She had, *not much to thank God for.*

Uprooting of the Family

The family house of my father's birth was where today Manbhawan stands. Father was living in that large house among 25 family members for the first 5 years of childhood and again after he was around 10. For 5 years he was living in the mountains with his maternal uncles at Bihebar, Kabre district. His experience of life in Bihebar changed him for good in many aspects of his life.

There was no school in Bihebar, the home village of Grandmother. But even after coming back to Jawalakhel at around the age of 10, Father had neither the opportunity to go to a school nor he had any job to do. He got married early; perhaps my grandmother hoped she would get a helping hand.

Juddha Shumsher, one of the most powerful men in the country who was to become the next-to-last-two Rana Prime Ministers, confiscated our sole property, the house as well as the dry land, where the family planted only maize, millet and mustard over the rainy season. This land was our only bread basket.

The Pandays developed a sense of fear, bordering on paranoia, towards the Ranas. We had reason to fear them. We were told to **not** accept any food in the house of the Ranas. For a long time the rule was imposed on us children, forbidding any kind of edible offered by the Ranas in the area.

That act of Juddha Shumsher was like a curse to his only adoptive son 'Manbahadur Dai', as he was called then, for whose sake Juddha Shumsher snatched our livelihood. His eldest son became an alcoholic and died in poverty. The second son, one of the two good intentioned ones, somehow managed to keep his head above water, worked hard in life but died of tragic disease and dishonour; while the third son, a gentleman, sold his property and migrated to Dehradun hoping to get something of Juddha Shumsher's loot in Nepal. He came back penniless and died in pain and poverty. The fourth suffered cancer of mouth and also died in pain. The fifth son had an ugly skin disease that confined him indoors most of the time. Of the second youngest we stopped seeing him; they said he went to the South. The youngest died in poverty in a small house nearby.

The common trait of all the seven brothers, except the second one, was that they never learned to earn their bread. Of the two daughters of Manbahadur Dai, the youngest, left her husband, a Shah of Kalimati, from whom she had twelve children, and eloped, with an elderly Brahmin from Kalimati, the tuition teacher of her children, from whom she got forcibly separated by her family only to live with her onetime domestic helper, Happey. My parents witnessed all these ups and downs of fate of once the affluent family in their life time. But the second and third sons of Manbahadur Dai remained Father's friends for life.

Juddha Shumsher had three weaknesses: a sharp tongue that could hurt the King, eagle's eye for 'beautiful and fat women' and a mouth longing for tasty special food. Perhaps he expected the rice grown in Jumla to increase his libido. He had a little ration of rice from Jumla brought to Kathmandu by the postmen to his kitchen regularly at the expense of the state.

Juddha Shumsher was not alone enjoying such a privileged lifestyle. Most of the ruling cliques had a regular source of delivery of what they enjoyed eating, from their private orchards of mango, banana, and orange scattered over the country. The state employed hunters around the Kathmandu Valley rim to deliver fresh cadavers and dried meat of wild deer (*sukuti*) and boars hunted regularly for their kitchen. They maintained cattle farms and farmed out for milk and butter on the mountains. I remember seeing, while taking cattle from my Mama-uncle, an old dry pond of skimmed milk on the Phulchoki Mountain.

Father Joins the Army

Just a few months before Father celebrated his 21st birthday his first child, my eldest sister Sita, was born on the 8th of January 1934. Right at this time, as an irony to my family, Grandmother had to see Premier Juddha Shumsher who lived nearby in order to try and get my father a job. To get access to him she first had to send him a gift with *84-parikar* (different dishes) she prepared at home, packed in a wicker-basket. All that did not come cheap at all for a family just making do. But she had no other possibility to reach Juddha Shumsher. One special pickle that Juddha Shumsher ate at lunch time, which she had prepared from of the root nod of *Dubo* the Barbados grass *(Cynodon dactylon)*, drew his attention to her gift.

She was called in to appear before him. She later said, that Juddha Shumsher roared at her,

So you are the Kajini of Sano Panday.

Although Grandfather's nick name was *Sano Panday*, (Little Panday), he was actually tall and strong.

What was it made of, and how did you make such a tasty pickle? Why all this trouble?

My son Naran's father died in the war in 1915. Perhaps you remember it. She answered humbly.

So what do you want me to do?

The pension money paid to me as his widow will be stopped because Naran just turned 21.

Go on!

Naran should be employed.

In April 1934 Father was 21 and with that, according to prevalent system, Grandmother feared losing her Veteran's pension coming from Grandfather's death. The family was in dire situation and needed an income. That was the reason why Grandmother went to that extent of bowing down in front of the mean man who was to cause so much pain to the whole family.

Ok, let your son join the army. He will be appointed as Jamadar-Subedar (Sr.Non-commissioned Officer) *in his father's battalion.*

Although my grandfather, the second son of Jagyabahadur, had made a name that perhaps helped Father a little to get the army appointment; no one would believe that Juddha Shumsher would do it free. Soon after the episode Juddha Shumsher confiscated our family land.

The eldest son of Jagyabahadur, Father's uncle Lt. Bodh Bikram had his eldest son Meen Bikram die without leaving a male heir, perhaps from the shock of having to be, literally, on the street. Lt. Bodh Bikram too did not survive the shock. The family started to squabble over what was left of their property. Having lost their all landed property to Juddha Shumsher, the cousins got at least their material property separated. My Grandmother and my parents apparently got nothing, without Grandfather at their side asserting his right to his property.

The families got separated and were miserably dispersed, went their individual ways, whereas the situation called for them to be living united. It was a fact that no rented place could accommodate such a large family.

The family was split into three groups, Bodhbikram's second son, our Mahilabuba Tripurbikram with two children daughter Ramu and the eldest son Rajbabu, migrated to Kantipur. Years later, when I could walk over to their place I met them in the rented rooms of a Manandhar family at Chikamungal, not far from Kathmandu Ganesh. Father's youngest cousin, Bate

(Shesbikram) with his mother accompanied by a lady with her little daughter remained at Jawalakhel in Gunche Rimal's house.

Moving Hither and Thither

When Father joined the army as Jamadar-Subedar in the Jabar Jung Battalion, he and the family could afford to rent a shelter. My family, with Grandmother, Father, Mother and my eldest year old sister Sita, shifted into rented rooms at Purnachandi near Gabahal, Patan in 1935. They did not have money to buy things they needed and wanted immediately for their new shelter.

My parents had just lost their second child, a son who did not survive his second year. My parents found the flat they rented at Purnachandi, inauspicious for them. They shifted again but this time closer to Jawalakhel, with two daughters Sita my eldest sister and the third child my elder sister Lalu around 1942, to Subba Kanchha baje Rimal's house at Taphalonha.

The beautiful house was just on one side of Taphalonha Bhairab shrine. It was an L-shaped house with wooden terrace along both wings of the house, facing south and east, on the 2nd floor. All the windows were wood carved, with *jhingati* roof (Kathmandu terracotta roof tials), *dachi-apa* bricks (traditional artistic terracotta bricks), and the chowk courtyard paved with *telia* (partially glazed) bricks. Behind the house was the clan deity of all the Rimal families in the area. The beautiful and artistic Rimal's house became my birth home.

The family had another son, me. One would expect the family would fare well in peace and harmony.

To everyone's consternation, Taphalonha was the place where Father fell for a Shrestha girl named Astamaya from across the road. What really annoyed me about my father was that when Mother was 6 months pregnant, with her 4th child and 2nd son (which happened to be me); he got other women pregnant in Taphalonha. Within around 15 months he became the father of two children. That I was one of them is irrelevant. It was just such an inconsiderate way to treat Mother.

My repugnance of this event has not diminished even long after Father passed away. The thought that I was in my mother's womb when Father impregnated another lady, Astamaya, disturbed me when I became aware of the event. Mother told me Astamaya died leaving a baby progeny, Gyana. I was about 6 months old when Gyana was born. Out of humanitarian obligation mother was to adopt the baby and raise her as her own daughter, because on Astamaya's family side they rejected their responsibility to raise the baby. Once again my mother proved great. Never did I hear that she discriminated against Gyana or said anything to her that would hurt her, or punish her for Father's and Astamaya's doings, of which she was godly innocent. For Gyana my mother was more than a deity.

Now with three girls Sita, Lalu, Gyana and a son to look after, my parents and grandmother were feeling bitter towards each other at a time when they were struggling to make ends meet.

The Rimal's Taphalonha house too became a cursed house to the family. Bitter memories were generated in the house. The family, especially my mother needed to forget and leave it behind and move elsewhere. It was an awful time for my mother again to shift to a new 'home.'

I was perhaps 2 and a half years old, when the family shifted the third time in the winter of 1946 to Thasikhel, rented a 'flat' in Rana's Priest Dataram Sharma's house, quite close to where our ancestral home had stood earlier. Ironically, the land the Rana priest got to build his house might have been part of the same land the Rana Juddha Shumsher confiscated from our large family in the 1930s.

That winter it snowed heavily. The first time I saw snow. I was standing behind the window, leaning on the *Kotal* (carved railings) bar with my eyes just reaching the end of the bar. There was a little pond designed like a star, a mimic of a Rana garden the Sharma had made. Father had bought me some gold fishes. I just saw how quickly the pond was covered with snow, and the garden and fields beyond, all lay under a thick cover of powdery snow. The fish pond was covered with a thick blanket of snow. My gold fishes disappeared right in front of me. I cried and cried. Faint memories of the sad day still hunt me. (The second snow fell around Jawalakhel in 2006, about 60 years later; I saw it in my own garden). We could not hold on to that house for long. It was soon time for me and my family to shift house again.

A year later in 1947, we shifted the fourth time to Jawalakhel to a twin-house thatched with rice straw. Father had saved some money and he could buy 5/8th of an acre of irrigable land and the twin house. For the first time my family had animals, cows, and some goats. Of the two identical farmers' huts, built with unbaked bricks with rice straw roofs, one we used as a stable and stored fodder and firewood. We stayed in the other. The kitchen and children's sleeping corner was on the ground floor while our parents slept upstairs in the one-room floor. The attic was grandmother's place, where she stored whatever the family could treasure—such as the outfit I wore for my rice eating ceremony, pension and property papers, my mother's wedding veil and Father's official head dress, the *chandtoda*—in a big wooden box.

I had a parrot I got from Father's friend. Every time there was a yogi visiting us the parrot would shout loudly, *chor Ayo chor Ayo*! ('A thief has come, a thief has come!'). One morning as usual I climbed the window bar to feed the parrot. The door of the cage was open, and the parrot was gone. As a solace a Myna-bird was brought to me. What a contrast of colour, the parrot green and the Myna coal dark. But I had fun with the Myna too.

One morning I found Sita sitting on the stairs and crying, with tears in her eyes, and Mother and Grandmother, telling her to shut up in sad voices. I was not yet 5 years old and was not to get a grip of the situation. Father was leaving in army uniform with a large bed roll, the *gunta* bedding on his back. His clothes, as I heard later, were tucked into it. That evening he did not come back. I was told,

Father has gone to Hindustan to fight a battle and is going to come back soon.

They were so sure that he would come back, but not me because he went to war. Grandfather too had gone to war and he never came back. Then it was my turn to cry and be sad that whole evening. In those days expecting news from Father was no more than a dream.

It was 22nd July 1948; Father was among the 10 brigades going to India to help them with garrison duties mainly in Banaras, while the Indians were to quell the sectarian conflicts brought about by Partition. After doing garrison duty for eight months Father returned home to the thatched houses. Soon after returning his troop was demobilized.

The Red House

I still wonder why Father was in such a hurry to demolish the thatched houses and build a newer house soon after his demobilization!

It must have been around 1949 that Father started getting construction materials, mainly pine timbers, from his maternal uncles in Bihebar. My maternal uncles in Godavari supported Father with adequate construction materials, labor, and food and financed the cash spending needed.

At the time the feed house of the Zoo located on the southern side was being replaced with a larger and stronger building. Then the director of the zoo was incidentally Father's friend Dadhi Sumsher. Father could have all the materials, such as roof tiles, bricks and beams from the old feed house. I am not sure whether he got them all free of cost or if he had to pay. Nor did we ever find out if Father brought some money from his tour of duty in Banaras. He built a three storey house, facing east. Thanks to the support from Mother's and my grandmother's families and not least from Father's friend Dadhi, Father could realize his dream of a *'unique red house'*.

By 1953 the nine room house with inner courtyard was erected. There was a stable, washing area and compost pits. In the inner courtyard places were designated for water jars, a firewood store and of course, also for his Geranium flower pots in large numbers. A seasonal flower garden for Father, right in front of the house and on its right side mother's vegetable garden complimented their individual tastes.

Behind the house was the sprawling crop land which over the dry season turned into our playground, a children's paradise. We were compelled to fence the land with thorny bushes. In earlier times the fence on the roadside had to be shorter than an elephant and *Hauda* (saddle used for elephant ride). That was the rule of Premier Juddha Shumsher Rana then. One reason being his habit of peeking into windows of folks houses with his eyes searching for 'beautiful fat lady' to quench his lust. But when Father was building his house the Ranas were no more in power, so he was free to build and design as he imagined.

It was according to Father's own sketch that he built his house. He painted the house red. Anyone passing by would stop to look at the house under construction. At the time, there wasn't any house being built by the common folk around the area. All the constructions were of Ranas and their kin. So when Father built his house it was the first of many to come.

One could see old houses made of red bricks, but Father painted the walls red, with terraces and an inner courtyard which must have attracted the attention of people passing by our house. Such elements in building were not used by common people like us.

Father used to promise me when we were in the thatched house that he would set aside a room just for me to use in any way I liked. Yes, he did fulfil his promise, but I had to accept it under one condition, never to hit a nail into the wall of the ground floor room. Only later did I understand why I had to follow his condition. The walls of the rooms were all plastered with a combination of mud, cow dung and rice husks called *liun*.

After the death of his mother, Bate uncle, who was in the army, came to live in our newly built red house with his newlywed young wife. We called her Kanchhiama. Many years later she told me she was a little older than my eldest sister Sita. She must have born around the early thirties. We became a large family. Especially, when Bate uncle came over for the weekends, we children enjoyed it immensely.

With the three story 'red' house with my room for my playing, my mother's behaviour of treating all equally in the neighbourhood, and her hand on us all the time, Father engaged in the Pioneer Battalion as an officer, and the land around the house giving essential foodstuff so that we always had enough to eat, the world looked very cosy and comfortable. We were basking the warmth of a little affluence. We the children felt the world stood still. We were not yet in schools. So life was just playing, eating and sleeping.

Father smoked from his shiny *hookah*, hot *chilim*, the ritual performed in his room as usual. After each meal mother and son would puff *tamakhu* together. Grandmother had her own *hookah* made out of coconut. I could hear them talk and update the day's happenings. Father seemed to have a very close rapport with his mother and shared much with her, but not much with his wife, my mother. Grandmother would listen to him and give restrained comments. I would not understand the context of most of what they discussed, nor did I try to understand.

Anyway, Grandmother would tell me what they discussed and explain it in simple terms in the evening for me to grasp. Father grew up poor but now he thought he was doing well and living well. Although he did not attend a school he learnt to read and write Nepali appropriate for his work as an army officer.

Things still looked good at home. We had a good house, with rooms for all and for all purposes, sufficient land to produce lot of vegetables and corn, as well as children attending schools.

We soon found out it was not to be so all the time. Fate that we were unaware of was deceiving us.

A Change in Fortune

One morning, a yogi came begging for water. I brought the water in a *karuwa* (a traditional bronze metal water jar) to him and I went back into the house. A little later mother asked me to bring the *karuwa* back to kitchen. I went out to the front garden. I did not see the yogi, or the *karuwa*. That was the only time we ever lost anything from our garden.

It was almost like a bad omen portending bad things to come. When things seemed to work well for the others, at our end the whole thing started to crumble.

Two of the grandsons of Juddha Shumsher, who confiscated all our family property to put up a mansion for his adoptive son Manbahadur Dai, remained as good friends of Father. The fateful tie up with one of them, a brigadier in the construction brigade the Pioneer Battalion, proved to be an unfortunate alliance. One bright day, the brigadier's epaulette was pulled off by the palace secretary in the presence of King Mahendra. Father told me the story of how it all happened quickly and how rudely it was handled by the Palace. Father witnessed it all.

Somebody, on behalf of the Palace, a certain palace official, Shahi, had a share from the timber trucked over the Tribhuwan Highway, (illegally?) into Kathmandu Valley. The man responsible to get it done was the brigadier. Something happened; in all likelihood it must have been the conflict in sharing of the benefits between the King, the Palace coterie and the brigadier that cost the Brigadier his lucrative job.

The officers group allied to the brigadier was sacked too, without recourse. That was the end of my Father's second career, but that did not affect his friendship with the brigadier.

We had again a difficult time making ends meet. It was not a question of how hard we worked. The sources of income just dried up, except that from our own garden.

The job Father had as an officer of the Pioneer Battalion after he was pensioned from the regular army back in the late forties was gone in the scandal of the brigadier above him. Father started to lose his head for the second time in his life. An ill-wisher of the neighbourhood started taking advantage of Father's situation.

Foes Disguised as Friends

Like all human beings, my father was not a flawless person. That gambling had been his pastime in his youth was known to us all along. He had other temptations too from which he could not abstain. I remember a friend of Father's at Taphalonha, a Brahmin with charming words and a smiley face. Father would call him jokingly, *Baaaabu!* He could grease you in no time and win over you.

We knew that Father was not satisfied with my mother, perhaps because of her strong personality and sense of independence. Father kept his distance from her. The clever *Baaaabu* took this as my Father's best weakness that could be exploited. By all accounts he blackmailed my

Father. Before Father could return to sanity, it was already too late to make a turn and he was trapped.

Father was also a good friend of the popular goldsmith of Gabahal, Purna Bahadur Banra. We heard later that, through Father's contact with the Banra, *Baaaabu* was able to get an interest free loan of Rs.300, 000. That was a good gesture on the part of the goldsmith. The amount of the loan was substantial in value in those days, when good land by the roadside was available at less than Rs.1 per square meter of land, compared to over Rs.100, 000 per square meter the same vicinity today.

Father started to frequent *Baaaabu*'s house, which was on the other side of the road where his friend Hari Prasad Rimal lived. Father used his connection from his time in the Pioneer Battalion to entice a soldier with promotion or money. We had seen him visit our house many times seeking Father's favour. Whenever he saw my mother he was mum and turned his head.

Whether he got favourable treatment in the army we did not know, but his promise to Father in return turned out to be very damaging for us in the family. Soon we learnt that *Baaaabu* hosted hospitality to a lady brought by the soldier for Father, as his mistress. Although the house was very small, Baaaabu provided a room for their sole use. That house became Father's second home. We were already living from hand to mouth and now Father maintained a relatively expensive indulgence.

Baaaabu had full knowledge of our family yet he implanted a reason for bitter brawls in our home for Father to tackle. Each quarrel was driving the family further apart. The fights between Father and Mother would at times get very nasty. At 14, I was aggressive on behalf of my mother. I know now that I was accusing Father of being guilty. I was verbally abusive, and broke contact with him then, when I came to know of his misdeeds and for bringing distress to the family.

Not long after that *Baaaabu* disappeared. My Father was facing bitter arguments with the goldsmith. Actually the goldsmith also knew the Brahmin and it was his decision, not my father's request to do so, to give the money to the Brahmin. *Baaaabu* just vanished with Rs.300, 000 from Purna Bahadur Banra, the renowned goldsmith of Patan and we never heard him come back to his family. Nobody knows what happened to him. He just disappeared. Was he paying for his sin? Sometimes I see his only son whom I knew from my childhood, and I feel sorry for him.

The family lay deeply split up into two entities. We were still in the red house designed and built by Father. But there appeared two worlds in existence side by side. Father's sense of responsibility was totally absent; it was completely unjust towards Mother and Grandmother. Mother and Grandmother were with us and that gave us energy to strive for survival and to chart our own future course again from the bottom up, if possible. It also meant a big responsibility to cope without anyone supporting me. My fate turned upside down and I was responsible in all matters for the family. I would not say it was a burden to shoulder.

Much later, after my years of 'wandering' and growing up, I tried to make up and make a peace with Father. I was constantly asking myself, was my Father wrong, doing all that he did to us? Why did he do all that? I was around 14 years old when Father again took a mistress. It was too much to bear. I used to shout at him. The words I used still haunt me with a little tinge of regret. That vocabulary I do not possess anymore. I did not want to punish Father. He had a difficult fatherless childhood, part of large family where he had to share everything with so many and never got what the other children got.

Looking back, I think his greatest contribution to me in particular and to us children in general was that he made us survive on meagre resources. Unlike many of our neighbour kids, we had little to eat, less to wear, poor opportunities for attending schools and less to enjoy in life. We had to strive, and be resolved to do something in life.

Exploiting his weakness for gambling was the easiest ploy for others to harm Father, a kind of giving him a slow poison. What this all led to is irreparable. Father continued gambling, took loans and his money was misused by friends. His mistress too must have been a demanding one.

Grandmother had long ago told us the story of *'insects biting our house'*. We kids just wondered how insects could destroy a house built with bricks, tiles and beams. Slowly we began to realize how Father's best friend conspired and intrigued to snatch our property: quarter of a hectare of land and the red house. The only asset we had.

The old lady, mother of my Father's best friend, Hariprasad, would invite Father and other friends to gamble with dice and pips or 16 cowrie shells. Her son Hari would participate too. But Father seemed to lose at every turn. How come? The modern day Casino is not any better. Father was somehow being plotted against to be a constant looser. Yet he would not wake up.

But when they thought that the property would be theirs with the gambling debt reaching a certain threshold, they asked Father to handover the property anyway. Father suddenly realized the stake. We were shocked and deeply hurt. Grandmother's story of the *'insects slowly eating up the house'* became so real to feel!

Father was not ready to hand over to the evil lady. He had to sell, but he sealed a deal with another person, Benibahadur Karki from Lagankhel, a Congress Party stalwart. Around December 1960, my father was forced to part with his life's pride and joy, the red house. What Father achieved was blown to pieces. The gambling and maintaining a mistress cost Father his hard earned property. It was his weakness to the extreme point. He was the one who demanded good food and the mistress, but the income was barely enough to sustain our own household expenses.

The red house was associated with memories of joys and pleasures as well as tears, mostly shed by my mother. For Father, Mother and Grandmother they were facing their second such devastating time. The economic downturn reached the deepest point. We were literally on the street, and realised we were without God.

Much of proceeds of the sale had to be used right away for settling all the debts and dues. He had virtually handed over his life's achievement to the man who had nothing to do with Father's debt. It was the old Rimal lady who brought to this down fall, but it was due to Father's pride that he did not give her the house, he only repaid all the loans taken from her for gambling and for his mistress. That day Father came back empty handed from the Malpot Land Management Office. Father had nothing in his hand for tomorrow. He had no job to attend but to go on taking loans from friends who still trusted him. That barely covered the household expense.

In 1961 the old house belonging to Captain Ganjbahadur at Kumaripati, which lay unoccupied became our new shelter, about a hundred meters away from our old rented rooms of Taphalonha. So we made a complete circle of a fateful life.

There we had only two rooms for a family that was now split into two. We were huddled together in two worlds; Mother, Grandmother and we children were in *patal* (deep underground) on the ground floor room, and the first floor, the *aakash* (in the outer space) was for Father and his mistress. I thought of all the ills about my father. In fact my odd feeling swinging between hate and hope for accommodation with my Father goes back to the time when I began to grasp mother's time of torture, while I was in her womb.

Did he hope to get a son again but not from my mother, because she had already lost one? It was not my mother's fault at all for my elder brother's death. In those days the chances of survival for a kid below 5 were very slim. Desire for another son would have been a lame excuse that nobody would buy, as his indulgence in other vices such as gambling and smoking was known to all. Womanizing was an addition to his doings.

Although he lost everything of his making and became a penniless he continued to hope for better and searched for a piece of land that had to be in Jawalakhel area.

Naran, the day your children are ready to start their life on their own, they will have some land to step into. When you are ready to buy a piece of land then come to me, and you will have it.

That was the word of solace given to my desperate Father by his friend former Brigadier Rana of the Pioneer Battalion. Did he want to come to terms with my father? Did he have guilty feeling all along because father had lost his job as an office under him?

Father found a quarter of a hectare of land behind the Mahendra Yubalay, at the corner of roads to Pulchowk and to Purnachandi at Rs.1 per square meter. Father thought it was too expensive and shifted his sight to the area on the southern flank of the Zoo. But the access was difficult, with only a meter wide path leading to the land. The houses around were red mud smeared huts. Though, hardly a kilometre away from the centre of Patan city, it was a completely rural setting like you find elsewhere far from the towns.

It cost Rs.0.8 per square meter. That was reasonable for him. His friend bought about 2250m^2 of land, with a dilapidated house on it, from a certain Laxman Thapa and handed it over to Father to live in. He told Father he would keep the land in his ownership, lest he gambled away. As soon as Father would be in a position to suppress his vices, such as gambling and womanizing he would hand it over legally to us. But we would have to come up united. He would sell back the land to us in the price he paid for. He did it in 1978. All three of us and Mr. Rana went to the Land Bureau in Patan together to settle the matter. It cost me Rs.5, 000, everything I had saved over the years.

I began to think of the holy era. Who would keep his word like him today? I changed my attitude towards him overnight. On the same day we divided the property in three parts between us two brothers and Father, in a judicious manner peacefully.

Life unlike His Love of Flowers – Father in Life

Father's love of flower gardens and potted geraniums: Father was kind of a 'curator' of the flowers at home. He would enjoy doing two types of gardening: planting flowers in the garden and raising plants in clay pots.

The flowers in the clay pots were solely devoted to varieties of the *geranium species*. I always wondered that there existed so many different varieties of geranium. He took hours to tend and nurture them: turning soil in the pots, clipping off sick branches and chipping off dead leaves and watering of the pots.

The flower garden was in front of the house, four plots each of approximately 10m^2 for seasonal flowers, laid out in *'French or Moghul style'* and two plots of similar size for mono culture of *Dubo* the Barbados grass *(Cynodon dactylon)*. He had been to India, in the late forties, so he must have seen Moghul gardens somewhere.

We did not have running water at home. Water had to be hauled from a natural spout, *gahiri dhara* some 200m away that had plenty of water pouring out, warm in winter and cooler in summer. That was a common water spout for the community use. The daily burden of fetching water home from the spout fell on Mother. That was in addition to her time consuming household and kitchen chores.

When I was big enough I was made responsible for watering the plants daily. Watering had to be done before going to school. Sometimes I would skip being with Father at the time he left for his office, so that he did not find me around to give the day's chores. Then I would have to face his mild wrath in the evening. I was not happy with the job. There were animals at home which needed water too, and for which too Mother was also responsible. It burdened mother and cost me my cherished after-school-playtime.

The outdoor garden was for us kids the best place to play different games. Many a time kids from the neighbourhood joined in. Sometimes we were playing in a rough way and did not take care of the plants. In the evening when Father would notice it, we were scolded and forbidden to play in the flower garden anymore. But we the kids took no notice and continued to play. Yet Father never scolded me in an angry way in front of other kids.

I was safe with him. In fact he was not angry with us kids. I do not remember any one of us getting thrashed, spanked or being scolded badly for damaging some of his flowers.

Father liked dogs. The last dog to be in his life was named Soni. Soni learnt from Father to do Namaste to visitors, but only when he told him to. Soni was a lucky dog; he got regular grooming, regular washing and medication. He was allowed to sit with Father. In his later years Soni preferred to sit on his bed. Soni was with him all the' time. Thus Soni was luckier than any of us kids for being so close to Father.

But once, some dogs mauled Father badly. What an irony! The attack almost took Father's life, and I was right with him. It was really terrible.

Father had a friend, called Mirga Rana, a born general, living nearby. That friend had inherited enormous wealth, part of which he invested in dogs and fancy cowboy attire we saw him going around with. He kept two massive Alsatians. Although they were kept chained, I was always afraid of them. One day, when I accompanied Father to his friend, the two dogs were loose. Both of them jumped straight at my Father, shoulder high, and started to maul him.

Luckily the owner was in the next room. One word from him made the dogs leave my Father alone, but not before he had suffered bites and bruises. The dogs looked much taller than my Father when they jumped on him. I was scared to death. Mirga Rana said the dogs had got their inoculations. He did not apologize or offer him help to treat the wounds. Father stopped going to his friend, and Mirga never came to visit him.

Father's Habits and Hobbies

In Kathmandu in those days, the only private mode of travel for the common folk was the bicycle. The horses were for the richer ones. The ruling class of Rana had motor vehicles or horse drawn carriages.

My father would find an old Raleigh bicycle, British made, discarded in the bicycle shops of Kamlachhi, for a cheap price. He would turn the old one to as good as brand new in function but not in appearance. He learned to repair his bicycle perfectly, and he kept a special tool box for the purpose.

He would avoid repainting, thinking people would be jealous of his 'new' bicycle. For him the condition of the two wheelers and the riding comfort given by the special large leather saddle, mattered most. He pedalled to any destination around Kathmandu city, to places like house of Gopal Buba at Lajimpat, or to Mahilabuba at Chinkamugal, to offices and the Patan area, his only world around, most of his adult life.

I saw him riding a bicycle almost throughout his active healthy life. But he never took me perching on the front bar or riding on the carrier behind him as many did.

People would know how good his bicycle was. I remember him loosing his Raleigh twice. Once he lost it while parked at the heavily guarded office compound of the Zonal Commissioner in Kathmandu. He again found an old Raleigh and put some effort into making it suit his taste and comfort so much so that people would believe him that he got back his lost bicycle.

But once it was me; I took his bicycle and rode off, by pedalling with legs between the triangle bars because the saddle was too high for me. Even then I could ride it far and come back home quickly before he noticed me.

One day the inevitable happened. His bicycle broke in two pieces at Jhamsikhel Chowk. On one hand I had the handle and front wheel and in another the rest. I pulled them home. I do not know how, but I did it. Father could not believe it seeing his bicycle in two. He didn't think a small boy like me could have done it. But he saw and noticed the weakest points on his old bicycle, and he was happy that it happened at home, I was unhurt and that it did not happen somewhere in the city or on the steep downhill '*Bhairav Shamsherko oralo*' while he rode it to Kathmandu.

Some of his habits and hobbies were something many would despise. We had a latrine hut in the garden, about 20m away. The closet was about a meter above the ground. Underneath the toilet floor was a big bucket placed to trap the excreta dropped through the lavatory pan. Almost every alternative day a vegetable farmer from Patan would take away a bucketful of it. But the farmer paid a price of Rs.1.5 per 38litre bucket full. It paid to empty your bowels! That amount of money then could cover the day's household requirement. What a world we had.

That must surely have not been the reason why Father collected everything in the toilet and let it fall into the bucket. He valued cleanliness. Very early and every morning he would take a Hookah, *chilimpato*, *tamakhu*/fire (sugared tobacco dough, pressed on a small plate of clay, put upside down to burn it with only charcoal heat) to the toilet. He would suck and puff out Tamakhu smoke while he cleaned the floor and brushed the latrine pan. He normally would take about an hour for the chore, before others needed to use the toilet. So everybody found a clean toilet and we were supposed to leave it as clean for the next person to use as we had found it.

Many years later, when I had children of my own, although Father was living separately, he was in the vicinity, at a shouting distance. He maintained good contacts with his children's children. Father liked to be with children. My daughter had special contact with him. There was a girl of her age, Indu in his house with whom she played the *gatta*-stone juggling game. In the north of Father's house lay our vegetable garden. We used to produce all sorts of green vegetables, cauliflower, broccoli, radishes, carrots etc. for home consumption. As a little girl Junamaya was an avid gardener. Father liked broccoli grown in our kitchen garden.

Father sustained friendship. Father was good at maintaining friends, and he had numerous friends around Jawalakhel. They each bore nick names like Pake (*KB Basnet's Father*), Quante etc. In his later years, when he was able to visit his friends and spend time playing Pasha-game he cultivated special friendships with two persons, the dentist Dr. Basant Bahadur Rajbhandari and Mr. Lokendrapyara Shrestha, who lived at a walking distance.

It was Father who mediated the wedding of Lokendra Dai's daughter with the second son of Đr. Basant. He was especially close to Dr. Basant Bahadur Rajbhandari, a commissioned palace dentist by profession, at Tafalonha, Patan. Father was weak in his dental hygiene, and also due to his excessive consumption of betel nuts, he started to suffer much in his later years. So his friend would always see to it that Father did not have much pain and not lose any teeth.

As if they were competing, my mother too was in a similar situation thanks again to the betel nuts she chewed for years, but she never got the attention of a dentist. Father never replaced his teeth by artificial ones. Mother had all her natural teeth pulled out. Hence, she could only smile with the false teeth that I got for her.

After the demise of both the Brigadier Rana and Dr. Basant, Father had only Lokendra Dai to turn to, as the friend. Lokendra Dai kept my father company when he was in pain. In April 2013, at the centenary celebration of Father we were happy to felicitate Lokendra Dai and Dr. Vijay Rajbhandari together with their spouses. Dr. Vijay, a dermatologist by specialization and the eldest son of Dr. Basant Bahadur Rajbhandari helped Father and often visited him to enquire after his health. My father was just Kaji Ba (Father) to him.

His Failing Health

Father, a small person, with a lean and thin body started getting weaker with diabetes, high blood pressure and asthma. He was sick for almost ten years with these ailments. We were extremely worried.

Then an opportunity came along. I visited China twice in 1985 for prolonged periods which I could also use searching out Chinese medicine for Father that I had heard about that would be his last chance. For another 10 years he lived without suffering, eating and moving around meeting friends as a normal old man. In October of that year I could also bring the wonder medicines for other senior Pandays Sirdar Bhimbahadur, Subarna Jung, Dambar Jung, dai Prembahadur and former PM Nagendra Prasad Rizal, from Chengdu.

We believed in the ominous constellation of the figures 8 or 12 to cause changes in fate. It happened to my Father. In his lifetime he shifted his abode 12 times within an area of hardly a kilometre in diameter, from his birth house to his house where he spent his last days.

Rescuing a Fellow Creature at Pashupati

The 1ˢᵗ of March, 1996 found my father hospitalized. Seeing Father not much worse in suffering that morning, I left the hospital to come home to eat and have some rest. Two hours later I received a phone call,

> *Father is already at Aryaghat, come immediately to Pashupati Temple!*

I could not believe it. That morning I still had hoped that Father would get over the worst, and now within two hours it was over.

Lots of thoughts crowded my mind. I even suspected foul play. What could I say? He was gone. I was not by his side at his last minutes and last breath. It was March 1st, 1996 four days before the 34th Clan Festival at Gorkha when my father Lt. Prem Jung Panday Kaji breathed his last at the Army Hospital Chhauni. He lived 82 years, 10 months and 11days.

I must see it as a pure coincidence that his Father, Lt. Jagatbahadur Panday Kaji too died around the Clan Festival time, in the 1915 war in the NWFP of British India.

Father's body was lying at the Brahmanal of Pashupati at the bank of the holy river Bagmati. I tried to keep his feet away from the Bagmati water, against the tradition. At that season it was more polluted than at any other time of year. I was waiting for our priest to come to perform Father's last rites, but he sent a message,

I have an appointment elsewhere. I am unable to come.

On the other side of the river there was a platoon of Army Band from the Rajdal Battalion in Lagankhel, waiting for the last retreat for Father as an officer, but the pyre had to be lit first. They wanted to finish their duty and did not see why we were delaying the whole process. But we were still searching for a priest.

This is also one reason why I declined performing the annual Shraddha ritual that benefitted only the priests. In my mother's case I had long introduced a new system. It is not a question of whether Brahmins are good or bad, that is another matter. I never followed things that could not see the value of.

What in the meantime was happening that brought the cremation area alive? Suddenly there were noisy living creatures all around.

A baby monkey came running towards us with its hand holding its stomach, crying, went towards the body of my father and lay down holding my father's feet. Many dogs ran chasing him, shrieking and barking aloud. I quickly grasped the situation. They had injured the baby monkey and they were going to attack it again.

Oh that is a bad omen, a bad omen! The monkey should not have touched the dead!

Came the shouts from the yogis and beggars loitering around and others, like the flock of crows.

I could just not help being angry at them. A few hours earlier that had been my father, alive and human, how could they see him as a bad omen in this holy Pashupati temple? Yes he lies lifeless but he is not alone here, we all are with him. He still is on this earth for some time today. I could not take the slandering of my father, I shouted at them,

You are the bad omens, you loveless creatures!

I had been fighting against such prejudices and double standards from the moment I got my holy thread at my maternal uncle's house in a group Upanayan ceremony in Godavari when I was only eight. I was against all this dogmatic adherence of touch-ability or untouchability between the people excluding them from our culture.

Today when I saw the situation of the innocent young life of a monkey, I lost my patience. They almost hindered me rescuing a monkey in distress, in the name of, my father 'as the bad omen.' I knew how I should face and react towards society. I don't care a damn what their backbiting would be tomorrow. For me the 'today' of this monkey baby was far more important and worthwhile to think of.

I chased the dogs away from closing in on the monkey, went straight to it and took it in my arms. Then only I saw how deeply and badly mauled the monkey was by the dogs. Its stomach lay outside of his body. I had to push its bowel into his body and with a piece of jute bag, the only thing that came into my attention, wrapped it and went along the Ghats looking for a man to take the monkey to a vet. A youth stood before me, more out of curiosity. He agreed to take charge of the baby. I gave him some money and told him,

> *Please take it to a vet in Tripureswor, get the stomach stitched and treated as the vet finds necessary. Take a taxi and hurry up! You should come back as soon as possible. We have to set it free here in the forest.*

He went off. But we could not begin Father's last rites because we were still looking for a Brahmin priest. After about two hours the youth came back with the baby monkey, bandaged and still. I prayed that he would live and that nothing bad would happen to him anymore. I had never before prayed so much for anybody. The day was for me just sentimental, deep in sorrow and somehow a desire to do good to all was coming from my heart. Perhaps this was something I could do for Father.

As soon as the monkey was freed in the nearby forest; a man dressed in shirt, a vest and a pair of trousers, with his pigtail swinging, murmuring prayers, looking all the while a gentleman priest came by in front of me, contemplating, with a book on both of his palms, reading and walking slowly passing by the Ghats. Was it just a coincidence? I gathered my courage and said to him,

Guru, our priest could not come, would you be so kind to help me complete my father's last rites? The army platoon, you see on the other side is there waiting for the last retreat in his honour. They are in a hurry.

He was more than happy to help me out of my quagmire. I was looking for a piece of stone; he appeared to be a full image of God!

We needed to lift Father from the Brahmanal and in a little last procession we were supposed to carry him over to our ancestral burning place, Ghat that we had made ready. On that Ghat somebody else had placed a body. They rudely said,

In a democracy there is nothing like your clan's ancestral Ghat. We came first. You can come when we are through.

We had been there a long time waiting for a priest. I had no energy to argue over such a trivial matter at such a moment. We hastily prepared a new pyre and placed him on a *ghat* on the southern side by the bridge. I felt sad that I could not have an ancestral pyre for Father.

I requested the godly Priest,

Please be, brief as I do not want to keep you here longer than necessary. Whatever is in our Vedic tradition I'd like to follow and no more. Is that ok with you, also?

Accordingly he started to instruct me in what I needed to do as Father's eldest son. I asked him, if everything was in the Vedas.

I wanted to make sure every bit of the last rites was done according to Vedic rites of passage. I placed a burning oil lamp and the Tulshi seeds in his mouth. The priest murmured Mantra. The army band fired a volley of bullets, blew the last retreat with a pair of bugles, and with the guns upside down, they stood still for two minutes and completing the army's part of the last rite for a soldier, the son of a fallen soldier.

Somebody threw a piece of a rolled paper over my head on to the chest of Father. I did not turn my head; at that very moment I was contemplating on Father's face for the last time. I picked it up from Father's chest, looked at it, an old piece of Nepali paper rolled, something written inside, it looked yellowish in colour. I soon assumed it to be *janma kundali* of Father.

Guru, is the janma kundali too to be cremated according to Vedic tradition? I asked.
No, not at all! He answered decisively.

So I pushed it into my shirt pocket. My brother and nephews just stared at me empty. Perhaps they were thinking I did something that is taboo. But they too were in no mood to drop words from their mouths.

We went three times around Father's pyre. I lit the pyre with my brother touching my hands. The last rites of my Father were completed as per the Vedic tradition, but without his *janma kundali*. I realised I had rescued it just ahead of the flames which would have consumed it and obliterated his Zodiac history.

My nephew Lava and I kept on stirring the fire. Within three hours Father was just ashes. And in ashes he disappeared. I was wondering why had it to be in Father's turn that he could not lay on his pyre, the clan's own *bhakari Ghat*. Surely things had changed from the time mother got the '*privileged place*' for her cremation.

I had never seen his *janma kundali* let alone touched it. He too might have kept it under lock and key as his mother traditionally did. After the death of my grandmother he never ventured to open it, the Pandora's Box of Disclosures of his Fates and Secrets. Did he fear the truth? For the first time, fifty years or more after my birth, it came to me, the *janma kundali* of my father. But it was at the very sad moment of my life. It was worth being treasured. What an irony.

That day I was the one to salvage it from his funeral pyre. Had I been so lucky as to light Mother's pyre, could I also have salvaged her *janma kundali*? What words were written in hers? I could have come to many of her personal facts about my rebellious mother. Were there things that I could have corrected on her behalf, even after her death to help her?

I decided to look deeply into Father's. Perhaps I would come to know some corners of his zigzag life.

My eyes were trying to convince me Father had left us all, his world. But my heart was not convinced. I have at least his *janma kundali*, not lost all in ashes. Now I have the *janma kundali* to solace me for life.

Somewhere deep in me I felt lonely; in the silence of this cremation ground, the dark moon seemed to rise making everything look darker and scary, in front of the afternoon sun.

My brother, nephews Sonam and Kalyan were observing from the *Sattal*-shelter nearby. I knew Father and Brother; the two had feared dead bodies. Father did not have to perform all this for his Father. Nor did he go to war to feel all the tragedies and overcome the fear of death. But for his mother he had to do everything as per the tradition. How did he do it? Now even his dead body was no more. My brother still feared death. I knew it was natural for him to stay a little distance away from the cremation.

Way back in December, 1980, when we were to take out the dead body of Father-in-Law from the morgue in Shantabhawan Hospital and place it on the jeep to take it for his last rites and cremation, neither Father nor Brother could come forward to help me do it. They stood away from me and the dead body. They could not even look at it.

So that day my brother was with Father's body. I knew he was as scared of death as ever and I could not wonder more. But this time it was an obligation to suppress his fear. He did not have to do much he just had to touch my elbow, so to say, symbolizing his participation. It was up to me to do everything, being senior to him.

All these thoughts came into my head only after Father went into ashes and his ashes to the river, to eternity. I thought of all his deeds and habits. Father had spoiled so much through his indulgence, his behaviour and his health condition in the later part of his life. How his destiny changed! Was my father any way wrong, doing all that what he did to us? I knew he grew up poor, deprived of a loving father being around him, he could not attend school. Did that drive *my* enthusiasm to make it in life?

In life he did not have to worry about his family. Except for his daughters, the elder Sita and Lalu, and the younger Gyana, all the other four of his children got the opportunity to attend schools. Surely, many loved my father. But during his life time I was the one to be his shield to take the first sharp blow of the tyrannical society. Many were not aware of it.

I mourned in my own way: avoided public appearances, and curtailing movements both inside and outside the house during the mourning period. I kept things cleansed, wore rubber footwear, slept on a blanket over a heap of straw. So I could satisfy myself: following the tradition and rituals, adjusting to suit time and my conviction, I persuaded my brother to follow me.

Like others, and yes me too, I loved my father. For three days I stayed on his *'kiriya.'* I did not see the meaning of 13-day *kiriya* in the tradition of Arya-Khas communities. Don't we mourn the loss of life of the dear ones for a long time? How about the thoughts and reflections about them? What are they, if not mourning? Will they vanish?

The Family Priest Violated Rituals

There is a reason not to forget the event. We had the Shraddha, commemorative day for our grandmother and grandfather. We had things prepared and laid everything ready for the priest to commence the ritual. We had to wait for him to come. Time was passing, sisters, nephews and cousins and their tiny tots were home with us to celebrate. But they had to have patience because no one could eat till the end of the ceremony.

He arrived at two in the afternoon and not nine in the morning as he was expected. The priest was a Bhattarai from Lainchaur, our family priest from ages past. He turned up with things hanging on both sides of his bicycle handle bar. He was munching a betel nut. We asked him why on earth he was chewing betel nut when coming for Shraddha.

He had conducted one Shraddha in Tikhedewal at a client's house. He had even eaten milk rice. All forbidden things to do. He was supposed to wait till he finished the rituals at our house, at least for that day. Sure, he could have felt hungry but he changed the cultural rule to suit his situation. Was he so weak a priest? Or he did not take the rituals and us seriously? He forgot we had hungry kids waiting. Before he could take seat to do the *Shraddha*, I told him, in front of all:

Guru, This Shrad-dha is going to be your last one in our house. When priests do not follow their duty we clients alone cannot keep up the culture. Perhaps you took only one pious meal yesterday, the Ekchhaki. But you cannot perform Shrad-dha ritual with your stomach full of food eaten to your taste. We have nothing more to say.

For today, please just do the minimum of Karmakanda as you can, because we prepared for as promised to our Pitri. We know it was not right, but the sins should go to you. Please do not try to come back to us again.

Mother and Father kept quiet, raising no word of objection to my 'rudeness.' Their silence was apt to signal me I did it right. That particular incident encouraged me to think of challenging other anomalies in our culture.

I was thinking of the priest, how angry he could have been. But it was his mistake. Breaking the link with us was tantamount to loosing client in other Panday families too. From that day on we broke the age old traditional bond with our Bhattarai priests. My parents never talked about the incident.

A Dream of My Father

After the break with our family priest Father never invited him again. When he needed one he contacted a Brahmin from Tikhedewal who was good enough for the kind of ritual ceremonies Father believed needed to be performed. This priest failed to come to Father's side for the last rites of passage. Inexcusable!

I was happy that even without the lousy Brahmin from Tikhedewal Father had honourable last rites. God's will! Was the monkey seeking refuge on the feet of my Father a messenger from Heaven? Only after we treated its wound did we find a priest to start the last rites for Father. Was it only coincidence?

Today, foregoing the traditional Shrad-dha, an annual ritual to honour the dead, we make it a point of bringing gifts to elderly women, cows and sick men of Baglamukhi temple in Patan on Father's commemorative day every year.

Despite his tumultuous time in life, Father and I re-established and maintained intimate contact during the last 32 years of his life. I feel grateful. I feel privileged to enjoy similar contacts with my own children, open, straight and loving.

On April 20, 1913, we celebrated Father's centenary birthday together with friends and relatives. The following night I had a dream of Father talking to me,

So you are becoming spiritual, he said in the dream, *since when did you think of that?*

So he saw all this during the day! Did he come to visit us on that day and how? People say when we do something for our Pitri, they pay a visit. We, the humans, do not see them. They come unexpectedly, in un-thought of guise. That day, on April 20, 2013, the programme was coming to an end. I had been telling my guests about the life and struggles of my parents, especially Father's before sitting down to lunch.

There came a gale of wind and heavy rains. The change of weather was so sudden, from blue and sunny sky, all of a sudden, in the hot month of Baisakh it quickly became cold and people who came in their light finery shivered. My friends and relatives got alarmed. All tried to seek protective corners. That lasted for only about half an hour. That gave an interesting moment to our guests. As they huddled together in different corners they did not budge and took time to chat and do catching up till late, but we liked it.

Five days later, the event was for remembering Father's annual kind of ritual of organizing a *Satyanarayan puja* on his birthdays. Mostly our relatives attended it. On this day also a sudden change in weather happened and the guests scrambled with their plates and took refuge in rooms and shuddered. But there was no rain as it was on the 20th April. The sun was bright and all were cheerful.

Long Way to Graduation

Wondering about the cause of myriad difficulties in my youth amid scarcity and struggles at home, I come to 'one conclusion' that it was my hesitation to take up just any job opportunity that came by. I was prone to playing truant rather than taking life seriously. No wonder my fate too played truant with my life. On the one hand I had a very free life to enjoy as I remained a naïve boy for a long time while on the other the difficulties at home were multiplying. Yet searching for means or an opportunity did not occur to me early enough.

What I never wanted to be was a bureaucrat attending a regular 7- hour job, a refuge taken by many of my friends. That was my weakness. Neither, could I be nailed or tamed like a prisoner of compulsion in poverty; stuck up in a dogma as politicians are to live without conscience, or die for a veteran's pension (it was still an irony for me to join the army albeit for a 6 years stint) for the family like my grandfather or became a lecturer tending a crop of rowdy students of a spoiled generation. Such lay outside my taste.

My rebellious mind sought to fly into far horizons always with confidence, with wings of hope spread wide, searching for newer destinations. Thanks to God's generosity I could feel the size and shape of the world, very early on in my life. The exposures fired my imagination further, leaving a constant hangover of the wide world I had seen.

I was almost pushed into politics in the mid-50s, at a very early age. That was when I was actively involved in defeating the Rana general who stood for the Mayors' post in Lalitpur Municipality. I was not aware of it until the last minute, and I was saved. I changed my taste and my mind searched for a new horizon.

Viewing in wonder, as a child, the beautiful constructions of the ages past, surviving vagaries of nature and man's war mongering, with all the elegance and spirituality in my home town of Patan inspired me and I knew one thing I wanted to be was an architect, surely not a nature enhancer. However, my weakness in mathematics and inadequacy of knowledge in other fields would not allow me to go for architecture.

This is also a story of me, of what I wanted to be and what it turned out to be for me. To wish for and to make it in life seemed to be two different planes not overlapping so easily. You see such is the life perhaps many live through.

Yes, eventually the time came for me to choose a profession. I got a chance to be an agricultural expert. That was my hidden wish for my profession. I must say, complementing my mother's constant encouragements and support I also needed my will and sweat, and luck stood firm throughout.

They say one who does not try has no luck. In my case I was not one to sit still, so luck must have rewarded me. It is not a new story but it is worth perusing. I will try to hang out my life on the laundry line to be exposed and hit by hot heads and stormy minds.

The changes that I witnessed or felt in my life within one generation may not be felt by the next generation on a similar scale and nature. Some changes I was confronted with were fundamental. I grew up from only being able to travel as far as I could go on a bicycle. Some relatives found a mole on the sole of my foot and said,

You ought to travel around the world!

I did it in jet planes flying in and out of the Valley on journeys that would take me to the far corners around the globe.

It was a time without radio. Now dozens of Nepal TV channels and hundreds of FM stations are beaming the voices and images of my country across the world. They also have brought many nooks of the world to me in my room. Is not that marvelous for the ones who take it positively? It can be different to others.

The changes were not only of a physical nature. The changes in the nature of relationships within my family were eye opening. Of course, the changes were not always soothing. I must say it needed a lot of energy to adjust and needed mental stamina to cope with some of the negative changes.

It was a discovery of my own self going along with the pains and problems within the family relation. So I feel I have to tell the story for the next generation to know and let them draw conclusions in their own terms.

I differed with the society in basic but fundamental areas of living life in Nepal. A misfit perhaps to live in this time! But the legacy of my mother and father was strong enough to leave a lasting impact and imprint on my thinking and behavior. Such, I thought, I should share too.

Growing Up at Jawalakhel

Mother had lost her second child, a boy when he was only two. Amid sorrow and disappointment, there was a void in the family. I never came to know his name. My parents only hinted that I had a 'big' brother. They just wanted to forget that he came to us at all. The third child was again a daughter, Lalu. As I heard there was no regret having another daughter. But she turned out to be a completely different person, with a lot of empathy, positive thinking and friendly to animals and people alike. Tears would roll down her cheek within seconds of her loud laughter, and not always for feeling sad.

Mother went to see an astrologer who predicted that she would have a boy child again, but he would not survive if brought up at home on her lap. That was the worst she could hear. She did not want to have another traumatic time losing another son. But the inevitable happened. In the year 1943 August 30, Monday early morning of New Moon on Father's Day, *Kushe-Aunshi*, I was born at Taphalonha, Jawalakhel. Mother would not dare to be happy for her fourth child! An *Aunshiya* son (born on the last day of the dark fortnight of the lunar month) was not necessarily the best omen for Mother, or so they would say. For many I was born at a time and on a day, very auspicious. Such auspicious new Moon takes place only three times a year, Father's Day, Mother's Day and the day of Laxmi, Goddess of Affluence.

For Mother at last she had a boy, and that mattered. As Mother told me she was not at peace because of the astrologer's prediction regarding my survival. What could she do? She sought his help and got hints of the actions to follow.

Jyapu heritage my destiny

Mother followed the astrologer's advice. As was the time honored tradition prevalent then, I, a baby boy, was ritually handed over or '*sold*' to a *Jyapu* (Newar farmer caste) lady, Nhuchhemaya. I became a *Jyapu* boy for all intents and purposes. There was no shame to the clan. It was a socially accepted practice, conducted in desperation with hope for the best. For my Mother and the family, I survived; that was important, at least for the time.

I grew up, in a *Jyapu* house, in the front street of Patan Dhoka Ganesh. I was *their* son. I was privileged to have a hand-woven outfit made by my *Jyapu* Mother. It did not matter which family I spent time with to stay overnight.

Even when I had crossed the age of 12 and was living with my biological mother, I remained an adoptive son of Nhuchhemaya. When I visited '*my adoptive family*' I used to get warm homecoming hugs. My school from grade four onwards was the Patan High School, less than 100m away from my adoptive family. It was easier for me to visit them fairly regularly, especially over the halftime school breaks, to get some food.

My foster '*Jyapu* parents', made their own clothes and shawls, all home spun. Wool was mainly used for the shawls, while all the other items were of cotton thread. The wool came from their own sheep they kept. I got a set of Nepali clothes annually, until I was 12. I was proud of wearing that home spun cotton outfit that was warm in winter and relatively comfortable during the summer time. It went well with an earring on the upper part of my right ear lap, as many *Jyapu* lads had, with a small blue stone. How could I not look like the other Jyapu lads?

Since I survived the event foreseen by the astrologers I was growing up well. Mother now had reason to trust the astrologers more. So she visited them every now and then for consultations. She seemed to have trusted them all out because she went to them with my *janma kundali* and asked about the potential evils to befall me and how she could avert them.

Even when I was doing homework for the regular examinations she would be worried that I would not make it. The astrologers, rather annoyed, once and for all told her,

Your son will make any exams in life a success. Now, stop worrying about him, for good.

That was it. In fact, that was the case in almost all exams that I attempted even though I did not work that hard. She stopped going to the astrologer with the same worry.

In every family festival, I was part of the *Jyapu* family. And the family was part of ours. I am proud of my heritage, to know and live with the *Jyapu* traditions, if not for life. I do not now remember much of the home other than their chores, food habits, the house and location, progressive values and their handloom work. I respected and appreciated them very much. Over time many of the Jyapu chores, cultures and social mores must have undergone changes and influenced by others. However, four events or rituals of the Jyapu family remained ingrained in my brain that I need to communicate:

Jyapu youth were raised to be progressive in social morals. Before they would decide to marry a couple were allowed to spend nights together in isolated field-huts constructed for crop watching, away from home, all by themselves. I was told it was a kind of '*couple compatibility test*.' Once they fall in love they may play music and hold each other's hands or put arms around each other's shoulder or waist accompanying their parents to and on return home from field work in the evenings. They did not care how the 'puritanical' communities like the Brahmins might be shocked. But the diverse communities then were living in a balance of tolerance and acceptance.

Despite the '*test*', the relationship between the two was subject to universal factors such as age and behavior of the couple, economic situation and the relations between the in-laws. The harmony in marriage in our area depended also on the relationship with families and relatives.

Things may not run smoothly in the married life as desired. When the situation goes beyond repair, at many an occasions the *Jyapu* lady takes initiative and decides to leave her husband. The child may live with the father. Once she decides to leave the family 'for good', she puts an unbroken betel nut under the pillow of her husband in the night and leaves the house very early in the morning before the husband is 'awake'. She takes all her ornaments, traditionally made of silver gifts from her parents. But that may not mean that the marriage could not be rescued. The husband may try to win her back. But promises are costly.

The third impression I have of the progressive nature of the *Jyapu* lady was her life after the death of her husband. Babucha was my best playmate. He lived near our house, south of Na-tole at Patan. They would do share cropping with us on our land at Jawalakhel during the cultivation of potatoes, garlic and onions, over the winter and spring seasons. He did not go to school. I never asked him whether he ever did go. I was too naïve or unconcerned to be interested in such things.

His father was much older than his mother. The couple worked in the field and we two friends, played with dust, stones and imagination on the dry field while they were around. We had a heavenly time together.

One day Babucha and his mother came without his father. I asked him why, and he told me that his father had died a week before.

But on that day when Babucha and his mother came to our house I was surprised to see his mother without a trace of being a 'fresh' widow except for her sad face.

Unlike *Brahmin* and *Chhetry* widows, she did not show any change of attire. She wore ornaments, the *kundali* (Jyapu's typical gold earrings), the red *tika*, the bangles, Silver-chain around her neck, the usual hand woven, black frock, the *patasi*, with red margin: nothing that showed she now was a widow. I accepted it without a question, as their tradition.

The following winter, one day *Babucha* came alone to tend the crop. He said,

> *I cannot play with you; I need to work and reach home before nightfall. I have to cook my own meal. I am alone, all alone at home.*

I felt sorry for him and I was sad I lost a playmate for the time. I then became curious to dig out more of his story. I was now interested to know how he would live.

> *My mother got married to a Jyapu man at Pulchowk, not far from our home at Na-tole. She lives with her new husband.*
> *Can't you go to live with your mother and the new father?' I asked.*
> *No I cannot leave my house. There is no one to look after it, the grain, and the field. It is my new destiny that I have to live with.*

I became no less sad, and he looked deeply unhappy telling me all this. But that was also the moment when I became interested to watch the *Jyapu* more intensely.

The fourth thing that impressed me about the *Jyapu* way of life was the egalitarian way the meals were shared out. One morning I stayed on to share a meal with *Chhabahale* Dai, with my youngest *Jyapu* 'brother' Hari and his mother and his five sisters.

The cooking was done with rice straw as fuel. Cooking with rice straw was tedious. One needed to tend the fire and push new bundle of straw into the open fire place in quick succession. One could not leave the fireplace not even for a minute, lest the fire went out quickly. That is what people meant when they would say, '*logne swasniko jhagada paral ko aago*' (quarrel between spouses is like a flame for only a brief second).

The food was ready, a simple rice and vegetable meal. Hari's mother spread all the plates around, for us. The size of the plates differed according to who was to get what portion of the meal. She first placed rice on the plates. The portion was divided according to adults and children; according to who was going to do what kind of work in the field that day. The rice pot was emptied and she *rang a bell* inside the pot and placed it on the ash heap, upside down. The same was done with the cooked vegetable. There was no second serving to come. It was so fair, I found.

Back home, whose ever turn it was to cook the meal, my mother or Grandmother, not only ate last but after everybody else was satisfied. Some would even ask for a third serving. What was left, if at all, in the pots was eaten by the cook.

Sometimes it paid to cook less tasty dishes in order to have something left in the pots. That I found was always punishing the cook. In our case it was usually my mother who was to eat last. *Jyapu* possessed higher social values in life than us *Panday* I presume!

Immersed in Spirituality

I was ignorant of the different religions. I was not even aware of the concept of religion. My devotion or my faith was not associated with one particular religion or one form of deity. I could not see differences between religions, or that the different forms of deity mattered. I never had a religious class to augment or sharpen my spirituality. I only had faith in God! In the later part of my life I realized that devotion to spirituality was for overcoming temptations and to empower myself to subdue my aggression, as a born Leo (*Sinharashi*), always seeking kicks and adventures. When I overcame my temptations many found me naive of day-to-day intrigues so that people could try to take advantage of me.

I started to do *puja* regularly at home early on; took it as my divine duty. My parents were glad that I did it. But the *puja* of Lord Bhairav on the southern side of our house across the main road and 200m on the other side to the north towards the crossings of Purnachandi and Pulchok took time from my morning strolls. To reach to the two Bhairavs, just two little shapeless boulders, far from the imagination of the artist(s) who sculpted the fiercely erotic *Un-Matta* Bhairav of Pashupati Nath inspiring feminine frigidity, I had to face the rising sun which made me feel I had the blessings and protection from the Bhairav, the deity for physical strength and inner security.

In the years of my absence from home I felt I was slowly being unplugged from my culture, estranged from friends and uprooted from my heritage. So I decided to be back to where I came from, to whom I belonged, without condition.

I have no imagination of the kind of face I carried around, even looking in the mirror at my image; some feared seeing me, others were cautious of me. It was not possible to know what was in my appearance that scared others. What was hidden behind my face? Somebody at home told me I was like a 'tiger'.

I knew whom and what to trust. I wanted to be good to others, including animals and plants. For me they were an important part of us or we were an important part of them.

'Amusing' Moments

Growing up among six siblings was a fun. I was free from many chores my elder siblings performed and was free to play with my friends who would gather in our house. I sometimes wondered why so many kids from the neighborhood came over to play in our garden and with me and my siblings. The elder siblings had their playmates from their age groups.

We got frequent visits by our Gadai Fupu, Father's distant sister. She was the best story teller I have ever met.

Whenever she asked me what I wanted from her I would wish for only one thing: that she tell me a story. She could spin out tales of fictitious characters, and the scary deities. She would tell them in a voice to enliven the tales with the atmosphere of the story that sounded not immediately frightening at all, even the ones with demons and ghosts.

Being 'a hard earned son' (because of the astrologer's prediction and the ritual of adaptation that I had to undergo in a *Jyapu* family), I received extra attention and love from my mother and grandmother. I was conscious of their feelings towards me.

The Pet Birds: I could have anything I wanted as a pet during my childhood. While we were living in the twin house with the straw-roof at Jawalakhel, I got a parrot. It was able to mimic our words. We would lock the cage at night and hang it outside the front window, facing east, with water and some grains in little pots. It was always happy to receive us in the morning and remained talkative during whole daylight time.

I don't know exactly who taught it to say human words. It must have been my elder sisters or neighbors, while I was away at school. For every time a beggar or a *yogi* came on morning round, the parrot yelled to warn us: *Chor Ayo Chor Ayo*! (Thief comes, thief comes!) We knew what to expect from his yelling. We would come out with a handful of grain or coins to give to the beggars.

One fine morning I discovered that our parrot was gone. We found the cage open. It could not open the cage itself. That morning we found the padlock on the courtyard. How come we did not hear anything at night, somebody climbing on the front roof and reaching the cage? Was it perhaps stolen by a *yogi* or a beggar, who was hurt by its yelling *Chor Ayo Chor Ayo*? Somebody took it away and killed it, perhaps. I was having so many different thoughts all in sadness I did not want to have a parrot anymore, not anymore in a cage I promised myself.

My parents convinced me that a myna would not be a problem to keep. Unlike a parrot, it would not pick up our words easily. We could train it the way we wanted it to speak, and not let others do it.

I wondered why it had to spell peoples' words at all! Did it not have its own voice? I did get a present, a dark bird with yellow beak, like a *sarong* bird except for the color of the feathers. I had expected it to be more colorful than the parrots. So a myna is black! It did not matter. I could make friends with it too. That was still in the straw roofed twin house where we lived for a few more years. I forgot how we lost the myna too.

When Father built his first house, the red house, around 1950, of the several promises made to me by my parents, a Chinese duck was one and I got it. It was dark with a little purple, on its feathers, and the dark red comb was beautiful to look at. Father got it from a friend. It was slow moving around but it was not afraid of people. It enjoyed our company. It would follow me in the courtyard. I loved him.

One day it got very sick. It would not eat or drink. No one in our house knew what was wrong or how to help it. There was no help available, as the veterinary service was far from our reach. Mother, as always could not see any animals suffering. One fine morning she said to me,

> *It will not recover. You should kill it and not let it suffer any more.*
> *Mother, I cannot commit a sin, can I?*
> *I am the one who is telling you to kill it. The one ordering the killing carries all the sin and not you.*

That was a different Mother. How could she give me an order to kill a living being? She was the one in our house who loved animals so much. Hesitatingly, I said ok. I should not let the beast suffer more. She gave me a *khukuri*. I was supposed to hit it once on its neck with the sharp bladed *khukuri*. I was used to handling *khukuri* but only for cutting branches of trees. I closed my eyes and hit it with all my might. Instantly the head got separated. The body lay on a pool of blood but still throbbing and slightly moving up and down. I had a traumatic time for days and was tormented for a long time. That was the first and the last beast I ever killed in my life. But the guilty feeling persists to this day.

It was an irony and contradiction to my fate and feelings that I took a foray to jungle battle fields during prime time of my life. But I was spared from the killing fields. Today it gives me things to reminisce about and regard sin in conjunction with the Maoists' excesses. So the sinners are the leaders who order killing, are they? No not the army of young followers, who carried the murder weapons given by their leaders. When will justice be meted to the real sinners and guilty?

It was in my uncle's 2-room-flat in the house of a Manandhar family at Chikamungal, Kathmandu, where I saw different types of pigeons. I requested Father to bring me some pigeons. Over time I had three types of pigeons: a swarm of *malewa* (the wild one, hill pigeon), *seto parewa* (the white ones) with feathers on the foot, and the *chhirbire parewa* (the red-white), and a pair of white doves (the *dhukur*).

The *malewa* would bring friends every evening, some would say 'mistresses', to stay overnight at our house. Their preferred place for roosting was the tile roof cornice, by the terrace. For the white pigeons I had wooden pigeon house made on the lower terrace. In the morning they would fly down and dance around on the *Dubo* (*Cynodon dactylon*) grassy courtyard my Father maintained, meticulously.

But the problem with the Rosa white pair was that they preferred to perch on a bamboo hanging horizontally. They could not roost; all the eggs fell down on the store floor in the attic. But they were the best flyers. During the dry season, letting them fly after school time was really amusing. They took up to 3 hours to get enough flight, and dived and landed on my arms or shoulder. I really enjoyed it.

Cats and Dogs: My fun with the pigeons was time consuming. It required my full attention and I was taking less notice of my cat, Suri. That cost me dear. One day early in the morning, as usual, I went to the attic storeroom to feed my red-white pigeons. On a flat basket, a *nanglo*, the two of them were laid close to each other as if a human hand was behind it, they lay on their backs, and their gullet pouches (craws) eaten up.

Who could have done it? The cat looked guilty. Suri followed me to the store room, as if she wanted to show me the ghastly trophy. I checked my Suri the cat. She still had some blood stains on her fur around the mouth. I was never so furious with her as at that moment. The pigeons were the best flyers I had. They were semi-wild, and with their red-white spots looked very lovely and behaved very friendly towards me. I could hold them in my hand and caress them. My whole fun of having pigeons at home was gone with their life!

That evening I pushed Suri from the attic window to the garden below, as punishment. She landed on her four legs and ran away. A few days later I saw Suri on the tile roof of the neighbor Mritunjay's house. Mritunjay was the Bengali teacher brought to Nepal by the Ranas to teach their kids English. I wondered how Suri sneaked into the house and climbed up to the roof! All the doors and windows of the house had remained shuttered for ages, after the big Rana, Juddha abdicated. There was nobody in the house. We used to call it a 'hunted house.'

My challenge was to get the cat down and back home. All my persuasion was in vain. She could not find her way out. I mobilized friends, opened the main door by force and reached the window on the top floor. I had carried some food and water in a cup for her. She came over to the window where I could catch and hold her. She was hungry and very thirsty. She was just happy to be home again, and all was forgiven.

Then one chilly morning following winter, I cried and cried! Everybody came to the north side of the house. Suri lay dead, apparently without any wounds or evidence of beating, under the plum tree, below the house eaves. She was just dead, how could it be? We speculated that it might have been the *Huticheel*; a kind of hawk. If it casts its shadow on a cat, they say the cat dies. That happened in a moonlit night! The cat had 'heart failure.' She was stiff and cold. For me the reason why she died was that she did not take the punishment I meted out to her lightly; that she was depressed and died. I carried a guilty feeling, and I was sorry for her. But when she was alive I loved her and had a lot of fun with her.

During my childhood we had one or another kind of dogs and cats. Father loved them and they were close to him. My cat, Suri, and the dog Kali (Alsatian) got on well with each other. Kali and *Suri,* both would eat their meals from a large plate and each had its portion separated for them to share on the plate, peacefully.

Normally, Kali would finish up quickly and would be begging Suri to leave some behind for him. When Kali came close to Suri's portion on the plate she would give a loving slap on Kali's face. Kali did not mind. But surely Suri would leave a small portion of its food for Kali before going out to sit and lick her paws. It was always a very amusing moment for me, that I never wanted to miss it.

Over time Kali was closer to me and had to be chained before I left for the school, two kilometers away. Hours later, Mother would set him free. One day, it seems, Kali protested being chained every day before I left for the school. He barked loudly and Mother thought he needed to do his call-of-nature rounds. But he just disappeared. They could not find him in the garden, in the house and also not in the neighborhood either. They all got worried.

At my school that day, head down, tail pulled between its legs, a big dog slipped into my 4th grade class room at Patan High School, Patan Dhoka. My eyes were fixed on the blackboard. All the students and teacher started shouting loudly, 'Kukur Kukur!' in panic! The dog came straight towards me and sat under my desk, put its head on my lap. I looked at it: it was my Kali. I was wondering how it made it to my school and to me; she had never left house before and never had walked that far.

On the way to our school one would find many stray dogs. They would attack any new beast coming into their area in a pack. Kali must have played nice with the stray dogs too and did not pose a threat. I was happy that he managed to reach me without a bruise. I assured the teacher and colleagues that they need not fear my Kali.

On our way back Kali brushed my legs with her head and walked quietly. The stray dogs did not try to hound him other than to give him some loud shrieks. Mother, Father and my sisters were relieved that Kali was not lost.

It must have been a year after the school episode that I had a big surprise. One day, I came back from the school only to find Kali nowhere in the house and garden. All my sisters stood frozen and looked in the other direction. I feared the worst and started to cry.

After he came home from his office Father told me that a good friend of his from Birgunj was here and had taken a liking to Kali. He wanted to take Kali back with him and Father could not resist. Just like that, so easily he could take my dog! I cried even louder and longer that afternoon.

Then Father promised me that he would bring a nice dog which I would surely have fun with. Not long after, he did fetch one. It was a Golden Retriever, named Holi, from a friend in Tripureswor, in Kathmandu town, across the Bagmati River. He became my friend in no time. We would go for long walks and run around. He would carry a stick in his mouth with which I could scare stray dogs closing in.

A few months later, one day, we heard a dog barking outside the house gate. It could not be him! But the barking was quite familiar. I could not wait to open the gate. Surely it was Kali at our house door! Everybody wondered how he made it; over such a long distance, over a distance of hundred and more kilometers. Father told me how his friend from Birgunj had taken him.

The two of them had taken a ride on an open truck sitting on the pile of goods to reach Birgunj. Father assumed Kali memorized the route, the smells, landscape etc. Later I learned that dogs, cats and pigeons are good at it, and have a good homing instinct with a built in biological smell detector and a bio-compass in their bodies.

He looked well looked after and had also put on some weight. I was overjoyed to see him. I did not let him loose from my arms and sight. He was so happy to be home. We saw some change in him as well. He was friendlier to all of us in the house and not only to me as earlier. It looked like he had missed us all! He went around sniffing and looking for Suri too.

Now keeping both big dogs at home was out of the question. So Father contacted his friend in Kathmandu and asked him to take back his nice Holi, the Golden Retriever. Father's friend agreed. I hugged Holi and said good bye. Kali lived with us again with his favorite cat Suri, cows, pigeons, ducks and hens, till her last breath.

The Bowl with Fish: I was perhaps around eight years old when Father had brought home some goldfish. We had to change the water regularly. One day when I was doing the ritual, the glass jar fell down; the water spilled, fishes flowed out and were jumping and panting in panic. I had no idea how I should rescue them. There was no glass jar and by the time I could get a pot and some water it was just too late for the fishes to survive. I cried for a long time. I promised myself, I would never again have fish in a glass jar, in fact not in any pots. It was just too cruel.

The Fearsome Fights of Bulls: One of the few entertainments available at Jawalakhel during my childhood was the bull fights. It was not organized by any man. Sometimes at most the bulls were a bit provoked or encouraged to fight by the people who had nothing worthwhile to do. It was the bulls' instinct that inspired them to play the robust game for supremacy their way.

The most famous bulls of Lalitpur and their soldier-entourage made their homes at Jawalakhel and Patan Tundikhel. I did not exactly know where the bulls of Lagankhel stayed for the nights, perhaps under the open sky even in the coldest of the months, but the ones of Jawalakhel had permanent shelters built for them, and the garages of chariot wheels and *Dhoma* of *Matchhendra* (the long large crooked log placed between the wheels, depicting the Bhairav deity) were available for them. During *Matchhendra* festivals, usually in summer, they had to vacate shelters for the devotees for about 4 days.

The bulls of Lagankhel were led by a massive Jersey bull with the loudest roar. The fights of the bulls of Jawalakhel were led by a sturdy black Zebu, slightly smaller than the one from Lagankhel. But it behaved all the same as if it was the strongest and biggest of all bulls. The roars had to be as loud as the Jersey bull's.

Both groups had followers and spectator bulls. Some, the *Acchame*, were almost dwarflike others were massive, tall and fat. Some were red, black or white. They would walk in tandem, the smallest following the bigger one in a procession of 6-7 bulls. They too would run when the lead bull ran. It was a scene worth looking at.

Each one of the leader bulls would challenge the other. As soon as a group of bulls felt energized, it took some followers and went on a rampage to challenge the other group of bulls. That started happening mostly at the end of monsoon, by which time they had accumulated enough energy in their bodies from green fodder. They would walk in the middle of the road in a column, with sniffing and snorting. Then they ruled the street.

The roar of the lead bull would make us expect a challenging fight in the making. The grassy grounds of Lagankhel and Jawalakhel were the best place for the fights of the bulls, but after each fight the grass suffered, since the hoofs were dug sometimes deep to get a good hold on the ground. After the fight was over the defeated bull would run away fast. The smaller ones of the group would join the victorious group, until a new challenger emerged and established its own group and defended the turf and territory. So it went on.

A comparatively small but mighty white lead bull of Jawalakhel once lost the defensive fight. While running away it fell into the well located in front of the St. Xavier School at Pulchowk about 100m from the Tiger Gate of Jawalakhel, which had statues of sitting leopards on top of both pillars. The fire brigade rescued it by filling the well with water and the bull floated up, people pulled it out and saved his life. The historic well is there at its original place till today, in front of the St. Xavier school.

New Matchhendra Festivals Using an Earthen Pot in the Garden: Most of the winter was normally dry and dusty. After the fields were ploughed, we could play in the maize field without any rules to follow, nor any one restricting us. In my case it was our own land.

The Matchhendra Festival was the biggest one in Patan when the image of the small red god was pulled all around the town and later taken to the neighboring village of Bungamati. We friends would gather and make a road to mimic the road to Bungamati by stamping the soil. We would use our 'kataro', an old earthen pot from Khokana village used for making yoghurt and would make wheels of clay, dry them and start erecting the Matchhendra chariot, with the upper part made out of reed stems. We had plenty of reeds in our garden to erect the chariot. Mini idols of Matchhendra were sold during the main festival and we had one to put in the chariot, to make it a true Matchhendra *Rath*. On a given day we had the festival: '*Hoste Hainse Ha Haaa!*' For many winters, that was the game we played and enjoyed.

'Not so Amusing' Moments

The Water Mill: I was perhaps around 10, when I had a long holiday and spent it in Bihebar, with my father's maternal uncles. The youngest of them had a water mill that operated right in front of his house. The stream was good and lovely to watch as it cascaded down the valley.

The water mill impressed me a lot. I spent most of my time in and around the mill playing with its water at the intake of the mill. I was there almost every day. I do not know how I did it but once I shut its exit flow and let it go into the mill wooden penstock pipe. There was a cry. Inside the mill there were ladies who were sweeping the milled flour and collecting it. The water in uncontrolled volume not only turned the wheel but also sprang up to the milling room and damaged their just milled flour. I had a time to explain but the ladies demanded replacement, and they got it.

Punished, for Cutting a Moustache: Father's distant relative, whom I used to call Thulba, was taking a midday nap in Dadhi Rana's house. I respected him, perhaps more because I feared him, and kept my distance from him. His long moustache made him a frightening figure and this attracted my aggression though in fact Thulba was a very loving person.

I wanted to test whether he was sleeping. He was lying on his side, asleep and snoring. He would not budge. It was good that he was fast asleep. Every time he snored his moustache moved up and down. It looked so funny. I thought of showing him what I could do to him. Armed with a little pair of scissors, I went to work on his moustache very carefully. But I could only cut the left part of the long moustache short. The other side was partly covered by his cheek and I could not do it without waking him up. Then I went into hiding.

I was watching him from a bush in the garden. He came out of his room trying to touch his moustache with both hands. On one side he could not find it. He looked really funny. Surprised, he went quickly to look into a mirror, came out furious and was loudly challenging,

Whoever it is who cut my moustache will have to suffer.

My laughing broke out; he heard me and came right to me to confront me. I could have hardly imagined and expected the wrath he had against me. It seemed I had hurt his pride.

So you rascal damaged my years of work and my pride.

He started to beat me but, unexpectedly, not that badly. However, he reported it to my family the next day.

The warning from my parents had a bearing on me, and I never attempted even to talk about other funny moustaches I had seen, like the ones of K.I. Singh. I had seen on him and his followers around Jawalakhel sporting the *KIsingh* brand moustache.

One morning, K.I. Singh as the Prime Minister, came to make a surprise inspection of the small AM Radio Station at the North East corner of Jawalakhel Zoo. We kids were playing on the grassy ground. We were curious to see a Prime Minister, for the first time in our lives, with the longest moustache we had ever seen. He came in an open Willis Jeep, in under vest and trousers. One soldier and a driver were with him in the Jeep, without dignity. That was a bad omen for him; he was PM only for 129 days from 14th of July 1957. There was one staunch follower of K.I. Singh near our place; we all shouted at him *KIsingh, KIsingh!* Later, in the early 1970s, K.I. Sing became district chairman of far west district, Doti.

The Holi Festival and the Man in White Punishing Me in Silence: It was Fagu Purne time. We were playing with colored water. I had prepared a bucket full of red color and a homemade bamboo syringe out of reeds. I stood behind the gate lurking. A man dressed in white was passing by. I was attracted by his white clothes and thought it would give a good splash of red color for me to enjoy. I let him go further down towards Pulchowk until I could see his back in full. Then I went out with the syringe full of colored water and pushed it behind him till he looked like he was painted red from his back to his legs. The spray was substantial, and it was dripping.

He turned to face me, the culprit, holding a still dripping syringe. He opened his eyes as wide as he could do and came towards me. Shivering, I ran into the house. He followed and caught me by my collar. He was merciless. He thrashed me so much I've never forgotten it.

My mother came to my rescue and begged for pardon. It was my mistake. I did not know that what he was wearing was mourning dress, and Mother explained that the white outfit meant he was mourning his mother or father's death. That was a sin I committed, I could not have regretted my act more. He left our house without a word.

Horse Riding: My first lessons of horse riding took place on the *Jawalakhel* ground, where Rana horses would be grazing. Some horses were partially invalid and unable to do service, but for us skinny kids they looked strong enough to ride. During my childhood years, it was my fun to ride horses. Naturally, none of the horses was equipped with saddle and reins. The horses were just abandoned by the owners. So they were on their own and mixed with the cattle while grazing around Jawalakhel. I had the chance to ride them one by one.

I remember once, riding a white one, tallest among the horses, I had to jump to be on its back, by holding its long mane. My first shock was to come as the horse galloped fiercely, and I was scared to death. It took me straight towards the door of the watchman's hut, *paleghar* of the zoo.

It was open. I bent down forward almost sticking to its back and entered through the door, its upper part was barely few inches above my body. There were two watchmen shouting, from the room inside,

Watch out!

I thought I could now raise my head. To my surprise we had just entered the room through the first door. There was another door to follow that led to the Zoo garden. Before I could duck a bit I hit the door bolt of the upper part of the second door, and I got a fitting punishment for my trespassing. It just dug my head. The horse was heading towards the deep circular Pelican pond on the left of the zoo. In panic I jumped down a few meters away from the pond. The fall did not hurt me, but I was covering the wound on my head with my palm and saw whitish liquid flowing down from my head reaching my eyes and nose. I noticed I was seriously injured. It was almost the end of my days of joy. How could I face my mother?

I had to pretend at home that all was well with me. It hurt so much that even after the healing of the wound I could not comb my hair properly. When Mother wanted to help me comb my hair, I avoided her touching my head, in case she would ask me many questions. I did not let her give me a head massage either, which she very often did for me when I was small. The tragic ride was kept between me and the white horse as a secret event. But my wish to go on looking for a ride was always there. I had not learnt a bit from the deadly ride into the zoo.

One day a friend of Father came on horseback. It was afternoon. Father and his friend were chatting in the living room on the first floor. There was nobody else in the garden. The horse was chained outside the small gate, on the road. I went closer to the beautiful, tall and attractive horse. I could not control myself. It had a saddle and everything for a rider still on its back. I could not have expected more.

I untied him, jumped on his back, pulled the *lagam* (reins), sat immediately on the saddle and took control. The iron stirrup hanging on a long strap was too long for the legs of a kid like me, so I inserted my feet into the strap loop.

The horse did not like me neither did he find me a good rider. He was sniffing loudly, rejecting me, trying to scare me. It started to behave wildly, but that did not scare me either. Then suddenly it galloped towards Pulchowk. When we came to Pulchowk, it galloped further wildly and ran down the slope towards Kopundole, over to the Bagmati Bridge.

I felt he was intent on putting me down and throwing me overboard to the river below. It could not and so it gave up. But I had no control of the horse. It galloped on to Tripureswor, to Tundikhel and made a long round of Tundikhel before stopping at where today the army HQ is located. It was tired. All over its body it had like the foam from soap sweating and wet, panting and hot. But it stood quiet. I got down and started patting him and thanked him in my mind. He understood my gestures. It even looked at me, lovingly I guess! His eyes were communicating.

After a while I mounted again. It made a light enjoyable gallop, and slowly we galloped towards Jawalakhel and both safely arrived home. I put him at the same place as before so that Father's friend would not notice it. Or so I thought. Father and his friends were still in the room, chatting by now over two hours. I thought,

'Now that I am home; they won't notice my mischief. I am safe from punishment'.

That was childish; not abnormal for a kid like me. A few minutes later, Father and his friend came down to the garden. The friend was leaving. When he saw his horse so tired and exhausted and full of soapy and foamy he shouted,

Hey! You my boy!

Me?

What happened to my horse?

I was dead scared to tell him. He insisted that I tell him the truth, why the horse looked awful. When I started to tell him what had happened and that I almost fell down but clung on to the saddle, he was just shocked. My terrifying ride to Kathmandu Tundikhel was just unbelievable to him.

But Father told him that I was not a liar. How come Father supported me? He was unaware of my riding adventures on the grassy ground of Jawalakhel and the incident that had almost killed me, from which I suffered for a long time. I had not even told Mother the whole story of my nasty horse rides. Father's friend congratulated me.

> *You know kid; my horse has never allowed anyone else on its back, except me, let alone galloped that far. You are a good rider.* I was elated beyond doubt.

Riding a Motorbike: As usual Father's friend had parked his motorcycle outside his house at Ekantakuna. He had kept the engine running, for his ride to his office in Kathmandu.

It was a Honda and was almost noiseless, always in the best condition. When I saw it the first time, I was determined that I would ride it one day. That was when awaiting the results of SLC exams and I was barely 12 years of age.

I had never touched it before with my fingers. I had only watched the man how he would kick start and drive out. I thought I had enough skill and guts to give it a try. That day, after I passed the SLC exams I said, *it is my day*.

Time was running out. Before the man came out to ride it to his office, I pushed it to the road and started it and drove off. I knew where the brakes were located and how to apply them.

The first shift of the gear was good and slow, I did not know it had more gears to be changed as per the speed gained. So I did not have to worry about gear shifting.

I had just arrived at the crossroads of Mangalbajaar from Lagankhel. There was somebody on a bicycle coming towards me from the Krishnamandir side. I thought he was turning left towards Sundhara and I rode on. But the guy suddenly turned his bike towards the direction I was coming from.

Bang! We collided. The whole thing was happening in front of the District Police Office; promptly they came down to get me. There I was in police custody.

I had to sign a paper that I would bear the cost of repairs of the bicycle. In the meantime the owner of the motorbike came to the police looking for his bike and got it back in good condition, only slightly scratched on the front mud guard.

The brunt of the accident was on the fragile bicycle. The police did not let me go. I sat at the window and hoped to see a familiar face to come over and free me.

In the afternoon, Kedar baje, uncle of my friend Bindumadhab who had a clothing shop at Mahapal, was walking below the police window. He was an acquaintance of my father. He was surprised but readily agreed to bail me out, with his signature.

I had some small savings because at the Coronation of the King Mahendra, I had been one of the 25 scouts selected to participate in the ceremony, march past and help with the crowd. I got a reward of Rs.25. I had kept the money in my piggy bank. Mother knew about it.

But now I had to use it. It cost Rs.13 to repair the bicycle (Rs.8 to replace the wheel rim, Rs.4 to replace the chains and RS.1 for labor) in a bicycle shop at Nagbahal gate, Patan.

The Awe, the Pain and the Fear

There were occasions combining my visit to my eldest sister Sita at Sanglekhola. Her husband took me to the high hill above Tokha and we would gaze at Himals over Rasuwa Nuwakot. I would be so happy to see hills behind hills and, behind and above hills the White Mountains. My expectation was for a wide world, large plains. Sometimes I felt betrayed by the hills for shrinking my world and narrowing my horizon.

In the early fifties the red house was under construction. The roof work was under progress. One bright morning Father was on the uppermost part of the house that was ready, planning for the roof structure and checking the work so far completed. He was placing beams, and I wanted to join him. He was hesitant, but I insisted, so he pulled me up.

But it was no fun standing on the unfinished wall perching and balancing. I was terrified to be so high up and wanted to get down quickly.

I jumped down and landed on a piece of wood that had a nail sticking out, about 7-10cm long. It pierced through my right foot and I saw the nail come out the top of my foot; the piece of wood was under me, and the pain was immense. I could not even yell it hurt so much. Such was the pain; it is engraved in my brain till now.

Mother called a shoemaker. In the absence of a proper hospital, the shoemaker separated my foot from the nail on the wood. I do not know whether he used any medicine to disinfect and treat the wound. That would have been too much to expect from a shoemaker. After a few days, the foot was swollen and emitted a bad odor. The shoemaker came back with his *banko* (leather cutting tool) and cut the wound on the sole, puss came out, and I could see layers over layers of skin. Over time it was not painful. The sole was numb, but the wound did not heal.

The cut the shoemaker made was deep, and it was not going to heal. After I got a pair of cotton shoes and a stick, Mother took me to the Patan Hospital at Lagankhel. With it began my first of many visits and journeys to the Patan Hospital, where today a mental hospital is housed.

It was the year 1955, as a boy of 11, that I developed the habit of going to watch the Bagmati river flood oozing out of the Chovar Gorge. The smoky water vapor rising from the mouth of the gorge and the surging flood almost touching the suspension bridge over the gorge attracted me between the fear and awe I never imagined before. That water could be so crushing and catastrophic, was beyond my comprehension.

Once a big wooden trunk locked with a large Tibetan padlock, came rushing down, at another time trunks of trees. So many things came floating down. I got scared at the time when a dead body appeared above the water and went floating by. Yet I was too interested not to pass the floods, every day after school. A run to the bridge was not a distance to scare me come what may.

There was another occasion when my fear and my desire to see and experience things reached an awful point. A DC-3 plane, from the 2nd World War era, had crashed during landing at the Tribhuwan airport, then called

Gaucharan. It was noon, and I was in the school. The news of the crash reverberated into our ears in no time. At the striking of the gong I dashed out, not telling others where I was going. I do not know how I ran over the fields and paths to the crash site, south of the tarmac, below the wall. The plane had turned 180 degrees hit a house slashed it into two by its right wing working like a Khukuri and settled towards the north of the farmer's house, ablaze. When I reached I could still see smoke and some fires.

That much I could watch. I had no fear. But when the police personnel started to pull out lifeless torsos without arms, feet and head, burnt black and smelling, and spread on the ground nearby, all that was left of the 11 of the passengers, I had no idea with what to compare the image flashing in front of me. I could think of the buffalos or goats slaughtered by the butchers at Kasaintole. They started to take the torsos away.

For the first time I was not only frightened of what I was looking at, I was extremely terrified, shivering and crying deeply, noiselessly. My curiosity was not to be suppressed. I was wondering what would happen to the dead bodies. I followed the police and others.

Unknowingly I was in the funeral procession. The bodies were placed on eleven *ghats* south of Pashupati temple along the river. Nobody could identify who was cremating whom. For the dead it did not matter. But for the relatives it must have been extremely painful.

There was the smell of burning flesh, and the smoke over the sky belched from the 11 pyres so close side by side that one could disturb the other. People mostly onlookers, friends and relatives were all in their saddest mood and silently mourning. In the crowd one could not hear sobbing of the closest and dearest ones. For my age it was just too much of a shock.

I reached home before dark. Then I had to explain to Mother, change my clothes and take quick sluice from the bucket. The images were imprinted in my brain. But sleep was not going to be the same for nights. Night after night, in my disturbed sleep, I shrieked and babbled of my fear of the torsos. All that kept Mother awake and she would admonish me again and again.

Why on earth did you go there?

My inquisitive nature was also my curse in this tragic event. I promised I would never go to see another crash if I could avoid it.

As youth whenever I had some little time to play truant, I would go to the cave of Chovar. I thought it was a big deal to enter the cave. I was not alone. My friend Munindra Rana-Magar often came along.

Sports and Games

As a young boy I played football, table tennis and a bit of hockey. Football was my favorite sport during my school time and Ping Pong much later. Football then was played mostly during the rainy season on the Jawalakhel ground in front of the Jawalakhel Zoo. We avoided the game during the dry period. That way the grassy ground remained undamaged, so we had a nice grassy, slippery ground for the annual games and for cattle grazing during the rainy season.

During the winter the ground was used by grazing animals. All the local cattle and abandoned horses occupied the grassland. Sometime we would also see jackal roaming around among the cattle, in the middle of the day.

After getting injured I stopped playing football with much enthusiasm. It happened because a rival was just jealous after I had made a goal against his team. He stepped on my foot and pushed me backwards causing a very painful and lasting sprain I could do nothing about.

During the monsoon season the River Bagmati would swell to a treacherous level of murky water, but the youngest daughter of Subba Kancchabaje, Bindudidi, would take us kids to swim there anyway. We would just wade into the river without a second thought and oblivious of the danger in the flood water. We had learnt to swim in the river very quickly.

Yet, I remember once being swept down by the river from Sankhamul to the Bagmati bridge of Kopundole, on the Lalitpur side without touching land or fathoming the depth. I was scared and feared for my life. I did not know where the others had reached. Somehow I managed to hold a small branch strong enough to support me under the iron bridge. From there I marched home wet and virtually naked. I think I still had under pants on, but I'm not sure. I learned the others had left the river earlier. Thank god, we all survived.

In winter we would swim downstream to Kalmochan. The water was clean and there was not much to wade into, but the white sand, warm water and fishes tempted us to lie for hours on our backs, half submerged.

Catch Me Games of Winter: *Telakasa* (run and catch me), *Lukamari* (hide and seek) and *Kathikasa* (stick chase): Three types of this game could be played on an open field. One with open eyes: There was a *dum (untouchable)* who was the defender, and his object was to touch one of the others to make the player next *dum*. It was slightly strenuous. Another was the *dum* blind folded and seeks to get hold of other player and the rest of the game was similar to open *Telkasa* but it had to be in much smaller ground and so less strenuous. The third type of *Telakasa* is *Lukamari* when all the others hide and the *dum* goes to find any one, who then becomes the next *dum*.

Kathi kasa: Each one of us would hold a stick as tall as we were. The *dum* would be selected in various ways. There would be a chanting of a child's lottery song to find a person to drop his stick on the ground. The stick would be left on the ground. The others would try to flip it up with their sticks, hit it as far as possible and run. If the *dum* touches the one tossing the stick, the *dum* is freed and the person who was caught would become a new *dum*.

When we had *Kathi kasa* it took us all the way to Lagankhel, about two kilometers, and back. There used to be a WWII vintage American Ford lorry which was hauling rice straw from *Harsiddhi* village for the palace animals once a day. I do not remember any other private vehicle plying the 15m wide road. It was virtually a grassy field all the way to *Lagankhel* and with only a few houses right and left of the road. That remained our playground for years.

Educating Life and Life in Education

Not only were we kids coming together for games and sports, we also devoted Saturday mornings pretty frequently to keeping the playground tidy. I was leading the youth of my age of Jawalakhel. Every Saturday morning we would come together and clean the playground. We even picked up pebbles, as we would be playing barefoot. Paper and litter were eyesores. All did it willingly. That was part of the camaraderie we developed.

We also came together to read poems, stories and essays composed and written by us. Much impetus came to the literary program after we established the first library at Jawalakhel, the Addhyayan Griha. Fattebahadur Thapa, Purnabahadur Rana-Magar, Basu Rimal 'Yatree', and me; we had 'rented' a little abandoned house in front of the sweet shops of Jawalakhel. Although the ground floor was damp and not so friendly it was the best we could get. But it was free for the purpose of running a library. The upper floor was used by a Khadka family, whose son was a vehicle driver to a rich man nearby. They looked after the library's security at night. The owner of the old house Mohanbahadur had vanished to Dehradoon ages before, following ex-Premier Juddha who had rescued him and his brother from Gokarna temple where they were eking out living as orphan kids without family identity. Juddha Sumsher gave them a name sounding similar to our family, without legitimacy to do that. Mohanbahadur's family thought we were related, but that was not so. They had lost the roots of their ancestry.

We went from house to house to collect books from parents and young people. They donated, voluntarily. We accepted any kind of books, but we had to be a bit choosy. Books for children or as part of school curriculum or literature were our favorites. There were not many bookshelves. A simple system of running the library was worked out. It only mattered that our friends read. I had brought along a little knowledge of getting a 'library' organized beginning at home.

Very early, Father allowed me to make use of the east facing ground floor room of the red house he built, for all my *'playful'* purposes. There was a wall cupboard. I used the cupboard for my first *'library.'* The books for it came from my own collection, old school books inherited from relatives, from Father, cousins and some from my playmates. Unlike now-a-days the school books were not altered or amended for years. Re-use of school books was an accepted practice by necessity. It made schooling affordable for many like me. Altogether I reckon we had about 20 things to read at home, yet we had a system of lending and receiving the books back. The first most and vociferous user was my sister Renuka. I was very strict. She was not permitted to open the cupboard and take a book out on her own.

At Addhyayan Griha, we managed it mostly turn by turn among us few friends committed running the library, voluntarily. We produced a monthly handwritten literary note book, with contributions mainly from the youth of Jawalakhel.

The inauguration took place followed by cultural events, such as reading poems, stories and essays. We had invited Mr. Satya Mohan Joshi (living now in his home at Patan aged 95), to inaugurate the library amidst multiple cultural programs and exhibitions. I remember going to the American Library at New Road and begging to borrow the photographs of the UN buildings and assembly halls. We were becoming aware of the importance of the UN. Satya Mohan supported us; he was our hero then too.

Establishment of the Mahendroday School: Jawalakhel had three faces. The motor-able road was lined by twelve Rana and Shaha palaces. Their owners were rich from the wealth gifted by the Rana Prime Ministers, who dipped their hands into the state treasury as their private 'cash boxes.' The palaces were widely scattered with large walled compounds, with circular park ways and strong iron gates. Each could be reached by vehicle or by buggies.

The other part had houses fairly well built with walled compounds but none with gates for vehicles. These belonged to *subba* (lower ranked civil officer), *hajuria* (private secretary), priests, English teacher, and the blue color henchmen of Rana regime.

Behind the back of these palaces and walled houses were the red smeared straw roof mud huts used by poor servants, smiths, Magar and shoemakers, for all purpose the slum or servant quarters of the Ranas and their henchmen. Father owned his first house, twin red smeared straw-roofed mud huts at Jawalakhel. Years later I found a similar trend at Islamabad, in the new and planned capital of Pakistan. The societal cleft was there too, which I did not expect in an Islamic society.

The schooling opportunities were also in relation to societal status. The Rana kids got the priority to attend school. There was one at Patan Dhoka built specially for them. Even after the Ranas were sent packing and were out of power, the schooling could not improve even in the new setup. Some of us, as the first generation school going kids around in the post-Rana time got to attend the schools. We inherited the best facilities of the school; it had a scout master, a drill instructor, an art teacher and weaving classes, a rose garden, large play grounds, and game opportunities, besides having enough teachers for all subjects.

We saw a great number of kids in the red mud brick huts who never got to school. The fate of those at distant places like Chovar or Bhainsepati was much worse. In 1955, together with Subba Purnabahadur Rana (*'Kanccha Dai'*), Bhairabbahadur Khadka, and Subba Fattebahadur Thapa, I established a primary school with grade one to begin with, in bull sheds at south east corner of the grassy ground outside Jawalakhel zoo where today *Satsangh* prayers are held. We named it the Mahendroday Primary School. This was not the first school I helped establish.

Way back when I was in the lower grades at Patan High School, I had started a school for little children from the neighborhood. Was I just playing around? There was a house in my immediate neighborhood, where the owner,

Dorbahadur Pande (no kin), had kept the ground floor and the front courtyard unused. I asked him if I could use it.

It was a fun teaching little ones to make them repeat what I had done only a few years back in my primary classes. It was a pleasure to be with the kids. Two of my friends of the same age group from the neighborhood also participated to 'teach.'

The Mahendroday School was run on voluntary service. Although we did not ask for fees we had a hard time getting kids enrolled. We visited poor Dhobi parents at Dhobighat, shopkeepers of Nakhu, and reached farmers living as far as Bhainsepati and the Chovar area. The red mud brick houses around the palaces were our special targets. Parents were not happy about our crusade. But we were determined to bring their kids to the school.

During winter the classes were held on the grassy ground outside sheds. The rainy season caused havoc to the teachers and pupils. The shed was open on two sides. When rain and wind lashed we had difficulty keeping papers and straw mats, as well as the kids, dry.

We requested Yubraj Rana, the grandson of former Prime Minister Juddha Sumsher, living in a palace (today it is the Administrative Staff College) nearby to donate his Dhansar (paddy godown), almost a 100m long house to 'our' Mahendroday Bidhyalay. We took his refusal as an insult. Well, education was never a priority of the Rana families anyway, and they would even deny it to common folks.

After some time we were able to use the Jawalakhel *Shivalay*, the marble temple. The Ranas whose elders had built the temple protested. We had no time to listen to them. Then we got some more youth volunteer teachers.

The Tibetan Refugee Centre started a Bhrikuti Tibetan Primary School near their carpet weaving center. Over time, the government recognized both schools. The two schools were merged by the government and renamed Mahendra-Bhrikuti School. The school is located near the Ring Road Chowk of Jawalakhel, less than 400 m from the place where we created the first primary school of the Jawalakhel area.

The Terror of Yakthumba

There was a time when Yakthumba (a Limbu by ethnicity) ruled the street. The *Muktisena* (Liberation Army under the Congress Party) whose chief he was, were barracked at Lagankhel.

Every morning his troops were on foot marching with music and bugles while ahead of them Yakthumba rode on a white horse swinging his baton and passed through the Jawalakhel roads almost every day.

Whether out of sheer need, because of the poor government's failure in the 1950s to pay them salaries, or whether they were an undisciplined criminal minded rogue army like the PLA of the Maoists, they created havoc in the localities. Robbery, rape and looting became routine for some time. The incidence of a rape case at the *Halwai* shop at Jawalakhel created panic in our little community. This was the first time that I came to know of that such a thing could happen in our society. The culprit, a soldier of the

Muktisena had entered house through the first floor window. The case disappeared in hush-hush. Numerous housebreakings were reported. The nights were scary. State security apparatus was nonexistent.

Our community felt a sense of solidarity. We were united and organized to protect and defend our families '*from the police force.*' An irony of events, it was, just after the 1951 political change!

Committees were put up. The one at Taphalonha was called *Mritu Sanskar* and *Tol Surakchya Samiti*, in which Dr. Basant Bahadur Rajbhandari was the treasurer; I was the secretary, other elders like my father participated as members. We collected monthly fees of half a rupee per household. Fortunately, there was hardly a case to support through the *Mritu Sanskar Samiti.* In fact we had seen the security of the area as the main purpose and gave priority.

We worked out a plan of action. We were to have 4-6 people in a group and two groups would do the duty in shifts every night patrolling the area. The round was made with sticks, *latho,* and lanterns in our hands, we shouted, *Khabardar, Khabardar*! The patrolling started after about 4 pm till 4 am.

I was fairly active in community related social work at the age of 12. Not only at Taphalonha I was also the secretary of the Bhanimandap Committee (which we call by error today Ekantakuna) at the other end of Jawalakhel. Purna Bahadur Rana, who later became district judge, was the Chairperson of the committee.

Revolt against Tyranny

When we were in 4th and 5th classes, we used to play the 'catch me if you can' game and hide and seek. It often was in the large exam hall where many benches were placed one upon the other. The benches would be pushed and shoved or dashed· down on the stone floor under the tin roof and wooden ceiling and the noise they made in the large hall was like a small bomb going off. Mr. Lokman Singh was the Headmaster at the time.

The noise would still be echoing in the hall, when the headmaster would appear and lift his glasses a little up and stare at us. That was enough to make us shiver. He was followed by his trusted loyal school assistant, the Paicha, his assistant from Chyasal, Patan. One of his jobs was to collect cane rods for the headmaster and other teachers at the end of the annual Matchhendra chariot festival. The chariot is normally dismantled and the canes used are discarded by the Matchhendra Trust.

That day he had the thickest of canes on his shoulder. All who could run fast, escaped. Rabi Shah (brother of Airline Capt. Bobby), Umesh Sigdel (son of Master Netra Nath), YB Bista and I would be taking the brunt of the canings on our backs. Not only that but we had to lean on the wall with our back and knees folded for the rest of the school hours. It was awful. But we did not stop playing there.

On both sides of the gate of the Patan High School there now a garden with rose varieties collected during Rana time and loyally maintained by the school. It was during the midday break we played '*Catch Me If You can*'. It was not much fun to play between the rose bushes. Somehow YB Bista picked a rose and broke the branch while doing that.

The newest news reached the Headmaster in no time and in no time he stood in front of us with his trusted Dongol Paicha, the waiter. There was one classmate who pointed his figure towards Bista. That was enough. Without further question YB got blows on the calves of both his legs. The calves promptly got a terrible swelling. They looked as if they would burst and the blood would come out like a fountain. He cried in such a painful way. I cried too. Many people who heard the shrieks came to see him. The school was quiet and soon all the classes came out. I went running to inform YB's mother at his home, where now the UN building stands. His family members came in panic. Arguments flared. YB was taken away from the scene for treatment. Lok Man Singh stood there like his cane, stiff and without remorse. He looked terrifying.

Right in front of him we the students decided to go on strike with one demand in our mouths,

> *Headmaster Lok Man Singh, Must Go!*
> *Out with, Tyrant Headmaster Lokman Singh!*

Siddhilal Singh took charge of the crowd. The next day we stood outside the gate and stopped anyone, student or teacher, entering the school compound. There were some students who climbed over the wall and attended the classes, classes without the teachers. The teachers had to go back home. My task was to stop anyone trying to enter into the school compound through the main gate. Slogans and 'corner meetings' and provocative noises, all these were new to our eyes and ears. It was Siddhilal he who launched the crusade to oust Lokman Singh.

It was really ironic. We used to tease Siddhilal as the son of Paicha, *the subservient assistant to the Tyrant.* I think he was deeply hurt by this accusation against his father. Of course we had started accusing the Paicha (school waiter) of being another tyrant. Siddhilal perhaps thought his father was a victim of Lok Man Singh who exploited his loyalty.

In this case he found the *alibi* and did not care about the job of his father. The slogans would come out of his mouth so spontaneously,

The feudal Lokman, must be sacked!

The Education Department wanted to negotiate with us. But we were determined to oust him. Our insistence paid off. Assistant Headmaster Lalit Bahadur Shrestha of Kopundole took over. He was not particularly benevolent either, but he used only his finger to rub our ear-lobes, far kinder than thrashing with canes. We had won the battle.

I think this event encouraged Siddhilal to change his thinking and became active in leftist politics. We were to have future run-ins throughout our student careers, and I was not surprised by his extremism in the later part of his life. He was a home brewed communist. I too was involved in the event, but I did not become one of his political sympathizers. I think he had legitimate grudge against the so-called feudalism and fascism. My belief is that to qualify as a communist you 'have to be hurt', in diverse ways, in your very personal life.

Siddhilal enhanced his social prestige among the school students. But his father must have cried silently at home. He hurt his son, lost his job and many students (most of them were from Patan) despised him. Siddhilal's seven years in jail and the underground life he led for ages must have made his father lonely for decades before meeting death.

Siddhilal could have asked his father what he thought of all the mess in the school. Loyalty was punished.

Years later we were to meet again on the benches of Patan Degree College. With his left leaning views it mattered to him to spoil our reunion functions that I was in charge of. In our literary contest he even demanded that I pull out the contest.

From Failure to Success

Carrying a blackboard larger than my body, I was on my own, guided more by Mother. I remember starting to learn Nepali letters with the help of Father's friend, Sambhu Rimal of Taphalonha. I joined Tri Padma Bidhyasram located in an old two story traditional building at Nagbahal for grades 1 to 3. The medium of teaching was the Newari language. It did not matter as I was well versed in this language, growing up around Patan.

Although it was the male privilege to go to school, one of my neighbor boys seemed never to make it. His parents did not want him to be educated. He was jealous of me and would be lurking at his door that I had to pass by going to my school. Sometimes he would snatch my slate (the slate was obligatory in the school then), throw it on the ground and break it into pieces. I had to make up stories to tell at home about how I broke a slate every now and then. Then the guy was taller and stronger than me. I do not know how many slates he broke by the time I could challenge him, physically. Eventually I was able to defend myself against his jealousy.

After my first primary schooling was completed, I joined Patan High School in grade 4, and continued till half way through Grade 9. My schooling was left to me to make it or break it. Mother was sure of success but Father was less interested. I was good in all subjects and got the highest marks which qualified me to be the Class Monitor in all the classes up to grade 9. But there was an exception; throughout my school days I failed in Nepali language. My name was put on roll B, failing in one subject. Nepali was supposed to be my mother tongue. But my Mother too was fluent in Newari, so were Father and my sisters. My failure in my supposed mother tongue made me a laughingstock in the classes. Was my Nepali learning subjected by my fluency in Newari, which is so fundamentally different linguistically?

Only in the School Leaving Certificate qualifying test from the Tripadma Bidhyasram in Mangalbajaar and in the SLC exam itself (the Iron Gate exam) did I score 'just a pass marks.'

Everybody reminded me that my mother tongue was supposed to be Nepali. Yet in our family almost everybody could speak Newari fluently. In the market places with whomever we met, we communicated in Newari. I too was fluent in Newari. My first primary education took place in Newari medium. It seriously affected my performance in Nepali subjects. I used to call my knowledge of my Nepali language '*Nepari*' (Nepali+Newari).

I was good in English lessons, thanks to our English teacher Mr. Bishnu Raj Jha, elder brother of my friend Keshab Raj (joined the Foreign Service and later became Nepal's envoy to France). Mr. Bishnu Raj Jha had the knack of conducting his classes strictly in English, while talking or in writing on the blackboard. No other word was allowed to be used. So, naturally we were better off in English lessons.

But every day my Nepali teacher Uddhab Duwadi from Mattar (today Imadol) used to throw my exercise book from one corner to another. My performance never got better. He was angry with me. How many times did I have to pick up my book from the dusty floor?

I rebelled against my Nepali teacher. But before he could take steps to expel me from the school, I left Patan High school when my class nine was in its midterm. Going back to my first school, Tripadma Biddhyasram I met my earlier teachers who were still there. They recognized my difficulties and were very sympathetic towards me. I was allowed to apply for the pre-SLC Test examinations that would take place the next winter.

Try, if you pass the Test then you will have it if not then we let you join class ten.

For the next six months it was an uphill climb. I did pass the pre-SLC Test exams. The door to the SLC exam was ajar. I think I was one of the 2500 students who appeared in the SCL examinations. Without getting through the SLC, the Iron Gate to further studies, nobody would be eligible to enroll in the college. I could shorten my high school time by almost two years. Until now my parents had no clue of what I had done.

The age requirement for SLC exams: I wanted to register for the SLC exam. In 1955 AD and while filling up the required forms for the SLC exam at the Patan High School, I declared my age as 12 years, as Mother told me I was that old. It almost denied me the opportunity, because I was too young for SLC exams. I did not have an official paper to prove my age, except the *janma kundali* Mother kept confidential. Mr. Lalit Bahadur Shrestha, the new headmaster of Patan High School, suggested that I be 15, 3 years older. If I wanted to do the exam then I had to agree, so I became 15 at the age of 12.

I had taken tuition class, to enhance my Nepali and mathematics with the officer of the Department of Education, Mr. Krishna Das Tamrakar, at Patan during the winter. He was a good teacher. It was always at night, when Mr. Tamrakar had time for us. By the time my friend KP and I were returning home from the tuition classes, it would be midnight. The season was normally very cold, and during the dark nights it was eerie. We were becoming feeble from overwork, but we were determined to make it.

KP had no reason to jump classes or leave the school and take the SLC exams. I needed to save face before the teachers of Patan High School, not him. Out of solidarity or out of 'I can do it too' kind of thinking, he joined me in the adventure. He was a god friend of mine very early on.

I decided to appear for the next SLC Exams. I was deeply hurt but not discouraged by what the Nepali subject teacher did. He had run me down every day in the presence of the crowd of my classmates. That was unfair of him towards me. Instead of feeling ashamed, I began to feel fired by enthusiasm to show him the results of my efforts. Although I passed SLC in the 3rd division, it was as I expected, with the marks in Nepali just the bare minimum required. In all other subjects I got high marks. It did not matter. I made it.

My Nepali teacher Uddhab Duwadi would not laugh at me anymore. My high school Nepali teacher Duwadi and my class friends of the grade 9 at Patan high school had teased me for attempting an impossible thing.

I had put so much effort into it. That cost me dear. After the very last day of the exams I had collapsed outside the school. My friends Buddhi Bahador Budhathoki, KP and Madan Dhakals carried me home, delivered me to my mother. One can imagine Mother's mood then! I was simply sapped of my energy. It must have been the stress and the challenges I faced for the SLC exams that was so much in my heart. But it was worth it.

When I left bed, I was weak, perennially hungry and thought of nothing but food. Everybody in the family was suffering for me, not only me. I wanted meat all three times a day, and that went on for months. It was awful for my mother to fulfill my wishes that the family could hardly afford, so regularly. Grandmother would make the midday meal for me.

Slowly my craving for meat was so reduced that I started to hate it. I did not want anyone even to say the word meat, and I became strictly a vegetarian. But I was fit.

Within a few months I recovered well and was strong enough to resume my sports, mainly football on the Jawalakhel ground, now that I had time.

Almost six months later the results were out. I was deeply moved by the result of my dear friend who accompanied me in this voyage to jump the class. He did not make it.

How unaware my father was of my schooling came up when I gave him the news that I made it in the SLC exams. He was with his friends in the living room. They too were surprised. Father had perhaps never mentioned to them about my schooling. I realized he was oblivious of my schooling. His response made me sad in a way,

What, you did SLC? How come I did not know you appeared in exam?

My success in the SLC exam changed me. I had made it! I was flying, not walking on the ground. Nobody in our family ever made it that far. I thought I could do anything I liked. Every objective I held looked attainable. I became more ambitious. Nobody would be angry with me, even if I did some mischievous things! A series of truancies began.

No more vegetarian

One day, around 1956, a year after I became vegetarian, I found that Father had left for the Terai on a hunting trip with his army colleagues. I had still not recovered from the sickness brought on by serious fatigue after my School Leaving Certificate exams.

I asked Mother how far and where Father had gone in the Terai and any other information that she had about him. He would be somewhere around Amlekhganj. That made me think; if I went there, I could have my first train ride. Mother knew I was planning my first solo journey. How old was I? About 13, not more! She consented. Not long after, I went to the Tripureswor area looking for a vehicle.

I found a lorry, that was laden and leaving for the Terai. I requested the driver to take me to my father, an officer I said, at Amlekhganj. I told him, I did not have money, but he agreed to give me a ride only on the back of his truck saying that he would not be responsible at all for any eventuality!

The ride over the Tribhuwan Rajpath was very rough. This was the first time I was leaving the Nepal Valley. I had no idea how the countryside looked. My whole attention was to get a good grip on the sacks I was sitting on. I was too afraid to look on the sides. I remember seeing here and there steep slopes. It was scary. Over the whole ride I was clinging on the goods on the truck. The ride mixed with homesickness and feeling loneliness was no fun, even for a first timer like me. I had no contact with the driver sitting in the driving seat front and below. He would not hear me.

I knew that I was covered with dust from head to foot. The truck screeched to a halt and the driver came down to tell me we reached Amlekhganj railway station. It was dark.

The truck driver told me to leave his truck. I had no idea what Amlekhganj looked like and where to find my Father in this ocean of darkness with little lamps twinkling like the distant stars. I started asking people in the shops at the railway station. There were only few huts with oil lamps, but they were shops, that much I could make out. Dimly lit oil lamps gave a scary feeling. I felt like crying.

The driver mentioned that we had arrived at the railway station, but I did not see a train. Had I really arrived at Amlekhganj? I began to have my doubts. There was a veil of darkness. I went from one shop to another looking closely for a friendly person to ask where my Father was staying, but they would only ask me things which I did not want to talk about, like where I came from, why I was there etc. It was not their business to ask me but to tell me where my father was in Amlekhgunj.

Except for the station buildings and sheds, there was nothing but dilapidated huts. With each hint I came closer to where Father was. I had no lamp. I followed a kind man who showed me where the hunters could be camping. He took me back towards the direction I came in the truck for a while. There was this government house under the big pipal tree that I could see only the next day.

I was so happy, tired, dusty and hungry but the feeling that I had found my father in such a strange land was enough to cheer me up. I entered what the kind man said was the government guest house.

I called,

'Father, Father', in the dark.

A response came from a dark room. They were all huddled in one dark corner. Father came out and wanted to know how and why I followed him.

Mother told me you were at Amlekhganj. I want to ride a train. It will be my first train ride.

The meal was ready; an oil lamp was burning dimly only in the camp kitchen but it was not enough to distinguish things placed on the plates. Father asked what I was going to eat.

Of course, rice and some vegetable, what else?

The vegetable was too hard to chew. All in the kitchen laughed. Father said,

Now you can eat meat again.

No way!

What you just ate was Sukuti, the antelope meat dried and roasted.

So after one year of becoming a vegetarian I again became a meat eater. For that I had to do penance the whole day.

At first I was so sad, but somehow I did not hate it. After all, I was hungry, thirsty and tired. For hours I had gone thirsty. I remember drinking water only at Tistung and Hetauda bazaar. The truck driver did not offer me anything to eat. In fact I did not eat anything for the 12 hour long ride. I had no *paisa* and I was too proud to beg him for food.

The next day Father placed me in a train carriage. The train pulled through the *Charkose Jhadi*. I was a little afraid of the wild animals and wondered where a tiger might be. But the window had bars, so no animal could jump into the cabin.

The *chhuk chhuk* and the whistle of the steam locomotive, all new, and the train racing through the jungle and the farmlands into Birgunj were so romantic. I cannot describe the fun I had of that first train ride.

Following Father's advice, I searched for Ramudidi in Birgunj. She was the eldest daughter from the first wife of Tripur Bikram, our Mahila buba, and was living with her husband Chautariya at Chhapakaiya. I was pampered for a while and enjoyed their hospitality.

Long way to Graduation

After the SLC early in 1956 it took me five more years to pass my Intermediate of Arts (IA) examinations, a two years course from the Nepal National College (later dedicated to Prof. Shankar Dev Pant), at Ranipokhari in Kathmandu. The reasons behind that I shall come back to below. I had joined the NNC, immediately. But somehow I felt I had not seen enough of the world to start college life.

So in 1958 I played the truancy of my life, but I never regretted it. All along I carried in me my determination to study higher and higher whenever time and opportunity permitted.

The day my demon in me woke up, Mother must have cried. At home unexpected things were happening much to my consternation. The daily eruptions of quarrels were unnerving not only me: my grandmother suffered a lot as well as she told me later. In the center was the subject of Father's mistress. We did not speak about our tensions. Yet Father was unhappy that I was distancing myself from him. Yet I was not seeking an escape from it all. It was not in retaliation for Father's misdeeds that I left home; for that I felt I was too strong to do. The two things just happened to occur simultaneously.

I also did not want to abandon my mother at her time in distress. It would be unfair to her. The situation at home collided with my long hedged ambition. There was my urge in me pushing me hard to decide:

> *Go and seek adventures now! Do new things and go to new places!*

It happened like this. Adhikary, KP and I were sitting on the grassy ground of Jawalakhel. Adhikary started to tell us stories of heroes of war. I listened intently. What he was telling was so interesting and new to me. I thought the life in the army must be adventurous!

He was telling us that there were boys going to join the army. At Paklihawa, near Bhairahawa, there was a camp and the officers there were recruiting young boys for the British Army. After that KP and I talked it over. KP had finally passed his SLC exam, and I was enrolled in the Nepal National College at Ranipokhari.

We decided to go to Bhairahawa, near Lumbini and try the recruitment tests. I had once tried to reach Birgunj and ride a train to Raxaul when Father was on his hunting trip to Amlekhgunj area, so I seemed to be the expert to guide KP to reach Raxaul station. We planned to take a minimum of belongings so that nobody would know we were venturing out far and for long.

One fine very early morning both of us made a trip to the trucks going to Birgunj side. In those road-less days, to go east or west in the Terai, you had to go via the more efficient transport available in India. We went over to Gorakhpur to Nautanwa by train, then took a bus ride back to the Nepal border at Sunauli. We stayed at a local hut at the Sunauli border bazaar and made it to the Paklihawa camp next door, in the morning.

The recruitment was on. There were boys queuing up to get tested, chest and height measured, running stamina, medical checks etc. I passed all the tests with ease, but somehow poor KP could not make it. Or was he rejected because of his Brahmin status? Nobody explained to him.

This was the second time that we planned something of importance in our lives together, and the second time he would not make it. I felt sorry for him though he did both attempts willingly on his own. I told him that the next opportunity I got, I would return home for good. He would tell my Mother the same. He went back home taking my belongings to deliver to my mother.

How Mother would take the message I knew from what she had told me about her astrologers, whom she had shown my *janma kundali*, and who predicted that I was destined to be a man of travels. I would end up travelling far and wide yet come back home to settle for good. I believed she did feel assured that I would not vanish, nor could I be harmed.

My determination to continue my education by any means was still very strong, though my life took a sharp turn. I had still not done the IA exam when I left home and left the college to join the army. That was in 1958 AD. I had just celebrated my 15th (biological) birthday. Nowadays they would not allow a 'child' to join combat service. But I had the certificate from my school saying I was already 15 years old in 1955. The camp did not have a technique to find out the actual age of a boy. Physical size and fitness were primarily the best tests.

The initial intake was for 3 years in the British Army, unless extended. After two and half years I got a six months home leave in 1961. I took the leave opportunity to appear for the IA exam. After 3 months of preparation I passed it. As the battalion I was in was leaving for a UK tour of duty for two years in 1962 and I was selected to go along, I thought it was too early to call it a day and leave the army. I would see more of the world if I went along and stayed in the army for another 3 more years. I seized the opportunity.

Then the second part of my adventures began. It started right at the end of 1961. The battalion I was in left for the UK for a two year posting, by sea on a 23,000 ton vessel. It took more than 3 weeks to reach Southampton harbor, with stop over at Colombo, passing by Socotra, with a day each at Aden and Port Suez, through the Suez Canal and Bitter Lakes, passing by the island nation Malta and a day at Gibraltar and the shaky ride over the Bay of Biscay. We were stationed at Tidworth, near Salisbury. Andover was nearby. The farthest we were allowed to go for excursions and marketing, with permission granted, was London and Salisbury, returning to the barracks same day.

We were the object of curiosity; I think the new generation of the UK never saw so many Nepali faces together. A new generation of people on the street had perhaps not even heard of the hard times of the Gurkhas contributing to the security of Great Britain during great wars by the people of Nepalese origin from Darjeeling, Sikkim, Assam and Dehradun in India as well as the mountain lads from the Kingdom of Nepal.

Black and white TV was just being tried over the transatlantic cable for direct beaming. There was a book by John F. Kennedy, in hard cover and I was attracted by the title of it: *Profiles in Courage* (published by Hamish Hamilton, London). It was so tempting to have a copy of the memorial edition that was released in 1964 and I bought one without counting a penny as soon as it was out. My English language skill was getting better from the interactions with the English officers, at the market places and from the pub goers where I was playing ping pong almost every evening. I thought I could read the book, and I still have treasured it on my bookrack at home.

It was awe inspiring to read the pages 146-171, to think of the cases in this book for opinions in critical junctures of life. Senator Edmond G. Ross of Kansas, with his 'one heroic deed' saved in 1868 a President (President Johnson, successor to President Abraham Lincoln) as an institution for posterity. I found his courage most tantalizing and quality unmatched, and I refer to it whenever stint of courage is required to make a hard decision. Almost 94 years later, John F. Kennedy credited him for his courage that saved 'the nation', in consolidation after the terrific war for separation. Kennedy not only admired courageous people, he was a war hero and embodied the same quality. His fidelity to principle was admirable.

I think it was on November 22nd 1963; 98 years after Abraham Lincoln was shot, we saw in real time view live, midday at Dallas and evening in UK, how President John F. Kennedy was cut down in the prime of his powerful role and youthful vigor. It was a heart wrenching scene. I think I was one of the millions, crying in front of the black and white cathode ray tube. As a soldier I had an ulterior reason to cry. I was not supposed to show it. TV is a cruel tech-beast I found. I was living an ocean apart, yet it made me witness the gruesome act of a cruel man, live. I felt like I was right in Dallas.

JFK had saved our lives. That is what I thought of, after 2-weeks of staying in high alert and standby as a soldier with all the knowledge of destruction and fallout from nuclear wars, the tension, and the fear; with the thought of losing people I loved, my parents. I, the adventure seeker, came to feel that I was never so much in love with myself. I was afraid to lose everything in case the Cuban Missile Crisis crossed the threshold of ultimatum. I feared I would never see my kin and kith and my country again. I had thought of all the ill of Khrushchev and Castro and all the hawks on both sides of the Atlantic.

We survived the crisis, thanks to JFK. We all believed in his charisma blended with courage. He did not shun, to rebuff for posterity, the communists' conspiracy to destroy democracy when the time came. For one act of his conscience he was my hero too. When I was writing these words between Nov. 19th and 21st, 2013, I realized it was sadly on the occasion of JFK's 50th death anniversary.

There were light moments, and technological marvels were unraveling, to inspire me with awe. The first heavyweight championship boxing match to be telecast live over the Transatlantic TV cable was being fought in the USA, and we had huddled to watch it at Tidworth. Cassius Clay became our world champion.

Nothing was boring about the experience, except for seeing almost only white men everywhere outside London. There were many first time experiences, for me such as riding the Underground train, visits to numerous sites worth visiting such as London Zoo, Madame Toussads's Museum, The Art Gallery, Stonehenge, Barnstable, Plymouth or Cardiff. A small tea party on the Buckingham Palace garden behind the palace (flanked by two 20-storey buildings that annoyed the British Royals we heard), a visit up to the door of 10 Downing Street, Westminster Abbey or the Tower Bridge.

The regular parades, the target shootings, the army maneuvers, the barrack life the time passed with breaks. Sometimes I visited the Royal Nepalese Embassy at Kensington Palace Gardens. I had established a friendship with Col. Jay Pratap Rana, the military attaché. The Ambassador of Nepal never showed up. I don't know who was there as our man. I remember once seeing Crown Prince Birendra visiting our Tidworth barracks. In a dark overcoat, a boyish man treading the hard parade ground upright to the Guard House and replying salutes gave me a little impression of the man who was to be our king.

As I could speak his language fairly well then, the English medical officer in Tidworth barracks and I became good friends. He was a learned man and an officer and I was a soldier. The difference in rank was not important for him outside duty hours. He had purchased Hagen's Nepal book. I had known Hagen when I was a child, but I did not tell the officer about him. He showed the book to me, and I wondered at the beauty of my country in pictures for the first time in my life. That was the first book with color photographs devoted to Nepal, and it made me proud of my country.

One particular part of my military life I have not yet shared with many. That was counter-insurgency training and excercises. Over the Maoists conflict era I had to restrain the very few ones who knew about it from telling it to others, in case it would make my life difficult. A thirty-three weeks long course on guerilla warfare was a technique used to flush out and eliminate the hit and run enemies menacingly active from their hideouts in difficult terrains. Much of the time devoted in the army courses was for covert operations and camouflaged actions searching out an enemy without a face. It was like searching for a needle lost in the haystack, finding a guerilla in the jungle or the city streets. They would blend in the landscape, in urban or jungle areas, so too the soldiers had to do the same to protect ourselves from them.

At the time, Sukarno of Indonesia was threatening Malaysia, including Sarawak and Singapore, which were yet to fully recover from the years of jungle warfare against the Maoists led by Chin Peng in the remote areas of Malayan peninsula. They now faced another menace, jungle warfare in Sarawak in the dense jungles of Borneo in Pontianak. So they said, anyway.

Fairly remote, the Pontianak area was an Indonesian territory but far from its administrative or policing ability. Having been trained in jungle warfare, we got airlifted to Sarawak. Over River Batang Rajang, Sibu Kuching, Lundu, on boats I think we spent months in the so called *'jungle warfare.'*

I felt I matured through witnessing deaths; my tent lost 6 comrades in one battle, out of 8. I was deeply saddened by their sacrifices. I was in the camp HQ, my duty kept me away from 'frontline' skirmishes though several times I went to the 'front' by helicopter, at my insistence at least to see for myself what it looked like at the front. I had to insist to be involved.

Somehow I was beginning to see some drama staged to train the soldiers with '*live bullets*.' There was no sort of panic, haste, emergency standby of the officers to soldiers etc. that we expect as a convention of warlike situations that the eminent battle front warranted. At the front it was nothing serious to look at. The stage was set for guerrilla warfare. Who was on the other side? I was beginning to discern that something was being kept from me. I was one of the few who could note in diaries or write also in English to communicate. Soldiers like me were kept mainly for paperwork, even in the frontlines. They must have reason for it. I did not believe that there was a real threat to Malaysia and Singapore from the Indonesian side, apart from verbal salvos of Sukarno, a good orator and expounder of *guided democracy*, so they said.

Can the army concoct real battles to keep the army personnel fit for eventual deployment in real wars? Are wars sometimes staged to reduce arms stockpiles and produce new weapons to sustain employment and keep industries running? How big was the slice of the defense industry in the national economy of 'warring countries'?

My current term was to end early 1965. I was still in the Sarawak jungles and had only a few months left with them when I approached our commander Hickey. With Hickey, I had a close contact and we were frank. Sometimes we forgot our differences in ranks and army protocol. He was surprised that I had decided to leave the army and he wanted me to stay, he even promoted me immediately to entice me but I had made up my mind, a decision I had made 3 years earlier. He was surprised to learn about it. I was not going to change my mind. I gave him my earnest reply that I was going back to continue my studies that I had left in limbo.

He let me go. After a tumultuous trip from Sarawak in autumn 1964, by a relatively small army gun boat during the raging typhoon of the season, I reached Hong Kong and stayed there until discharged in the spring of 1965. The jungle guerilla warfare, the tense life, the camaraderie, and the trust and tolerance I could build with my simple compatriots away from home made me feel confident that I could trust my simple mountain folks. The closest friends emerged during the jungle life. There were none from the Terai taken in the army. That I missed, I did not have any idea what the youth of Terai were like.

I returned home to work to look after Mother and siblings, and also for college studies that I had interrupted. I started my bachelor studies immediately.

Years later I met Hickey in Kathmandu. He was at the UK Embassy. He invited me to his official quarters inside the British Embassy and we reminisced about old times.

Looking back I can say the '*six years of escape from home reality*' did not go in vain. It allowed me a kind of and amount of freedom to do and indulge in whatever I wanted and liked. I grew stronger in determination, fast in drawing conclusions, hard driving in effort during that period. I also kept my pen busy in writing under pseudonyms, played ping pong a lot of time, learnt typewriting, photography, games and sports, learnt to use weapons and forged friendship with diverse youth and learnt to value the importance of camaraderie.

I underwent diverse kinds of endurance tests there without physical and mental stress. I felt confident to carry out any assignment. The training conditions made me confident that nothing was difficult for me. I learnt to go without food and water for longer durations of task and training exercises. I could do any kind of hard work. I did not fall sick at all, and got only my wounds from basketball games, to be treated and healed leaving numerous scars on my legs. The only thing I did not like was the punitive system applied by the army. One did not have to err but got punishment when a comrade made a mistake.

I lived with different ethnic Nepali people, mostly Gurung, Rai, Magar, Limbu, Chhetri, Tamang, and Lepcha. That was the moment when I came to know Nepali people, away from our homeland. I was so naïve about my own people earlier that their diversity even outside Nepal astonished me, but I found the common thread of affinity between us: patriotism, it gave me joy. I could divert my energy away from youthful aberrations. I did not fall prey to juvenile delinquency as many would at my age. I was in a state of discipline that we hardly have outside the army. There were exceptions too. The army life is not a spiritual life. It also harbors ills of the society it comes from.

Of all feelings, the constant homesickness for my beautiful country haunted me wherever I went, travelling into distant countries and experiencing life on ships, planes, boats and ferries. In 1965, at age of 22, I came back home from my first round of stints in the foreign countries.

I was lovingly received back by my family. Mother admonished me with her tears of joy at seeing me back and remembering her feelings when I ran away. She made me promise that I never would boast of it to anyone as if it were my real adventure, which she did not consider to be anything great. It had tortured and greatly pained her over my years of absence, she would say. I was sorry for that. But almost fifty years after returning home from the *'mischievous travels'* I am writing about it on these pages.

I had hardly been home for 5 years, as the astrologer had predicted to Mother when, as a man of travels, I was in my second tour of life although not as an adventurer, that took me round the Earth, from China to Canada, from Nairobi to Normandy, from Aberdeen to Amsterdam and what not places. I feel I have settled now. It was high time. At over 70 years of age I deserve to stay put at my home, very close to the village where my mother was born, Godavari.

The change at home was more painful, more distressful and all were stuck in poverty. I did not earn money during my absence over the 6 years away from home. I could not help them immediately but I had come back with will and energy to do something for Mother, Father and my siblings.

I restarted my college life. I had to work too for my family to sustain their livelihood and take up family concerns, seriously. For another two years it was a combination of study and work with Walter Staub of Swiss Red Cross Society working for the Tibetan Refugees. I had difficulty finding my way to old friends. They too had changed. We had little in common. This was a big loss I had to accept. But that also left me free to find new friends in my jobs, contacts and in the college at home and abroad.

In 1967 I completed my Bachelor's study. The examination center for us was at Lainchaur School. I was sharing the desk with Prem Dhoj Pradhan from Sindhupalchok. I later heard him in Radio Nepal, singing Nepali songs, with less music but more with his captivating voice. That was unique. Many other singers I found had used musical instruments to drown their voices, even those with golden voices.

The job at the Red Cross office catering for the Tibetan Refugees paid me well. I could earn, Rs.450 per month. That was huge, considering what it could buy in gold: almost 18 grams (1.6 Tolas). At 2014 price it would be around Rs.80-90 thousands. That job lasted only about 2 years. But it still was not a golden era for the people in my condition.

Having completed the Bachelor's study, I took the job as liaison officer for Jiri Multipurpose Development Project in Dolkha district.

In April 1959, Nepal's first university was founded. I was one in the crowd marching, singing and dancing in the rain from Kathmandu Tundikhel to the site Tyanglafant, Kirtipur singing in the monsoon rains of Ashad, the famous song: '*It is raining but I failed to plant flowers, I must not be blamed that fell in love*', together with Nirmal Rimal of Dillibajaar, to be part of the foundation laying ceremony for Tribhuwan University in 1959. But ironically I never made it to the campus of the Tribhuwan University in Kirtipur in my life to study.

Dreaming of an University Education

I was deeply dissatisfied over what I had learnt, and what I could make out of my life, with my own *non-achiever* status. Seeing my fate being sealed with a BA certificate in Nepali, rudiments of economics and political subjects and my hands not able to do any creative and contributory work I looked around for a new opportunity. I was awoken by my exposure of years earlier, within and outside Nepal, and I needed to look for opportunities. The way I would see things was not the same as many of my friends were used to. I would question my ability. The saga of my long and arduous journey to university began.

It was long, arduous and quite a '*revealing trek*' through Jiri, Hawa, Jafe, Malu, Jhule, and Kabre, Namdu, Bigu in Dolkha over Thingsa La to Barabise in Sindhupalchok. The year was 1968, on 27th of March after staying overnight at Dhunge Swanro, I was passing through Patale village of Jafe with 60-70 households, in Dolkha district, when the interaction with Kasi Ram Damai changed my perception of rural poverty. I had a revelation that changed the course of my life. And what I saw and how farmers could be helped raised my thirst for knowledge. I saw my life coming to make a turn, if I could only afford it! I developed another state of dissatisfaction with myself.

Straight after my arrival at home, I went to see Mr. Paul Koelliker who was the boss in Swiss Association for Technical Assistance (SATA), at Ekanta Kuna. I tried to convince him about what I had seen in Patal, my determination and the possibility of joining a Swiss university. There was a surprise in store, a positive coincidence. To my surprise he said,

I've just had a letter from the Bund (Federal Government) to reply to, asking me to contact the Ministry of Education of Nepal for the last time, whether they would forego or accept our offer of a scholarship to send somebody for study in a Swiss university. The Bund has written several times to HMG. In fact there was no response from Nepal at all. When I asked the Ministry, they said they could not take up the offer as the process of selecting a candidate for a single placement was too difficult.

Mr. Koelliker looked at me with interest, and added,

Why don't you try to get this seat? Shall I write to the Bund that I have found an answer to their letter?

I told him that would really make me happy.

The idea of knocking on the door at Singha Durbar was dropped by SATA. It cut short the process and yet it could respond to Bund's letter in a positive way.

About a month later, the Ministry of Foreign Affairs of Switzerland asked for my CV, certificates etc. and my willingness, to study agriculture, a four years course for Diplom (equiv. MSc) at the Federal Institute of Technology (in German abbreviations – ETH). The Bund sent the papers I had submitted to ETH for their opinions. It found me weak in mathematics and other science subjects.

That was so. In fact I had not gone further than SLC level in these subjects. In my college years I had studied only economics and political science, only to learn late in my life that it was not a science at all but the art of lying.

I wrote back that I had not studied mathematics or science, but that I wanted to be in the university. They promptly replied that I could take a chance. My fate started to shine. What could I lose if I did not grab the opportunity? I was anyway a looser here at home. With a BA in political '*science*' and Nepali, I was going nowhere other than to try for a clerical job at best.

They would offer me a scholarship also for the preparations in Switzerland. I was required to be fluent in the German language, proficient in Math, Chemistry, Biology and Physics. My dilemma began. These were all the 'highest peaks of my life' to climb and scale. I had never tried any of these peaks ever before.

Together with ETH, the Bund put two conditions for the scholarship grants. One, I appear for an entrance exam, as per the requirement of ETH, and pass; two, the Bund required that I go back home on completion of my study.

Those were reasonable propositions or conditions to accept. In fact they suited me well. I had never thought of spending long years of my life out of the country. I had seen enough of the little world during my 'Escape from Home Reality' from 1958 to 1965, from sea to jungles, from world cities to Kampongs. I was not attracted by any of them.

I agreed to the two conditions of the Bund and their offer of a modest Federal Government scholarship. The acceptance letter came. I was supposed to be in Switzerland by September 1969. But I went there 3 months ahead in June and used the time to do some practical work as part of the 'hands-on' work in the farms in Aesch, Baselland and Aegle, Wallis, near Geneva, as part of the study requirement.

It was not easy to get a place in the university. I started to hear that ETH is for determined heads and talented students. I had the first, but only time would tell whether I had the second one too. ETH is the best University in Europe, if not in the whole world. That is what the Swiss perceived and I believed, because I was facing the toughest time of my learning career.

Even the preparatory classes were cloudy and I could not see the horizon. How would I pass the entrance exams? I had to show a minimum of performance with marks exceeding 4 out of 6 in all subjects. I was never burdened with any infusion of dreams and pressurized to achieve anything in life from Father's side. My mother had only trusted in my ability, thanks to her astrologer, that I would make it, so found no reason to push me to be ambitious. The burden was heavy on me alone to realize my dream.

The preparation of the entrance exams for ETH took place in Fribourg, 20 km south of Bern. The time between the autumn 1969 and Spring1971, was the most crucial time of my life. I said to myself:

'See! You have nothing to lose, kindle the light of hope, go, do it!'

There were six of us. The others were from Honduras, San Salvador and Nicaragua. The experience in the University of Fribourg posed a new challenge in my life. I wanted to succeed but I was not prepared for it. I faltered during the first year of preparation. Most daunting was the German language, with its complicated rules, but without learning all that I would not be able to follow the lessons in math, chemistry and the other sciences. But I was determined to try my best.

Yet, midway through, I too realized that I would not make it. The proficiency in the German language was a must. The basic knowledge required for the university in German language, Mathematics, Biology (because I got the scholarship for the study of Agronomy), Chemistry and Physics all to be taken up simultaneously was a very difficult uphill journey. I frequently prayed to Dakchinkali, to bring me out of this quagmire.

The Swiss Federal Government's scholarship office realized this and granted me and one other student, Alvaro Espinoza from Nicaragua, an extra year to make preparation for the Entrance Examination for ETH. The other four had to go back home. This time the courses were organized by Dr. Junod Schule near the very ETH, into which I was sweating hard to enroll.

It must have been sometime around 1970 in the middle of the second preparatory course when I seemed to start making progress. There was a happy surprise in store.

In mathematics I started getting a 100% of the marks allocated. The laborious difficulties almost killed me, but it paid. I got energized. Over time I learnt to play with math to sort out many difficulties during the study of diverse subjects.

The trend of success in other subjects, physics and chemistry followed. I was more optimistic and determined than ever before. In the end, I and Alvaro Espinoza from Nicaragua passed the Entrance Examinations with ease and were enrolled in ETH. After that I never had difficulty passing any exams.

In spring of 1975 I finished the 4-year course for the MSc. Alas! My mother died in February of 1975, just a month prior to my MSc exams which I passed with flying colors with over 90%, making me eligible to do PhD research (min. marks required was 80-85%), if I wanted to. All my efforts paid, but the sad demise of my mother cast a showdown on my joys. But she had dreamt of it.

I joined two federal research stations, Waedenswil and Reckenholz near Zurich for a year to gain some experience in research oriented tasks. Then in the autumn of 1976 I journeyed back home with my family to serve my country, and with that I fulfilled my obligation towards the Swiss Bund. I will always be grateful for their support. My first destination was the remote hills of Sindhupalchok and Dolkha districts and the assignments led me to the households similar to the Damai village of Jafe, in Dolkha which I had promised myself to serve.

After putting my knowledge to use in the remote mountain areas of Nepal for three years, I was to return to my university and obtain ETH-PhD (Technical Science) in April 1984. It was to be also a part of my adventure in life that I made it.

Was it just my luck backed by my determination to apply for a technical qualification, not knowing of the chances that had brought me this far? Somehow I was not at ease with what I achieved. If the Nepali Government had behaved in a more responsible manner, perhaps someone needier and more determined than I would have got the scholarship and served my country better. Such thoughts hunted me all along in the hills where I spent 3 years after my MSc.

Janma Kundali Recreated

When I was a small boy my Mother used to tell me that she would take leave from us all from this world when I reached a certain age, and that she would not live to see my success in life. But she had believed so much that I would succeed that she deserved to see what I made of her dream. I had to hear it so often I would not even dare to doubt it at the same time I was pained. Would it come true?

Second Son a Boy of Burden: Normally, if the eldest son is surviving, second son had not to bear the brunt load of the first son, as per the tradition. I had to take the role of the first son with that befell responsibility. With the responsibility, my freedom was to a large extent curtailed. It also made me more determined to make it in education and to be creative to fulfill the 'dreams of my mother'.

My original *janma kundali* was jealously protected by my Mother, because in those days one believed that a *janma kundali* could be misused by others disliking you to damage your fate. She died when I was away. I cannot say who was behind it, but I found my little room ransacked and lost many valuables after my mother's death.

Once during my school days, I needed a book on algebra. Father did not want to buy me one and Mother did not have a paisa. She pawned her small gold Mundra-earrings and 9-*gedi tilari* (worn by married women).

Then when I was earning sufficient for all purposes and my savings allowed me to buy gold for my mother, I had replacements made; tiger-headed gold bangles (*baghmukhi chura*). The gold ornaments were my little gifts to my mother in gratitude to her gift of books she provided me.

After Mother's death, they were kept for me at home in my cupboard as 'something of Mother to keep.' But to my sorrow the gold ornaments belonging to Mother were given by my sister to another person without a thought of what they had meant to me. That earned her a momentary favor. I have long forgiven her for that unthoughtful act, but I find it hard to forget the gold bangles with tiger's heads made for my mother. My *janma kundali* (*chinha*) and Mother's artifacts lost were a big loss to me. That was not a mere annoyance to forget.

Revisiting my *Chinha*: My Mother had instilled in me over the years a few hints related to my birth: I was born on a Monday, towards early morning, before daylight, on a Dark Moon (*kushe-aunsi*) night, with the Zodiac sign

(Rashifal): Leo (Sinha) and the secret name having a first letter Mo.

But I was interested in having the *janma kundali* reproduced. Armed with the hints left behind by Mother, my wife Sharada and I went, in 2007 to see an astrologer, an old Newar lady, with hearing deficiency in the heart of Kathmandu city. She cross-questioned me thoroughly.

She drew a temporary *janma kundali* and juggled with some figures on a piece of paper. She made me answer some questions to be sure of what she came up with, then she drew a final draft version of my *janma kundali*: it is Monday August 30, 1943, on Father's Day at 04:30, my secret name: Modi, Rashifal Lion. It was the confirmation to a great extent of what Mother had hinted then.

With the new *janma kundali* sketched, she started relating many events like marriages, number of children, my study I had completed in my life and all seemed to be accurate. This information reinforced me to accept her reading and let her complete my *janma kundali*.

She even predicted so that we would be successful in selling our house and land but had to wait a while and warned us not to negotiate a deal before 18th of October 2007. In fact the house and land was sold in January 2008. That was the 9th house I had lived in since my birth. The tenth place is Kitini, where I am now living with my family.

After the death of my mother, I had asked Father to find some new land for me where I could live when I returned home from my studies in Switzerland. Around the end of November 1975, Father wrote me that he found a nice green place at Kitini, in Godavari, with a small house on 3000m^2 of land, a peace of woodland with Alders, with irrigated rice land just below the maize fields. He was waiting for my nod.

At that time I could not put together the required money. It is such a coincidence, thirty two years later I shifted to a place quite similar to what Father had described, and almost the same area of land with a little forest mainly of Alder, the rice fields below and the maize field we acquired very soon. Was it the land Father had visited then?

Five years later I wanted to have my *janma kundali* reconfirmed by another astrologer. I gave him the same information my mother had left in my head. He was to work out a *janma kundali* and relate events that spoke of my reality in the past and present terms. There were two minor amendments suggested. It was Monday in the calendar but it is to be judged as Sunday, while the time of birth worked out, to be precise, 04:31:20, just before the sunrise. My secret name should have its first letter to begin with Ma and not Mo. How important was the vowel used is for the astrologers to sort out. But the new astrologer confirmed all the hints given by my mother.

Not only did the second astrologer even relate similar happenings in my life as the first one, but they were fairly accurate. I have accepted also the new *janma kundali* worked out for me. Thanks to Mother for her memory. She could not read and write so she had to memorize the details.

The only contradiction was with my official date of birth declared while making the citizenship paper and my first passport made back in 1969. I needed to have information to fill the application for a citizenship certificate, a precondition of the government before issuance of a passport. Naturally I turned to my Mother for information on my date of birth. Of course, I got the date of birth information from Mother. Had she feared that an evil person could harm me if my true information was disclosed to the strangers? Did she then concoct my personal details in order to protect me from evil minds? The date of birth deviated. It seems to have mattered. In astrological terms even seconds have value.

Struggles of
my Rebellious Mother

Mother was born a Silwal Chhetri at Manedanda, Godavari in Lalitpur District on Tuesday, February 23, 1915 AD, on the ninth day of new moon. Her father was totally bald, dark in complexion and sturdy, and despite his authoritarian look was in fact a kind-hearted man towards all those around him. Her mother was impishly attractive with a light brown complexion, and she complimented his authoritarian look with her soft voice. She was very friendly to look at, and was loved by all. My Mother embodied her father's determination to act and her mother's cheerful disposition, even under stress.

My Mother, the Maicha

She was a happy-go-lucky girl, whom everyone called the little Maicha. *Maicha* means 'little girl' in the Newari language, and in this case was used to mean *her parents' most loved child*. She had the privilege of knowing her parents better than any of her other four siblings. They were some of the most affluent people of the community. Her father worked as the personal assistant to the most notorious, shrewd and powerful of the nine Rana Premiers of history, Chandra Shamsher Jung Bahadur Rana, around 1901-29 AD. He enjoyed his power, but was conscious of the wrath of the Premier if there were to be any misuse.

Her parents also had a large piece of rice land and a small house, the Patana-ghar at Bakhundol, Patan (west of what is today the Engineering College at Pulchowk), where they stayed during the week. Her father attended his office in Singh Durbar five days a week, about 3 km away in Kathmandu. Singh Durbar, built at the turn of the century by PM Chandra Samsher, was the largest private building in Nepal, then.

Being the youngest and the most protected child, Maicha accompanied her parents on every trip to and from home. On weekends they would walk two hours from the Patana-ghar to be home at Manedanda, Godavari. The house in Manedanda was the largest in the village with carved windows and rooms for all purposes while adjoining sheds housed animals. Caged wild boars reflected the status. The paved courtyard was used for drying harvests.

Mother's four siblings--three older brothers Jhanka, Jhapat and Sahila together with her eldest sister Thuli-ama, (later known as Krishnakumari) stayed home at Manedanda to look after the animals and rice farming. The farming was mainly done by the family members, although there was a family of workers, the former bonded labor, in the household doing all sorts of chores.

In the rice planting season many households came together to help each other. The tradition was called

Parma, helping each other turn by turn to plant beginning with upper terraces. So the young lady, my mother was spared from dirtying her hands with dung and soil. Always cheerful and skilled in hunting with pellet-bow, a *guleli,* Mother had a very playful time in her youth. Her carefree life, however, was soon to reach a turning point.

Not yet 18, Maicha (later known as Premkumari) was married off to Naran Panday, my father (later known as Prem Jung) in 1932. Just a week before the Great Earthquake hit Nepal in the afternoon of 15th of January 1934, she gave birth to my eldest sister, Sita. She and her newborn baby survived narrowly while buried in the rubble. That was the start of her struggle for freedom, a struggle she entered with enthusiasm, right in her own house.

The veil she wore during her wedding hid not only the first tears of separation from her loved ones, but also veiled her destiny to come. It was the beginning of the tearful life that was to follow. I can now imagine, of all her cherished possessions, why she chose to keep her wedding veil, and preserved and entrusted it to me. It has been with me ever since.

The veil, from around the year 1932 AD, was of the finest embroidery, woven on the best cotton, with the most flowery, multi-colored Dhaka designs I have ever seen. Mother was 16 years old when her father imported the finery from British India before Premier Chandra died in 1929 AD. Such embroidery was not done in Nepal. Even today the veil is as fine, transparent and unscathed as it was. Considering its age, I wonder how good it must have been back then; how changed she must have looked under the veil. That was the only thing left untouched by my siblings after her death.

The experiences of parents are naturally not openly communicated to the children, nor are the happenings prior to their birth. I needed to take various paths to uncover my parents' lives. As an example, going to the astrologer with the *janma kundali* (horoscope: see Chapter 1), of my long dead father was one of the ways coming to know them. I was not at the side of my mother when she passed away, so I could not rescue her *janma kundali* and come to other aspects of her veiled life. How interesting it would have been!

My Sisters and my Mother's Relations with Her Own Sister

We were six children from my mother, four daughters and two sons who survived to adulthood: sisters Sita, Lalu, Thulikanchhi (Renuka) and Kanchhi (Dolma) and I, Kumar and my younger brother Janak and my half-sister Gyana from Father's first mistress, Astamaya Shrestha. Three more siblings, one brother and two sisters, did not survive beyond infancy.

My eldest sister Sita loved cinema. However, she was married off to a Kunwar (Jangbahadur Kunwar-Rana's clan) of Sanglekhola, Kantipur district when I was ten. Every time I visited her I had to make sure that I had first been to see a new film and learnt by heart the songs and story. She wanted every bit of the story so that she could tell the

Jyapu ladies who were her neighbors, as if she had seen them herself. I could hardly make sense of the Hindi spoken in the cinema, but I could tell the story as I saw it, and I could catch the melodies.

Sita had narrow eyes, could hardly open them in fact, and what we saw were slits like the Mongols have. We called her *chimsi*. She had suffered from smallpox when she was a baby, so she carried pockmarks all over her face. Lalu, my second elder sister had similar eyes to Sita. She would exude empathy and love towards people and animals. I do not think there was anyone whom she knew that she had not visited when they were ill or hospitalized. That quality distinguished her from my other siblings. Unfortunately, both sisters, Sita and Lalu became victims of the era; back then it was out of the question for girls to attend school both due to prevalent attitude of the elder generation and the absence of a single school for girls in the area.

Time and again I wondered why Mother was at odds with her only sister, Thuli-ama. I just could not understand what went wrong in their relationship. It seemed to me that after both had established families of their own, Mother at Jawalakhel and Thuli-ama at Jhamsikhel, not far from one another, they would be in good contact with each other. The two sisters could have started a new kind of family relationship.

Thuli-ama was married to Bista Chhetry at Jhamsikhel, had two sons and four daughters.

Mother made frequent visits to her sister, expecting perhaps for things to improve between them over time.

Such gestures did not seem to impress Thuli-ama, or bring about any change in their relationship.

The cynical remarks and verbal exchanges continued between the two sisters that even I, at my tender age, could feel. Sometimes, I heard Thuli-ama murmur, 'Pandays, the casteless, without social hierarchy, are not equal to us'.

She probably thought she was right. But I found nothing wrong about us and even felt proud of my clan's historical background and its proud heritage as unifiers and nation builders of Nepal. My ancestor, the warrior Khas Panday-Magar, as I learnt hailed from Sinja Valley, Jumla.

In 1980, I met an old Saru-Magar in Tansen and he told me of the Panday-Magar community living near his village close to Arebhanjyang in west Nepal. Years ago a nephew of mine, a colonel in the Nepal Army came across two young Panday-Magars whom he recruited for the army training in Butwal camp. So there are people claiming themselves to be Panday-Magar to this day. Whether we qualify or not; but today we tend to call ourselves the Panday-Chhetry, correctly spelled it is पाँडे in Devanagari. It is not to be confused with the Pande/Pandey, (Rajgharana)/Pandeya in Devanagari पाण्डे/पाण्डेय Brahmins mostly, who supposedly migrated from Kumaon of North India.

Our ancestors traversed through Palpa and reached Gorkha in the 16th Century. As one of the indigenous folk, *Adivasi*, of the western mountains, they evaded the caste system, maintained their own brand of spirituality, worshiping Mother Earth. The Masto Puja that is manifested in our once-every-12-year clan Diwali festival takes place to this day at Gorkha for all to see.

The tense relationship spilled over to Thuli-ama's kitchen floor where we all sat for meals. Thuli-ama made her sister, our mother, take the lower seating spot in the kitchen. The same was done to our father. Mother always found it unfair and discriminatory. It was a clash between two different mindsets: one inherently universal and the other narrowly local. Thuli-ama's treatment of Father was glaringly derogatory, degrading and disrespectful, contravening the prevalent social norms. Did she want, in a way, to ostracize my father for his cruel treatment of my mother? But it also meant indirectly ostracizing my Mother. Father was not even treated as equal to her daughters. It was painful for mother, and she often told me how much she was hurt.

Naturally, for us kids it did not matter where we sat to eat. We were anyway at the lowest rung in the hierarchy within the family. That was a different time, when caste and social status mattered much – not that Mother was affected by this.

Of course, for Thuli-ama, Panday was not just our family name. It encompassed all the Pandays (पाँडे) of Nepal. The irony was that in later years, two of her daughters, the eldest and the youngest one, were married off to our uncle, Colonel Bishnubahadur, and his eldest son Colonel Krishna. Her granddaughter was married into the Panday family too, to Bishnu Jung, son of Hem Jung of Dhalko, closely related to the Colonel.

Perhaps there were other reasons for Thuli-ama to put us in that social position. Did she despise Mother's thoughts and actions? Mother was different from other women, in many ways. I knew that Thuli-ama would not share the values Mother followed. Was Maicha going too far for her?

Understanding Mother's time in rebellion

My two elder sisters always supported Mother. I only followed them when I became aware of all the animosity, later. Mother did things we never would have done on our own in the area where we lived, or within the family. Women seeking independence were not tolerated even by other women, back then. Slowly, I began to see consistent, meaningful and practical patterns emerging in her actions and words. This not only surprised me, but also gave rise to opposition within the family and among relatives.

As I grew, I could discern and distinguish the changes taking place in the house. Her assertion for rights, against inequality and patriarchal hegemony, she believed could be manifested only through the education of girls. Years later when I understood it, I established a fund for girls' education. Justice would one day prevail to break the taboos in the caste and class systems.

I took up the issue of the caste system too during the training courses of progressive farmers (the successful farmers were called *Tuki*, the torch bearers named after the oil lamp). It was after the third progressive farmer training course that I came up with the concept of Tuki on 13

September 1977 to mobilize the local farmers for wider development programs in the remote areas of Sindhupalchok and Dolakha districts of east Nepal.

My Mother's ideas influenced me all through my life. For example, while developing a training system called Integrated Progressive Farmers' Training, conducted four times a year on four different topics, caste was an issue I raised slowly but consciously. The courses would last 15 days. But the classes and demonstrations needed to be held in the farmers' fields and the surrounding villages. A community kitchen was organised for the morning meals in the field.

In the first training course held in April 1977, at Thulopakhar of Sindhupalchok district, an argument flared among the trainees, on the very first day of the training session. It was meal time, and the participants were queuing up with their plates. The food was cooked by Kajiman Tamang and his wife whom I intentionally requested to take up cooking responsibility. For caste conscious communities of Brahmins and Chhetris, Tamangs are *Pani Chalne Bhaat Nachalne* (water acceptable, cooked rice not acceptable for so called higher castes).

Among the trainees, there was a man named Krishna Bahadur Mizar who was traditionally a shoemaker, and thus considered of low caste. Some of the others complained that he almost touched the rice pot with his plate. Immediately behind him was a Brahmin Meghnath Timilsina from his own village, Kaping. I was watching and hearing all this from a little distance in the courtyard. Then came a moment when I needed to intervene. I told everyone to place their plates on the ground and then to come back to pick up their meals when portions had been given out. That solved the problem for the moment.

Before this, there was a squabble in the morning while Kajiman was preparing to cook. One so called high-caste participant decreed that Kajiman Tamang could not cook his rice and maize dish. I told the participants, that Kajiman was going to cook, and if they wanted to eat they had better advise me how he could cook in a way that was acceptable to all. Then a wise man came out of the crowd of 18 men and shouted,

> *He should put some ghee in the empty pot, ahead of the water and grain, and then place it on the fire.*

Done! The ghee made from the holy cow milk is held as purifier. It was a tradition adapted for cooking food outside one's kitchen to be eaten with other people. So the contentions of the higher caste Brahmins were dealt with easily and everybody sighed in relief. We never again had a problem to do with the caste system. Over time, Mizar of the shoemaker caste became for years the best Tuki, a trained progressive farmer.

The legacy of the modesty of my mother was to be tested and appreciated. I tried to be true to her legacy. The first opportunity came when I was advised by a number of my friends such as late Social Scientist Prabha Thacker, Radio Journalist Krishnaa Tamrakar, entrepreneur Haridhoj Tulachan and relatives that I should not live alone. '*It will not be good for your health,*' they said. Prabha gave me the example of tourism entrepreneur,

Tekchandra Pokhrel, and how he returned to health with his second marriage. After a long contemplation, I agreed to follow their advice.

After I got to know Sharada better, there came an opportunity to let her meet with my son Arnico at my place. We invited her for a morning meal. We two cooked some rice and *karkalo (Colacasia esculenta)*, which many regard it as the lowliest of all vegetables. Both my modest dress and the food we cooked would have disappointed some, but it was not to be in her case. I saluted my mother!

But there was yet another test to be tried. Among the dishes at the wedding dinner were *dhindo* and *gundruk*, more 'lowly' food in the minds of many urban people. Some laughed about it; others seemed to be liberated, feeling it suddenly acceptable for them to try these dishes for the first time. Only a very few were just ashamed to see it. It was thought by some that the kind of catering presented at such occasions reflected the status of the inviting party. I did not believe that. For a self-made man who had undergone many ups and downs in life, nothing is for show, nothing is for prestige. The inhibition was long gone. I see it as a kind of tribute to my mother.

Both my mother and grandmother said that we were not supposed to eat poultry (*kukhura*), as this was the tradition in their families, but we could eat the wildfowl, *luinche*, from the hunt. The Pandays followed traditions brought into the clan by their wives. So we too were not the only ones in the community not eating *kukhura*. Of course, such rules were discarded over time, and many urban Brahmins and Chhetris became indiscriminate meat eaters. Besides our name and clan deity, Pandays have retained the tradition of eating wild boar at every auspicious occasion, like other *adivasi*.

Having left behind our ancestral niche in Sinja valley centuries ago, having failed to retain much of our cultural and religious identity and social ethics and norms, we became *janjati* to the other communities of Kathmandu Valley, following them in many cultural and religious matters and linked to the local social networks. We have become more integrated to the mainstream society of Nepal. An increasing number of our men and women marry those from diverse castes and families. That goes well with Mother's sayings, actions and social behavior.

Her Principles and Struggles against Social Taboos

In fact, Mother was developing, knowingly or unknowingly, assertive working principles, but with a benevolent heart and a smile on her face. Her principles were encouraging.

These were manifest in three principles, which I call Mother's Strategy for Survival Actions:

Gare Hunchha: Do it! With this she encouraged us to act. 'The things you want to achieve are possible only when you try.'

She would say, 'You will make it if you try, but never if you do not. Success or failure is a result of trying and trials.' This principle made me strive and take important steps in life.

Hane Marchha: She would tell us, 'Pull the slingshot (*guleli*)' and you may hit the target. But if you do not pull it, your hunt goes for nothing.'

Bole Tarchha: Speak up! But do it quickly. Nobody knows what will happen tomorrow. People may change their minds. People will only hear if you speak, if you do not, no one will hear or understand what you want. Those who understand you may trust you, but the ones who do not understand you may reject you.

Very early on, these principles helped me become what I have been and what I am now. Those were strategic lessons of encouragement and inspiration to me to cope and fight against prevalent injustices inherent in hierarchy in the society.

Hierarchy is manifested in social status (*adivasi to janjati*), within so called Dalits (*Mizar* and *Biswakarma*), domestic animals (cattle/buffalo, swine/wild boar), even deities, between communities, among family members (mother-in-law/daughter-in-law), married vs unmarried (daughters), among siblings with sons over the daughters, between relatives and between different cereals and meat.

My Mother believed that only an educated generation would take food, without segregating it into hierarchical values and prestige. Relegating of food was unacceptable to her. She would lecture us:

Food is the gift of nature, and a reward for your toils. It would be unfair to nature if you put one kind of food above another. The taste, aroma, nutrients, ways of cooking and eating habits may differ, but food should be food!

Mother valued rough and tough food, fiber rich and homegrown whenever possible. It suited her lifestyle and increased her stamina. She needed lot of energy for her chores: She alone was responsible for the cultivation of over a quarter of a hectare of partly irrigated land we had around our house at Jawalakhel.

She was rewarded by nature. She remained strong and healthy to do all of the work at home. As opposed to my father, she would not shy away from menial work. In fact, she believed that good health came normally through good and hard work.

She said the secret of healthy life, to a great extent, lies in the balance of three elements:

Tan (body/strength): Keeping fit: bodily health depended upon nature of activity, condition, shape and size of the body. These are influenced by thinking that creeps into mind, *man*.

Man (attitude/temptation): *Man* should control your words. What, how and when you speak about something may also harm your health. Hence, speak only when you need giving enough thought to consequences of your words. *Man, per se* is volatile, influenced by *dhan* (the material wealth at your disposal), livelihood.

Dhan (wealth/affordability): Utilize your wealth so it can lead to positive development. Earning is a medium with which you can afford to buy what you want: food, drink, and living condition. But it can also spoil your life and become the cause of your ills. Restraint in the use of *dhan* leads to harmony in your health.

Our body survives on food and water – my Mother would remind me of this all the time. That was quite something for a lady who had spent much of her childhood being with parents staying five days a week in the town. That was also something great for a lady who never learnt to read and write.

During her childhood, five out of seven days a week in town, she had rice, and even worse when coming home to Godavari for the weekends, she had rice as well. She longed to eat maize and millet. Although she hailed from a rice farming family, for her, rice was not the food of her choice. For many city dwellers, rice is a staple food of choice, and even more so for the rich, with rice commanding higher status. Such people very often despise maize dishes, but my mother disliked rice.

Maize was scarce, and it was thus regarded as an exotic food in her parental house. With just the kitchen garden for planting maize, the crop was eaten green, before maturity. She introduced the habit of eating maize to her family at Jawalakhel. We children were happy about it, because the maize tasted much better than the quality of rice available for us then.

There used to be heated debate over the menu at our Jawalakhel home. At times it became a matter of prestige and an issue of hierarchy who determined the menu. Mother being junior within the family hierarchy *Vis a Vis* both Father and Grandmother, not following the 'order, to cook according to their wishes' was against social norm. Mother would prefer to make different maize dishes for her and for the children, while grandmother and Father would get their rice and *dal*. Together with Dal-black gram, vegetable and pickle Father wanted to be served with *Masino* long-grained or *Marsi* short-grained rice: tasty, popular and prized varieties.

There were times when she was given cows or newly harvested rice by her brothers. In time she would exchange the rice given to her for maize in the market, keeping some to please Father and grandmother. This kind of behavior by my Mother caused a lot of dissent in the house.

For us kids whatever Mother cooked was tasty, and we ate with gusto because we were hungry all the time. We were required to eat mostly things produced at home and what was available in the garden. We did not have much choice to the day's menu, and we could not say which was tastier. The main point was that we got the quantity we needed to fill our bellies. That was important. Looking back I know that we were well nourished.

We had sufficient land area growing maize, beans and vegetables in our large plot of land at Jawalakhel. There was the centuries-old-system of small irrigation functioning that helped us to grow different food crops year round. Mother's loving hands would look after the farming and

Father's cash income from his job made sure we always had enough to eat.

We did not have rice land. Neither were we, the Pandays, permitted by tradition to keep a buffalo. Mother was happy about all this.

Damned Class and Caste Consciousness

The Brahmin-Rimal men (neighbors), friends of Father, would pop into our kitchen, usually when my mother finished cooking for the morning meals. Mother was good at making simple food taste better. She would dish out her best prepared from the available materials.

The Rimals especially did not want to miss the tomato pickle, Mother prepared! They would even try dishes with onion or garlic which were forbidden in Brahmin kitchens. Yet they would not eat rice cooked by us. We were *Pani Chalne Bhat Nachalne,* for them which meant that while they could take water from us, rice that we cooked was not acceptable for their caste.

Life was hard for Mother at Jawalakhel, surrounded by the snobby Rana, orthodox Rimal Brahmins, 10-Nami families (Giri/Puri/Mhanta..), bluffing Basnet-Chhetry and contact-shy Newars. Her way of doing things and dealings with people looked strange to many in the locality.

She treated, so called, *'low caste'* people or so called, 'higher caste' families, equally. Their wealth or poverty did not impress her. As long as they were nice to her she was nice to them. She could not be chastised by the so called high caste families because of her strong personality.

Mother was a generous person. No one coming to us needed to go away empty handed. She shared anything she had with the visitors. It could be as banal as dried red chilies from her garden, when she did not have anything better to share. Beggars or yogis would come to collect food and/or money normally in the morning hours. Despite the fact that we were struggling with our own chronic food shortages, she would share even the food cooked for the family with them when she saw them wanting.

Your ability to share what you have, even when you have very little to share, reveals your true character. Your happiness is bonded with the happiness of others you serve. For that you need good intention. Wealth alone is nothing.

Such outpourings were quite emotional to feel for us kids. At times she would lecture us at length over the value of a smile and kindness towards the others.

From her sick bed, in her last words of caution, she dictated her youngest daughter Dolma,

Make sure that whoever works in our garden is appreciated and adequately rewarded if you have to get their help.

That magnanimity, a god given gift, she possessed.

My Father wanted some of his clothes washed and ironed by Dhobi, from the traditional laundering community living at Dhobighat, nearby west of Jawalakhel. That meant there was a constant coming and going of the washer women (Dhobini), sometimes, with their husbands carrying bigger loads.

Mother made friends with the washer women. She took her Dhobini friends into our kitchen. She would not send them away without offering them whatever she could to eat. That was not acceptable to my grandmother, who was a Thapa Chhetry lady, and who was rigid and clear about her perception. Grandmother would very frequently get the shock of her life-time. Their age difference was hardly of two decades yet there seemed to be a real generation gap between them.

The Dhobis were regarded as a 'low caste' community and traditionally were not allowed to enter a Chhetry kitchen. One was not even supposed to drink water from their hands: *Bhat-Pani Nachalne*. Mother did not grasp that it was a taboo. Or did she do it consciously?

Well, she had a different upbringing. Growing up among shoe-makers, tailors and smiths (the occupational castes: *Bhat Pani Nachalne*) she frequented their houses, played with their children and ate their food. I remember getting Dasain Tika and food at a shoemaker's house at Khatrichhap in Manedanda. I thought of their house as my *mamaghar*, my maternal uncle's house. Her parents and siblings, perhaps, had a practical purpose to tolerate Mother's kind of socializing in the village. They did not want to antagonize the helping hands of the occupational castes.

The three occupational castes (tailor, shoemaker and smith) were kept in harmonious friendship and in close proximity by the farming community. They could not be hurt by words or through deeds, in the slightest, lest they would fail to support the villagers in important festivities or in crucial cultivation times. Without their especially skilled contributions, the farming community would not survive.

When the households in the community slaughtered a goat, certain parts or portions of the cadaver was given to them. The tailors would get the tail portion, the shoemaker the neck piece and the smith the head of the animal. Such was the tradition of sharing in a community of interdependence.

Mother was, in all probability, brought up without this precise tradition of discrimination between lower or higher castes. She found the caste system a social injustice meted to the most useful, laborious and productive communities. For Mother, the caste system was absurd and she felt that the notion should not have been allowed to persist.

The rituals and mores followed in the cultural matters and the sense of caste-hood understood by Mother and Grandmother lay, a world apart. The arguments and quarrels between them would have no end in their lifetime; particularly on the issue of caste.

Years later I discovered that I could not agree with her more. For me there is no such thing as a Dalit. This degradation of human beings is immoral. We have no right to call any one a Dalit; in fact it should be taken out of our social, legal and political vocabulary.

Father would remain silent and would not intervene in the duels, debates or discussions between the two ladies,

Mother and Grandmother. I did not expect Father to risk his relationship by taking sides with either.

In fact we did not know what his perception on caste-hood was. He was in the army where even in those days, tolerance a must to keep the soldiers under control was.

Mother had, as her best friend, an emancipated or freed 'bonded' lady Ghartini named Indri. She was regarded as slightly unequal at my Mother's parental home. They grew up together. Indri's wish was that she be married near Mother's place, and so it happened. They remained lifelong friends in proximity and supported each other.

Mother was adored by her friends from the so called lower caste groups. I began to deduce from her efforts and sense of spirituality that whatever beliefs one had should embrace humane values. Let people be what they are and let them believe in any religion, but whatever they do they should do without loss of kindness, without degradation, without segregation in castes, color or cultures. God treats all living beings equally and we all are his creation.

Mother was fluent in the Newari language and her nickname was, *Maicha* ('the little girl' in Newari). She would befriend many Newari speaking *Jyapu* (farming) families. By tradition prevalent then, even the Jyapu*s* were placed socially a step below Chhetry, *'Pani Chalne Bhat nachalne'*.

She had a special bond with one *Jyapu* family, Chhabahale Dai and his wife Burumaya. They lost their first child, a son. Following the tragedy Burumaya bore five daughters, one after another, perhaps hoping to have a son.

Only the seventh child was a son, born in 1961. For Mother's friend it was a gift of God! In order that the last child, a precious son, would survive, the astrologer had advised Burumaya to trick the evil spirits. She asked my Mother to 'buy' her son from her and raise him as her own son, so that the evil spirits would not take him away from her.

Mother had her own intimate experience going through similar trauma. That was with me, and I have written about it in the second chapter in detail. Mother helped her friend Burumaya to rear her last child, Harigopal. He survived, is now around 54 years old and lives at Chhabahal, Lalitpur town. He loved and respected my mother not less than his own natural mother.

He grew up to be a respected man conscious of his duties and family responsibility. Till this day, we think of him as our 'youngest brother', and we called his mother our mother too. On Dec 17, 2009 we participated in her 3rd Jankhu celebration at her '88 years, 8 months, 8 days and 8hrs of age' in the evening. A few months later she died a happy mother.

We had a unique relationship with the *Jyapu* families. We are thankful to Mother for bringing me at least closer to the *Jyapu*, who command my respect for their high social philosophy and values.

Educating Daughters!

Although, Mother could be considered 'literate' in coping with the kind of life she was leading, she remained completely illiterate in matters regarding reading and writing. Also because of that lack and weakness she stressed the importance of education:

Educate girls, it is important for advancement!

She seemed to advocate gender equality through girl's education in the sense that we talk of today. Many say only an educated mother is a guarantee for a girl's education. But that did not apply to my mother. Though she had no formal education, she had the will. We take pride in the fact that four of her six surviving children, two sons and two daughters, did manage to go to the schools. She saw that in her lifetime. Unfortunately, by the time two schools opened nearby specifically targeting girls, my two elder sisters and my half-sister Gyana were too old, had been married off early and left to face their fate. They too, like our mother, remained unable to decipher written characters.

In her times girls were forbidden to go to school. The older generation thought school would make them morally corrupt. Yet, I do remember Mother taking her two younger daughters Renu and Dolma, to enroll them in the recently opened Madan Memorial Girls' Schools at Pulchowk and Adarsha Biddhya Mandir in Mangalbajaar, both in Patan, a walking distance away. Renuka studied up to master's level and worked in a high school in Kathmandu while Dolma completed domestic science teacher training at Sano Thimi campus and worked as a teacher in a private school in Lalitpur.

Mother had the knack or a talent or a hidden gift from God for anticipation, making judgment of situations that she thought would turn out badly. One example I can think of, towards the end of her life, concerns the wedding of Renuka, my second youngest sister.

One day the priest returned with Vengeance

He came with a proposal for Renu's wedding. He knew of a certain Thapa family in his locality, looking for a bride for their eldest son. Mother was surprised by the gesture of the priest we had long avoided. How dare he do it?

After hearing all the nice stories about the Thapa man, everybody thought the proposal needed to be considered. Mother was not convinced. She opposed it. The groom was said to be bright and working as an engineer, and the family was not less than aristocratic in origin at Lainchaur.

The groom was an electrical engineer, respected for his ability to solve complex mathematical problems related to electricity, earning a salary even without regular office attendance. His office was mulling whether to retain him or not.

As it soon came to surface that the Thapa man had a past showing him not in a good light, as a husband though by education he was technically well qualified engineer. The Thapa family kept mum and hid his past and the condition of his health while negotiating with us.

He was suffering from a neurotic problem. He was proud of his only child Shraddha, a daughter from Renu. He was a loving Father but passed away early. Did the priest bring the entire proposal knowing fully the personal history of the lad to take revenge on us? Or did he try to get again in touch with us with the kind of middleman role he played?

Father had insisted that Renuka got married to the Thapa man. Mother felt that this was not the right man for her. Augmenting her fear was that the ex-priest had been rejected by the family years ago and he might have been seeking revenge. Unable to resist Father's insistence, Mother walked out of the 'negotiations.' I always wondered why she reacted the way she did. She had a fighting character. She must have had reason. Renu got married but the burden fell on me.

But instead of being involved again in a squabble with father, Mother retaliated by being conspicuously absent during days of 'final negotiations' with the Thapa family of Lainchaur between May and June of 1975. That surprised me. Why did she give in? She had always been a fighter for what was right and was not a person to give in or give up easily. I fear she foresaw some other problems to be faced had she insisted to her standpoint.

There were several ways to explain her behavior. For one, her health was failing. Also, she had no means of financing Renuka's wedding on her own. Father had not been supporting her. He was now living with his 'other wife.' Was she threatened? Was Renuka pushing her to agree to father's decision? Years later we saw Mother proved right, but for Renuka it was too late and her life was filled with struggle. Mother did not live to see Renuka's fate for she died 7 months after the wedding but Father lived to regret it.

Mother herself had had no choice. Married before she had even reached 18, she wanted to see that her daughter did not go through a similar ordeal.

Defiant Acts

In a democracy, today, we take it for granted that we all have equal rights. Mother was not so fortunate. She did not feel free most of her life. She had to carve herself a niche to exercise a little freedom. That niche may not have been broader than the family and circle of friends to begin with. Mother's constant efforts to have her rights respected did not pay off in her lifetime. Her problems only grew. But she continued asserting her rights, despite reality responding to her with harsher terms.

After office hours was the time for father to go out with his friends. On the one hand, you could consider the fact that after the day's hard work he needed time to relax. Where could he do that other than with his friends? But this time conflicted with Mother's home chores in the evening, since Father was regularly absent from home at dinner time. Mother had to wait for him to return home, sometimes until 10-11pm.

To show loyalty and 'love' towards their husbands (perhaps more submission or subjugation) women were supposed to eat beginning with the leftovers from their husband's plates. That required Mother to wait for Father before she could have her dinner. He would come home late, eat and go to bed. Then it was Mother's turn to eat what was left, wash up and try to fall asleep at odd midnight hours. She regularly got up by 4 am. That hardly gave her 4-5 hours of sleep. I remember Grandmother telling me a similar story about her own hardships as a young bride in the 25 member family, but even harsher.

I do not recall how long Mother accepted this as her duty. Nor am I sure how much she took it as her fate. But she was forced to endure this 'tradition'. We would see her in a somber mood in the mornings, perhaps because of the long wait for a cold meal around midnight, and lack of sleep almost every night. We feared for her health.

One morning, just before Father was to leave for his duty, an argument flared between them. Standing face to face and eye to eye Mother was trying to suppress her tone and Father was fretting and trying to turn his eyes away from hers. This time they were not arguing on a trivial point. From what I gathered it sounded like a mutiny in the making, an *'act of her defiance, unfolding'*. Now I knew she had not taken the whole thing as her fate. In fact it sounded as if it had been nagging her mind for decades. Was Mother conscious of what she was doing?

I have enough! If you can't figure it out, it is about me waiting for your dinner time.

But you've always done it for me. Why don't you want to carry on?

That's right. It was for you, not for me. I'm sick of waiting for you to come home late, night after night, waiting for you with an empty stomach.

So what do you want?

From today on, there will be a new rule. I'll cook the evening meal as usual and eat with the children. I hate going to bed late at night.

Are you telling me I have to follow a new rule?

Yes, if you take it that way! I'll leave your meal in the kitchen for you. You are free to come home whenever you want. If you need a hot meal, light a fire, and heat it up yourself. Otherwise, eat it cold.
Remember, if you leave the utensils unwashed overnight, you risk God's wrath. It is also not allowed by our tradition. You know that, don't you?

She meant what she said. The point had a chilling effect on father. He stood spellbound. Despite a stern grimace and staring eyes void of affection, his response was not forthcoming. Perhaps he saw his privilege on the wane. Normally, he was not overbearing to her even in his gestures. This was also true now. That was his character. He was always reluctant to speak his mind. He was never assertive nor did he express what he wanted. He would sink within his mind, a silent sufferer. Sure enough Mother's rule infuriated him.

That day he left home for his office without uttering another word. In the evening, the main door was left unlocked so he could sneak in without waking anyone up. Mother had left his meal in the kitchen as promised to him in the morning. What would he find? What would he do? We kids were wondering the whole evening. We fell asleep.

Father must have had shock of his life! Perhaps he had not taken her words seriously. Did he take it as a minor setback to his macho personality? We heard from Mother that he came home late at night as usual. When he got the same message the next day, mind you, it was a magic! It worked after the first night onwards, but unfortunately not in a positive way.

Father would not talk much and remained expressionless, mostly quiet. He never talked about the new order in the house, he just followed it. How did he feel about it? Father was a changed person to look at, much more serious than he already was with us and would listen to her in earnest.

I do not know how he took it in his heart. Was his male chauvinism offended? Was he angry with her? Did he think Mother was being rude to him? Did he feel his masculinity challenged? Did he become colder towards her?

Putting this little domestic incident within the context of time and place in which we lived; it was a first big step towards revolutionizing not only the household but taming the male domination, too. Yet, the change in their relationship over time confirmed my fear that he had felt subjugated, disgraced and had become revengeful in silence.

Was Father seeking an escape? Grandmother could not help him here. As a widow who had been the youngest daughter-in-law herself, she had lived through the past as a young bride suffering the tyranny of a large family dominated by male members long enough. She did not want to take sides. Perhaps she agreed with my Mother tacitly and felt the issue she raised carried value in the life of any woman.

Father grew quieter day by day towards Mother. At times he would not even notice her presence. We children were saddened by the outcome. Things did not stop there. Her assertions were beginning to manifest themselves covering wider areas and in manifold ways within the family matters.

In the society Mother was part of, especially in the Panday family, the movement of the women folk was rather curtailed and at time, strictly restricted within a defined circle. One could not think of seeing Panday women alone on the road in those days in town. There were different reasons for it. No other families suffered as much harsh treatment and humiliation as the Panday families at the hands of the ruling cliques of Shahs and Ranas, over 150 years. The history of Nepal is full of accounts of brutality of the rulers, particularly against the Pandays. To leave women folk exposed was tantamount to inviting social and political troubles.

But Mother made it a point to move around on her own accord. I was not aware of her asking for permission from Father or Grandmother, as expected in our society, to go out. Not that she was afraid that Father or for that matter Grandmother would say no to her adventure. Father knew that Mother would not in any way accept being told what she could and could not do. It was no use to argue with her, as she normally had better arguments to counter with. She did not try to justify her decisions or actions. She did what she thought was right for her and for the family.

There must have been disagreements between my parents over a long time. We could see some sort of change in their interactions and relationship. The change in their relationship was perhaps also due to intellectual disparity between them. My mother was wiser and more practicable despite her illiteracy. She had never made him feel it, yet he was at a loss.

He began to look elsewhere for emotional fulfillment. Yet when I showed an astrologer his *janma kundali* posthumously, it appeared that he did grieve that fateful night in February, 1975 when my mother died. Did he regret his treatment of her?

When we look at the contemporary, politically biased so called, revolutionaries today, we see blood stained hands and an evil mindset working against the innocent people destroying their age-old culture, community life, civilization and sense of nationhood developed over millennia. My mother, on the other hand, achieved changes without the politics of blood-spilling and vendetta. The difference I feel is that my mother left behind followers, at least in her children, to begin with. I vowed to carry on her legacy. She risked and strained her relation with Father in doing so. That was the price she paid on behalf of the future generation. I am convinced that the bloodstained revolutionaries of today will have no mourners and followers within the era of our life time.

One expects a revolutionary to be a person either hurt; socially, politically or abused by the family members and to develop feelings of vengeance; or a saint diverting human qualities to inspire others. My Mother was neither type in its extreme.

But she definitely was hurt. She was hurt and abused in many ways by her own husband. The excess of Father's womanizing was the first wound inflicted on her. She must have felt miserable and frustrated countless times with daily strife. She revolted within the family while over time I noticed she was no less a revolutionary in her own terms and time. My mother stood out because of her actions and thought. She was a determined housewife and shaped her household to her terms. Mother revolted in a passive way within the family, by inspiring us with her ideas and actions.

Chronicling of Mother's Last Days

Her last words which she dictated to my youngest sister Dolma, reached me only on Dec 5, 1974. She enquired,

Is my son Kumar coming home?

She feared she would not see me before leaving this world and said her last day was approaching. It was her last wish to see me come home and meet her one last time. That was three months before her death. On the other hand she expressed the wish that I not come because of the expense. Why could I not leave Switzerland to be by her side? It is again the money that denied me the deep satisfaction in my life. I have to leave this guilt behind, one day, but when?

Between, Nov 30 - Dec 1, 1974 onwards, her health worsened. On 19-20 December 1974, she put on with difficulty the best dress she had and walked around to impress the family that they needed not to worry about her. Everything about her was ok.

That was read by the family as the indication that the worst was to come. Alarmed, my youngest sister took Mother's *janma-kundali* to show it independently, to 3 astrologers in Patan and did not tell them that she was sick. Yet all the three astrologers agreed upon one conclusion: an approaching sad event!

Mother had started telling her children at home that she was approaching her death; that was two months before the astrologers' predictions. She started giving instructions to her daughters at home, how they should be managing the household. Her interest on the wellbeing of other people was not dwindling at all. In particular, she was worried that after her death others would not treat the ladies who came to help her in the cultivation well, and pay them what they deserved. Her sense and value of empathy was so touching!

A lady doctor frequented the Jawalakhel Library, the Addhyayan Griha which I had played pivotal role in establishing. She was there on Sundays and Thursdays and my mother was taken to her for checkups in the beginning of her illness, during the month of January-February 1975.

On Feb. 13, 1975, Mother visited a temple. In the evening she said she was unwell and went to bed. On 16th of February 1975, she seemed to be doing slightly better than she had been in December last. She appeared fit to move around as much as her frailty allowed.

February 17, 1975: What was new in her life and behavior was that she started frequenting shrines and temples, despite her loss of appetite and frail body. She walked over to Sankata, and Mahankal temples in Kathmandu city, 4 km away.

I do not remember that she ever was so spiritual in the past, so these were pretty unusual indications in her behavior. She even consulted the local shaman and that was unusual as well; in the past she trusted and always consulted astrologers. That was another symbolic gesture of 'someone at journey's end.'

On 19th of February 1975, her condition deteriorated. She could not sleep and would tussle and roll much on her bed, at night but the next day she put up courageous behavior as if she was alright.

A doctor had to be called in. First, Dr. Vijay, eldest son of Father's best friend at Taphalonha, Dr. Basant Bahadur Rajbhandari, came to see his 'Kaji Ama' and diagnosed her *'having asthma that had apparently triggered her high blood pressure'*. Then Dr. Sundar Mani Dixit was called in. He was at loss to diagnose her. He speculated and wondered, with his right hand touching his fore head:

It is so complex, perhaps a very bad disease she is fighting against, with a high blood pressure. All indications showed a mysterious loss of blood. What could it be?

Over the month of January she must have become seriously ill, perhaps diagnosed again with a 'high blood pressure and low blood'! I am still wondering why I did not get any information during the whole month of January 1975 about Mother. The only good hospital in the area was run by the UMN at Shanta Bhawan, Jhamsikhel. I had earlier requested Father and brother to leave no stone unturned to look after her, do everything possible, even admit her in the hospital, the cost should not bar them from taking her to Shanta Bhawan, and we would manage it. But she did not reach a hospital.

In the morning of February 20th, 1975 my brother wrote nothing about how serious she was. He only wrote; '*Let God be on our side that she should recover.*' She was taking in only liquid food. Renuka came in the morning after a long time from her home at Lainchaur. That night at 2100 hrs our Mother left us. She died of 'unknown sickness' and without being diagnosed.

She was born on February 23rd, 1915 AD and died on 20th February 1975--having lived a tumultuous life span of 59 years 11 months and 27 days--of an illness that even the renowned Dr. Sundar Mani Dixit was at loss to diagnose.

She chose the same *Tithi* to die as the *Tithi* of her birth; the ninth day of New Moon. She was born on 12th day and died on the 8th day of 11th month of Nepali calendar. People in Nepal take the figure 8-12 as a very ominous sign. God's will!

It took two hours for all the close friends, neighbors and relatives living in close proximity to assemble and prepare her funerary farewell. At 2300 the funeral procession moved slowly towards Pashupati, 5 kilometers away.

February 21, 1975: At 0100 hrs *Dagbatti* (fire the pyre) was placed on the pyre, *Antim Sanskar*, the rite of passage was completed. Her body was cremated at Pashupati Aryaghat on the clan cremation Ghat, *Bhakari*, and North of the main bridge.

By 5 am, it was all over and there was no trace of my Mother, except in the hearts of her kin, friends and relatives. That it took only 4 hours for the fire to consume her indicated how frail and reduced she had become over her time of sickness! Having born nine children, she was never sick during her entire life except for the last 4 months. Her suffering was, many said, not that long, compared to Grandmother and even Father in their times.

At 1100hrs Kathmandu time on 21st February 1975, Father sent me, the first and the last telegram ever: '*Mother expired*', and letters followed. In the first letter after her death he wrote me,

'*Be solaced, your Father is still alive. It is His will.*'

I do not remember what I jotted down and posted immediately for Father to write me back,

'*I can understand your deep sorrow!*'

Did he too mourn the death of Grandmother, the way I mourned the death of my mother? In a way I felt so unlucky that I could not be by Mother's side when she expected me so much.

She got *Kajkiriya* (rites to passage) according to *Sanatan Dharma* (ancient Hindu religious tradition) but the only son at home, my brother, had not received his holy thread but participated in the ritual with a *Kush* symbolizing the holy thread. A Brahmin friend of mine, Nanda Prasad Rijal accompanied him in the *Kiriya* rituals lasting 13 days. Father bore all the cost for the whole ritual, a last tribute to Mother, who had suffered immensely from him. A day after her 13-day ritual mourning with *Rudri*, *Hom* and *Daan* rituals, Father wrote,

You now need to console yourself that you still have your Father alive; not everything is lost.

The last time I met her was in 1973. Thus her journey that started in the rice fields of the foothills of Manedanda, Godavari came to an end tilling the maize fields of Jawalakhel. From a cheerful little *Maicha* to her parents and friends, to a brave lady who suffered a lot but maintained her posture behind her nuptial veil for the sake of her family and for the name of her clan.

I have not lost everything of my Mother. I still have her wedding veil, the insignia of my parents' most important social occasion, from the point in time when the knot was tied to establish their relationship and our being in this world. When we look into her life, all her miseries as well as the best moments of her life, at least with her children, happened once she got the veil to cover her tears during her wedding. Everything happened underneath and behind her wedding veil.

On the night of 21st February 1975, after reading the telegram from Father that reached me in the afternoon telling me of my mother's demise, I had trouble getting to sleep, what little deep and brief sleep I got was devoted to a dream of her.

Clad in snow white *fariya* (farmer lady's frock) and *chaubandi cholo* (typical Nepali blouse), the *sapko* (end part of *fariya*) covering her hair and in an unknown surrounding, standing alone not far from me, she was telling me with a soothing voice,

> *My son! Whenever you are in difficulty, think of me. I shall always be with you!*

It was at the Studenten Haus, Dietikon, near Zurich, when I woke up. I found myself almost choking with the thought that it was all in the dream. On my bed table lay the telegram from my Father, reminding me of what had happened the previous night at Jawalakhel. But the dream I believed was a reality to remain with me all my life. I do think of my Mother whenever I have some sort of uneasiness coping with hard times.

As a tribute to her thinking for the wellbeing of people who need support, on her death anniversary, February 23rd or on Ninth Day of New Moon, we make it a point that at least two old people, preferably both men and ladies, those 'forlorn souls' sitting begging in the temple area of Baglamukhi in Patan, get a full *Sida* of food and some cash,. With this I have come to terms with my bereavement, yet my love and gratitude to her lasts long after her death.

Living memories of my Mother

In life she was contentedly self-effacing. She wore simple clothing farmer style as in her parental village in Godavari. It seemed her life's purpose was to live simply, without barriers of caste, religion, dress codes or prejudice of food.

She could very well meld Panday-Kajini (the title given to the wives of Panday Kaji) sentiments with the trends of the common folk. It was a big departure from the so called prestige of the Panday clan which maintained some semblance of aristocracy (khandani), despite our difficulties making ends meet, no matter how hard my Mother toiled. She was humble in life and cared little for etiquette. Imitating others of her equals who boosted of the clan prestige was far from her liking.

For her the food was the Gift of God. It should be taken thanking God with a smile, no matter what food is to be had.

Despite fateful adversities in her life, Mother maintained cheerful expressions on her face in front of us all. She would normally rather be in a jovial disposition whenever we were together than to harbor outrages even when things went too far.

My last and the lasting image of her embossed and colorfully imprinted in my memory is her smiling face on an unblemished blue sky and the sparkling snowy mountains dancing in the far north of the Valley from the terrace facing the Jawalakhel zoo. We were giggling on the north terrace of Mataaneghar and she was laughing and was full of happiness. That picture is ingrained in me, and no other picture has superseded it.

She amused herself with little pleasures. She took pleasure from the kitchen jokes, or the company of Dhobini or Indri, the Ghartini lady, her childhood friend who lived nearby. These were immensely gratifying; ever since I have understood their way of looking at the world.

At, almost every meal, we traded jokes and she would invent more. The kitchen jokes had become our daily staple of family life albeit without Father around with us. Earlier even when Father was still eating from Mother's kitchen, he was normally absent during our joint meals. Either he had to take his meal early to attend his office or was out till late at night.

The best jokes received the loudest laughs. It was a fun and the food tasted much better eating amid laughter with her. My brother would not utter a word or raise his head up to participate in our jokes during the meals. Years later my sister Renu told me that he published a collection of jokes almost all finding roots in our kitchen, all that in a little book: entitled, 'Jokingly' (*Khyal Khyal*). Well, we forgot to apply for a home patent for our jokes, didn't we?

Mother loved farming and no work was too degrading. It was her lifestyle; she was proud to remain a farming girl. Perhaps she missed her part in touching the soil, planting and looking after animals when she was a girl. She had to be with her working father in the Patana-ghar in Patan throughout most of her childhood, yet even so, she was denied schooling.

At home in Jawalakhel she kept cows, goats and birds. I remember Mother looking after very old Kali-the cow till her last breath. She used to say, Kali for her was like a mother. We profited from her 'hobby' of being good to animals. I could also have my animals: cats, dogs, pigeons, ducks, rabbits, myna birds and parrots.

Whenever Mother couldn't milk cows while she was in menstrual period or not feeling well or away from home, Father had to jump in to milk. He could do that but was rewarded with less milk and more of kicks from the cows. We were amused thinking that Father got punished for never taking time to feed them!

Mother also churned butter. It was her most loved pastime. The *singmang* would be filled with freshly made ghee. She loved to drink *mohi* (buttermilk); *mohi* and *makaiko dhindo* (maize paste) went well and was the best food we could have during late summer.

Besides keeping cattle and goats she liked the company of cats, dogs and chickens. Both dogs and hens would follow her around the house; they understood her well and *vice versa*. Father shared her love of dogs. We always had dogs around. She looked after them as if they were her children.

One of her favorite hens came out early one morning from her cage with her back featherless and naked. All the feathers had been pulled off. Mother was alarmed and went to see whether others were alive. Outside the cage there were the feathers scattered all over the place from her favorite hen. It seems a jackal had tried to pull her out from the cage. Luckily, the jackal only got hold of her long feathers from her back.

We had three dogs living together with us. One Situ, a Tibetan Apso with light beige fur, was my favorite. Mother was looking after two dogs Jirel and Namche, both males. The first was a brown, somewhat long bodied, similar to Dachshund which I had brought from Jiri Dolkha and given him the name Jirel. He would be chained the whole day because he was super active and too clever. He would follow Mother everywhere in the house. She was the one he respected most. Jirel felt secure to sleep inside the house and never slept in the daytime.

Major Chakrabahadur Bista, a neighbour and relative, was Joint Commissioner (*Saha-Anchaladhis*) at Namche Bazaar in Solukhumbu district. Once he asked me whether I wanted a dog from Khumbu. He brought me a cute little dog from Namchebajaar. I named him Namche. Namche slept or stayed awake the whole day or night out in the open. Namche would not enter the house till morning to get his food. He was looking after the family from the garden and when required he would bark at strangers passing by the house at night. In a way he was never in the rooms and would not come into house even if you would call him to come in. He preferred the outdoor life in all weather and seasons.

In September 1971, Jirel died. It saddened Mother in particular. Jirel was for her like the youngest of her 'sons.' Three years later Situ, my Apso dog too died. I was very sad. I was absent from home while she was in pain.

Over the years Mother lost all her teeth. She was chewing too much beetle nut. Father did the same, but he had a dentist friend who mended and treated his teeth and jaws, whenever he had toothaches. But Mother went without any teeth for years and I found it ridiculous to see her smile anymore without the 'pearls'. When I could afford it, I bought her a nice set of teeth to fit into her jaws. It looked so funny to see her laugh again but with the artificial teeth which we were not used to.

Torturing the Loving Heart

Sometimes, as in any family situation, a son will hurt his mother unintentionally or unconsciously. Two instances come to mind: one was in a drama I had acted in the Dasain of 1957. We were four, Fattebahadur Thapa, Bhairabbahadur Khadka, Purnabahadur Rana and me. We wrote a drama and rehearsed to play on the ground outside Jawalakhel Shivalay. The drama was based on a social problem prevalent in those times. My role was that of a very sick son. There were hundreds of women who cried aloud hearing pathetic situations on the drama.

Mother did not appreciate my role in the drama. She had cried seeing me pretending to be sick on the stage. It was too real for her. But we generated good will among the people, and they responded lavishly and generously when we went on *Deusi-bhailo* rampage throughout the night in the following Tihar, festival of lights. We collected lot of money and used it for the school we had founded.

The second time I tortured her was when I wrote a letter from a faraway place, that I was suffering. In fact I was suffering from the deepest homesickness and it reflected in my letter. And that was interpreted as me lying on my *death bed*. In those days there was no direct contact possible. I deeply regretted my foolishness.

Mother on Treks

Mother was used to walking the 12 km distance from our home to her parental house in two hours with us kids. For her that was a pretty short, slow walk and too regular and monotonous to satisfy her need. I did not mind doing it, and as I grew up, I often accompanied her to Godavari.

While she was not interested in visiting temples, I was, and she would watch me go three times around a temple or a shrine with pipal tree at Godamechaur. She would just wait for me at a distance, bored with my slow pace to finish my round. I do not remember her coming with me to the shrines. But I would bring her some Prasad from the shrines.

There were long walks she planned, to travel over the high hills close to Phulchoki Mountain and go to the other side of the Kathmandu Valley into another valley with clean mountain streams and greenery around. They were so tempting. I knew I could always accompany her. My Father had done the same when he was a kid and living in Bihebar but as a cow herder. I on the other hand roamed Phulchoki Mountains as a kid, but on school holidays. How times have changed.

Mother and I often travelled over the hills from Godavari to Bihebar. In one of our numerous treks, we had just entered into the valley beyond the ridge behind the Godavari Kunda. She suddenly stopped, took me into her arms and said,

Something smells foul, the smell of a wild animal. It smells like a leopard.

I was afraid it would jump on me!

Mother, are you sure it can be a leopard?
Wait; there must be a leopard around. We need to be quiet and be careful. But we must not fear. A leopard after its meal is less dangerous, but I am not sure whether this one has eaten.

A few steps downhill towards Bihebar, we found a freshly killed cattle carcass. The leopard had had his day and must have been resting in the bush nearby. She assured me,

The leopard had enough to eat, so we are safe to walk away, but at a faster pace, my boy. It is only downhill now to the Thapa house.

I wondered at her and admired her; how brave she was. She was to me the epitome of courage. She knew animal smells and what to make of them! All that was so interesting to learn from her!

Though she would sometimes call it a 'temple visit' to a holy shrine out somewhere I was going with her the first time, I could see that it just did not fit, since she was not carrying the *pujasardam* (the offerings). I think she mentioned the temple, deities and *puja* just to please me. It was a trek for her pleasure and of course, mine too I shared with her.

She pleased herself with the long walks and satisfied my craving to walk and visit temples far from our place, so it was a compromise. What was important also to me was that she enjoyed the long treks and visiting relatives, particularly the relatives of Grandmother in Bihebar, where my Father spent his first few crucial years of growing up.

My first solo trek: My Mother's numerous hobbies and habits inculcated in me that 'hands-on' is just fun, far from shameful. Her habit of making short and longer walks, for days at a time, taking me with her for what we today call 'trekking', was infectious. It at least affected me more deeply than my other siblings.

I got this lust for walks by myself. Believe me, Mother was an avid trekker. I inherited the fun and value of treks from her. People say it is trekking that I got used to, but I take it as walking for a healthy long life.

The first time I ventured out alone on my own was after doing my school end exams in the winter of 1955. I was 12 years old. I got from Father his army overcoat for my first trek, and addresses of people he knew from his services on my route. The large pockets of the overcoat served as sacks to put things into and, the overcoat itself became a 'sleeping bag' during the nights and a raincoat under little drizzles. The first trek of my life alone took me over Sisneri, in Lalitpur district, Lankuri-bhanjyang, Bihebar, Roshi Khola and Panauti in Kabre district, the farthest out, then returning on the back of a truck over the old route down Sangabhanjyang. It was my first trek *par excellence*!

Most of the treks took place before our children went off to the USA for further studies. Many treks were undertaken when they were home on holidays. My wish was to have them feel like a Nepali first, get the taste of Nepali food, enjoy Nepal's magnificent natural beauty. Let them first experience life in Nepal, feel the struggles and face the challenges of a common person, yet live a blessed life that they would not get to the fullest in the industrialized countries. All these efforts paid. I never wanted them to dream of 'America, America' before they dreamt of Nepal. Now both of them are dreaming of future living in Nepal.

Over the past decades after my professional life I made many treks with my wife Sharada and my youngest son Somikumar Jung. We started treks when he was just over 3 years old in the winter of 2006. He walked 5 days. We remember carrying him on our back only for about 35 minutes during his first trek from Birethanti to Ghodepani and over the ridge down to Ghandrung and back to Birethanti. When he was 6 years old he could do the trek to Muktinath and walk 11 consecutive days. I hope Somi too starts dreaming of Nepal's other corners and dreams of the future of Nepal while working and living for Nepal.

It has nothing to do with my patriotism. I wanted to give my kids a home both physically and mentally, an anchorage in the rich cultures of Nepal, as my mother tried to do to me.

In Gratitude to my Mother

I wanted to work to preserve Mother's legacy. The times I lived were tough to cope with. But I am the product of the toughest times of my parents, especially of Mother. As a tribute to her, I started to concentrate our private support to the needy in seven areas: scholarships to needy girls, gifting books to libraries, activities in environmental protection, support for women's efforts, farmer's initiatives, contributions towards health education and ambulance services.

Her love of education of children I was able to compliment with scholarships which was of lasting satisfaction. Scholarships to girls and boys of Surkhet, Dhading, Lalitpur, Sindhupalchok and Dolkha districts were offered. Such were besides the schooling of siblings, nieces, nephews, cousins and needy kids in the neighborhood who could not afford schooling.

For decades contributions were made in time and money to the *Tuki*, the progressive farmers of Sindhupalchok and Dolkha districts.

In 1988 we donated money for the purchase of books for Shree Annapurna Pustakalay (library), located at Sami Bhanjyang, Lamjung.

The news covered by Kantipur Daily of the farmers who had pawned their land ownership papers (*Lalpurja*) worth 4 million rupees to pay for the construction of a 20km road to the district HQ Damauli, was so touching we called the district office and expressed our wish to meet the 'little gods of development in Tanahu district.' The district engineer organized a meeting to receive us with the local press and the farmers when we passed by Damauli on our way to Pokhara some years ago.

The old vehicle route to Damauli with much hassle and loss of time took a detour of 62km stretch, over treacherous alignment to Bhimad. The farmers did not want to wait to access the Damauli market with goods produced locally. The government had not responded to their needs for ages, so they took the initiative to do it on their own. We felt pride in their initiatives. As a mark of appreciation, we wanted to contribute towards their good work, and we did support modestly towards paying of bank interest.

When the efforts of reknowned Surgeon Dr. Rajesh Gongal and his team touched our hearts, both my son Arnico and I became patrons of National Ambulance Service #102 for life, the first time such a far reaching social initiative was launched. I hope many will participate.

Dr. Arjun Karki, Physician-Internist, and his colleagues came up with a visionary initiative to launch a health education program under the MBBS curriculum and established the Patan Academy of Health Sciences to make it a viable and an ongoing concern. We felt privileged to be associated with the concept from the inception. Patan Academy of Health Sciences (PAHS) was in its initial phase of preparation and planning, and our modest contribution could reflect a token of appreciation.

We contributed because of its vision and action towards making health services available to the neediest in the remote and rural areas of Nepal. The remote and rural areas were not reached by the conventional approach to health services. Compounding the situation the health workers were not prepared to leave the urban areas. They were perhaps not at fault, it was their education that did not inspire, enable or motivate them to go to the neediest. PAHS aimed at filling that gap.

It took quite a while for us to link the relationship between the achievements in life, diligence and investment in education and the will to contribute to society. I came to appreciate the contributions of my late mother. Her contributions to us were educating her children, making us love farming/gardening, eating home produce, visiting faraway places on foot and appreciating the beauty of the countryside (trekking!) and loving simplicity.

Everything was for sharing, that was Mother's principle that we tried to emulate as tributes to her thinking and acting and for what she did for us to become what we are today.

Part TWO

Kin, Kith, Neighbours and Strangers

Moments with Friends

After all, it was the Palace!

Kin, Kith, Neighbours and Strangers

Our place of birth, the community to which we belong and the environment in which we grow, the way we live – all of these exert their influence and shape our goals, determination and achievement. The individual stories about relatives, neighbors and friends reflect the context, place and time in which my family existed, indicate how much we differed from others and what influence these people had on me in particular. We are surrounded by relatives, friends and neighbors of all shades: some well-wishers and some harmful.

Some 'neighbors' may live far away from you, but seem so close to your heart. Then there are others in physical proximity, but who seem much farther away. Yet there are profound influences of friends, neighbors and relatives on our thinking, interactions and wellbeing, and even in the destiny of our families.

We tend to take those outside of our kinship as strangers. But the truth is to belong to somebody one does not need to have shared the womb, or to have a common clan or a common upbringing. We know we have found our people by being honest, and through this we might come across more of our people.

It might not be difficult to find an ungrateful family member who shared your mother's womb, so sometimes you might feel as though you would not die for your kin. Examples abound where the bitterness is not limited to siblings; their offspring sometimes inherit ill feeling.

Thinking of the people who live far from me, but are close to my heart: I feel they are my own people, and there can be no boundary between me and my own people. Close by or far from me, I find it difficult to write about them. There are things about them that are very sensitive to touch. I need to be cautious and shall be selective in writing about all of them. Many of the persons with whom I have had uncomfortable feeling or difficult relationships shall be represented by proxy characters or appear incognito.

Loss that could hardly be made up

The one tradition of my parents that I always enjoyed was greeting friends who would pass by our house in Jawalakhel. They would often be invited for *morning meal or khaja* or evening meal. Sometimes they needed to come over, and accepted what my mother could offer. Most of the time they were in a hurry, on their way to their offices in the government secretariat or the Kathmandu market, but the gesture was loved.

Nowadays, few would ever say,

Come and have [whichever meal] at our place.

That tradition or culture seems to have been lost.

Once I floated the idea of holding a friends' gathering with a simple lunch at my home out of town. My understanding was that such gatherings are good for us elders.

My friends from diverse backgrounds including journalists, lawyers, advocates, politicians, scientists, medics, soldiers, business persons and bureaucrats all said,

Good idea! When is it going to be? We will surely come.

However, missing was the response,

Well, it can be at my place first, why not? Let us do it in rotation.

How times have changed and behavior becomes introverted! The notion of reciprocity sounds strange in modern times. Has sensitivity given way to selfishness?

Shadow in Captivity

There were once five brothers. Their father, who used to call them by the nicknames, Kule, Dile, Thale, Batase, and Sunshane, was long dead. The names had been appropriately worked out by him, and their behavior and activities reflected much of what they were named after.

At home, their elderly mother was unwell. As she could not go up the staircase without assistance, she slept in a room on the ground floor. It was not so pleasant, and a bit too chilly for the old lady to feel comfortable, but there was a small bed to lie down, a little sunlight piercing through the curtain and a boy-servant assigned to look after her needs.

When I heard of her illness, I went to visit her one afternoon. She was alone, lying on her small bed, but not feeling sleepy. She had an FM radio; the sole medium of news and entertainment, or means to hear from the outside world. There was a color TV, but the vibrant palette of the Indian channels with gyrating lasses, violence filled scenes and the reverberations were too much for her age and docile life. Her frailty and sickness would not allow her to enjoy it, and so she gave it to her boy servant.

She was calling the boy to bring her a glass of water. The boy was in the next room watching the TV. I could hear the blaring, noisy sound from the room where the lady was lying. He would not budge; either he did not hear her, or he just ignored her call. It was so pathetic. I went to give a hard knock at his door. He opened the door with guilt all over his face.

You should never shut the door. And don't make any noise. Try to hear her every breath and do what she tells you. You are paid to do that job. Aren't you?

Her husband had always been very sympathetic to me, and he would communicate as if we were good friends. Things he was reluctant to tell his family, he would share with me. Actually, we were friends in a sense, because we could share the many ups and downs of our life, as it happens between good friends.

When he was alive she followed every discussion we had. Sometimes I took my children with me, so that they would learn how we were supposed or expected to pay respect to our elders. That was one of the reasons the old lady loved me so much: I highly respected her.

Look, I wanted to visit you, she told me.
I could take a taxi – that would not be a big deal for me. I am sick, but still think I can make it. But…

Her voice trailed off.

Why do you say, but?

What she said next shocked me.

I have been told by my sons, that I must not leave the house.

Why would they tell you such thing?

They are just paranoid! Although they do not tell me the reason, I assume they fear I might transfer my valuables to someone I liked or someone who loved me, or that people might blackmail me to sign a deal.

But do you own anything after your husband's death which makes them so suspicious?

Yes I do. I inherited what was left of his earnings (personal savings?). He had told me from his deathbed to keep it until my last day. Without it, nobody – not even my sons – will look after me. The world has become cruel, you know.

But how do you manage it?

My signature is still required in many matters. I will soon die, and they will be at peace and free of fear. I'm glad that you came, and I could at least tell you so much.

So they did not trust their own mother! They were keeping her in virtual captivity; in isolation.

Not long after my visit, I heard she had died. That left me with a dark shadow that follows me even today. Sometimes I wonder why I did not talk the matter over with her sons. But then, how could I? Never in my wildest dreams did I think that educated folk would treat their mother in such a cruel manner.

Grandfather misunderstood

Suspicion was the greatest weakness of the people in my neighborhood. For example, there was a family of my acquaintance that to all appearances was doing fine. The children were growing up well. The grandfather was very fond of his little granddaughter and wanted to be with her whenever time permitted. Many a time he went to play with her at her home, but often he was turned back at the gate without explanation. Time and again she sneaked out and went to play with her grandfather, although she was warned not to.

The negative effect of watching too many Indian soap operas or reading too many trashy novels is not to be underestimated. Over time, the viewer or reader tends to identify with the characters, and one starts to look at even the dearest ones with suspicion. This in turn generates fear.

In the case of the mother of the little girl, it was the stories she was reading and the TV serials she watched that made her insecure.

She had heard and read much about pedophiles, and it's likely that this material was exaggerated, oversimplified or generalized. Of course, one can understand her concern perfectly; times have changed. But our fears can hinder the normal development of a child, and reduce affinity and respect in families.

Fear that the little girl might fall prey to these assumed untoward intentions of the old man was constantly nagging at the mother. Even one's own grandparents were seen as a potential threat. I knew that he should not be suspected, and that the mother's behavior was unfair to him. We ought to know each other better.

Obligation Forgotten

On 16 October, 1983, during the Dasain festival, my father wrote to me in Europe, that he did not feel so joyous:

> *I cannot see any reason why your brother wanted only Dasain Prasad from me, but did not come in person to me to get the Holy Tika and my annual blessings?*

It is the tradition to take Dasain Tika as *sagun* and blessings from the elders, particularly from the parents, as part of a living culture. It is said such blessings and *tikas* could protect the recipient from unwanted eventualities.

Father was living on his own in a separate house some distance from my brother's house. It would have been a treat for him to invite him and offer a Dasain lunch, at least once a year. How proud Father would have felt! But it was never to materialize. Father noted that his daughter-in-law came to him to get Tika. Not surprisingly, Father's response was,

> *It would not be customary to give you Tika, without your husband coming to pay respect to me, to his father, first. Blessed be you, but Tika I will not give you. This would be against the family norm and tradition.*

He sent her back. That was a pretty defiant and unusual act on the part of my father. I did not know this side of him. I was surprised by his strong reaction. Was this a bad omen for my brother? Not long after Dasain Father wrote again that after Vijaya Dasami, while taking a meal,

> *He* (my brother) *fell down from a chair and had a cut on the head. He had to be taken to emergency ward of the Shanta Bhawan Hospital.*

Father had visited him in the hospital within hours. To reassure me, he said,

> *Fortunately the cut was not that deep.*

Even then, I was saddened by the whole episode and deeply affected by the incident for years afterwards.

Ungrateful, Wicked, Worthless

The reason I call anybody wicked, worthless and mean is that they seem to be devoid of self-esteem. It may sound very subjective. What I mean is not only that they are never content with what they get as free gifts, but that they never express gratitude even when they get all they can lay their hands on, as in the story of '*The Merchant of Venice*'.

This was the case of Peco, the *nouvou riche* brother of my friend Mukta, who was my closest neighbor until recently. One of his nephews, Kushe, settled in another district, while the senior Ranapurb built a house where he was raised and lived close to his uncle Peco. All the nephews and the uncle, as well as their wives, shared a common trait of thinking, behaving and backbiting for good or for ill, and remained very close. But the person who raised all Peco, Kushe and Ranapurb, helped in their education and professional training, supported them with property, financed their marriages and fulfilled their cravings was none other than Peco's brother, Mukta. The reason why I come to this point is that all three of them failed to appreciate the generosity of Mukta. One particular story related to me by Mukta was touching, and I was so deeply disturbed that I feel I should share it with you.

One early evening Kapal Bateki, the old aunty of Peco, approached the house of Peco, holding the hand of her grandchild. The house stood tall and its windows could be seen from a distance. Walking towards the house, she saw Peco peeking from his window of his 'high-rise' building. Peco hurriedly came out of the house and stood outside the garden gate, almost blocking it. At that moment Kapal Bateki and her grandson arrived and stood face-to-face with Peco who pretended to be surprised by their presence.

All three stood still or what seemed like an eternity, their eyes meeting, without a word expressed, just a meter away from Peco's gate. Words of greeting, let alone bowing down (as is the tradition of greeting very senior kin), were missing. Did Peco say?

Shall we go in; your daughter-in-law is home. Have some tea. You have travelled far. You must be tired and thirsty?

I am afraid such outbursts of kindness rarely came out of Peco's mouth. Or did he perhaps say,

Are you in a hurry to go elsewhere? Otherwise please stay at our home.
It is getting dark and we have much to catch up on.'

No, for such godly words had no place in minds eclipsed by the darkness of Kaliyug.

Kapal Bateki understood the situation – how unwelcome she was – and felt deeply hurt.

Well, my son I must leave.

Off she went, holding her grandson's hand and walking towards the main road further east, thinking,

Let God never make me see him again!

Mukta said she related the story to him when he met her sometime later. It seemed obvious Peco needed nobody. Such instances of insensitivity became common over the next two decades.

Missing gratitude

In one neighboring family, the father used to work at an unrewarding menial job in a government office. By the time his earnings would come trickling home to buy food, much of it had already gone to pay for the alcohol he consumed. He dispensed with a large chunk of his earnings *en route* between his job and home and in the time between salaries. Coming home drunk, he would thrash his wife, and every night we heard cries of distress from the neighbor's window:

Help, he is killing me, is anyone out there?

The violence at home and the misery reflected on the three children – two boys and a girl. They were suffering from malnutrition, lack of sleep and the loss of peace at home, and were ever hungry for parental love.

There was little possibility of schooling for them. The mother was a wretched lady. From head to toe she looked so poor – mentally and physically abused – and appeared many years older than she actually was. The eldest son was on the brink of becoming a professional thief. He was often in trouble in the locality for minor shoplifting.

Very early on, we were seeking ways to help these innocent children, first with some boiled eggs, which they had to come to us to eat, otherwise the mother or the father would snatch them away. Then we set aside part of our earnings for their schooling. The eldest ended up as a skilled technical hand from the USC training center at Patan.

The sister was diligent, and attracted attention from strangers. Before she finished her schooling, however, she had to get married, fortunately into a good home. It was quite early for her, but perhaps it was her rescue from the misery. Her second brother continued going to school, and did his matriculation. I met the boy three years after his school leaving exams, outside my house which he had visited every day for years to get his share of eggs, and collect school fees and clothing. He pretended not to recognize me.

I thanked God for helping the three children to finally become themselves.

Loyalty, *par excellence*

The future dictator, Juddha Samsher Jung Bahadur Rana, was building his palace at Jawalakhel in the 1930s. There was a big plot of land belonging to Jyapu farmers on the north side of Juddha's palace compound. He confiscated the land of his neighbors. On the south and east sides of the land, there was a traditional funeral path used by some Newar communities of Patan for funeral processions leading to the cremation ground at Baisnavdebi, by the side of the Nakhukhola, 2km south of the palace gate.

What prompted Juddha to not only confiscate the farmers' land, but also close the age-old funeral path and reroute it? Given his lifestyle, power and personal weaknesses, he needed more park spaces, garden areas and a bathing pool for his 'harem'. He already had a luxuriously furnished wooden house that could be rotated on a metal track. He had built a hill with caves and underground spaces in the East Garden for the privacy he needed, presumably, for his time with the ladies he had identified while riding an elephant through the city. He would tell his henchman later to go after the girls he had seen in the windows.

As a boy I remember splashing in the bathing pool with a hill with trees and ornamental plants on the confiscated land that became the North Garden (*Uttar Bagaincha*), where today the SC bank and Dingo Restaurant are located. The Juddha put up his horse stable there.

My father said, 'Juddha was suffering from a lack of money. He had numerous wives and scores of own and adopted 'sons' and their offspring in dozens to feed, besides an army of servants in his households. The lavish lifestyle of Juddha did not come cheap. Where did he get the money? He resorted to blackmailing his own boss, Bhim Sumsher Jung Bahadur Rana, who was to be the next prime minister.

Bhim was preparing for his Sindure Jatra, a kind of 'coronation' of a Rana prime minister. At the last minute, the PM's Kalki Pagari (a kind of crown) went missing. The auspicious time (sait) was approaching. Juddha, the commanding general under Bhim, told him he knew where the Kalki Pagari was. He could have his crown, but it did not come cheap. So mules laden with sacks of silver coins, left Singh Durbar and entered the Jawalakhel Durbar of Juddha Sumsher. Bhim then had his 'crown' delivered personally by Juddha, who had hidden it. Bhim had his Sindure Jatra, an inaugural procession. That cost him at least 300,000 silver Moharu.'

Even before Juddha hastily left Nepal for Dehradoon in 1945, according to my father,

> *He emptied the treasury by a staggering figure of Rs.130 million of silver Moharu. Then, the Moharu fetched a higher value than the British East India Company currency. But he staged a drama of appearing as a Saint Maharaj (Rajarshi) taking leave from powerful active life, wore a yellow turban around his head and went around Kathmandu Tundikhel on a four-horse drawn coach with a royal entourage.*

Father had told me of the event. Women, children and elderly men wept. There was much mystery behind Juddha's abdication in 1945, after ruling some thirteen years. Did he fear a deadly coup from Chandra's clan?

But to return to our story, not long after this jackpot win with the Bhim's Kalki Pagari', Juddha dreamt of a sage-like figure telling him,

> *You did something inauspicious. The funeral path should never have been closed and taken into private use. I will curse you. The curse will be that your grandchild will be born with only one leg.*

He woke up sweating and shivering. Shaken and alarmed by the dream, his first action in the morning was to order the reopening of the funeral path. The North Garden (*Uttar Bagaincha*) was then detached and separated completely from his palace compound. To his surprise, he found that his daughter-in-law was in fact a few months into her pregnancy. It was too late to correct his mischief. So the punishment, if it was to be believed, was imminent.

Juddha's fifth son from his legal wife, Surya, and daughter-in-law were living with him in the same palace. He had long arranged that the child from his son Surya, if a boy, would become a full-fledged general at birth, in his army.

Baby Yubraj, as dreamt by his grandfather Juddha, was born with only one leg. However, he grew up with a silver spoon in his mouth, and we heard he became the richest man in Nepal.

Yubraj, the single-legged general had many horses and other animals. He had horse-driven buggies and beautiful cars. He would go around Jawalakhel, dressed immaculately in a bow tie and a 3-piece suit. I was always impressed by the grandeur. We later noted that he had an artificial leg made of leather and metals. He could walk unaided, but would still limp a little.

He had a stable full of European cows. They produced so much milk that after making ghee, they would pour the skimmed milk (*Mohi*), into the drain. The keepers were allowed to give cow milk to whoever came to ask for it. When our cow went dry, we too fetched milk from his stable. Yubraj lived in the rear part of the huge palace.

The first hotel to come up in Kathmandu Valley in the early fifties, the Nepal Hotel, was located in the Yubraj's palace managed by an Anglo-Indian man, Mendies and the Russian Boris Lissanovic (1905-1985) at Jawalakhel. It contained the favorite dance parlor of King Tribhuwan. He used to dance there well past midnight, with the army band playing instruments in the garden. We, the hotel's immediate neighbors on the north side were not able to sleep. For us kids, it was annoying to go through this routine almost every night. Later Boris shifted the hotel over to Bahadur Bhawan at Kantipath, 'renamed' as Royal Hotel and became a popular 'gossiping and guessing corner' of expatriates and the tourists who trickled into Kathmandu then, where at present the Election Commission is housed.

Yubraj had a grain storehouse on the southern side of the front west gate. The long barrack-like structure was like the Durbar High School in Kathmandu. The largely empty building had long ago lost its purpose. There were two families living in there, Khadka the driver and Ustaj Gobindlal Shrestha, King Mahendra's harmonium teacher. The youth of Jawalakhel had asked him to donate the barracks to the Mahendroday Primary School that was being run without a roof of its own at Jawalakhel. It would not have cost him anything, but he rejected our request. That rejection was unexpected, and we promised to give him a message one day.

Despite his riches, Yubraj's life was full of unhappiness. He was living alone. His wedded wife had left him to live on her own with their only child a daughter in the East Compound of the palace, with her share of the property. Yubraj's daughter was married off to an ex-royal somewhere in South India. The father had not even been allowed to say 'goodbye' to his daughter.

The bridegroom was rumored to have rejected earlier one of the royal daughters of Nepal on the grounds of her appearance. That seemed to have hurt the royalty immensely, and though Yubraj had nothing to do with it, we linked the Indian royal's rejection with the government putting pressure on Yubraj. Soon, we noticed he was in big trouble with the taxation office. He was forced either to pay the government Rs.6 lakhs, or have his palace confiscated. He could not pay the government's *'ransom'*, the tax, and so he lost his palace. The large entourage of his household service was gone. He had to leave his birthplace though he was allowed to retain a small house by the main gate. We knew Yubraj was innocent in this matter. Could this have been royal vengeance?

Hoping it would help him regain status, he fought once for the post of Mayor of Lalitpur City. I was one of the active youths going around using loudspeakers and a microphone in support of his opponent Dittha Rambahadur KC, a very polite man, a friend of all youths. On the evening, when the votes were counted at the old municipality building of Lalitpur City at Patan Mangalbajaar, Yubraj emerged a loser. Mr. KC won with a large majority. The youth of Jawalakhel prevailed. The message that we promised him when he refused to let his storerooms be used by the Mahendroday School could not have been stronger.

After the result was announced, Yubraj went to the window facing Mangalbazaar Durbar Square. He grieved, and was weeping to his heart's content. Though I was in the opposition camp, I went to console him, but it was of no use. Perhaps he had not been allowed to weep even as a child. Now nobody barred him from crying, and he had a genuine reason to cry. After that incident, he wanted to mend the fence separating him from the 'social worker' youths of Jawalakhel. He would bring football gear (balls, nets, boots, jerseys and socks) and even a live goat to cheer us up. The goat was for the winning team. We had revived the Jawalakhel Football Club (established in 1934), defunct for over two decades. JFC was established mostly by Rana sons, among them Nar Samsher Jung Bahadur Rana.

We were witnessing a phenomenal change in an adult's life. Over time we saw Yubraj with new weaknesses, such as gambling and drinking bouts. He became an alcoholic. Many traders and even his own close relatives and friends fleeced him of his wealth, and then abandoned him. There were two supporters who remained at his side. A lady from his Durbar days stayed on with him. She later married him and provided loyal and trusty companionship, looking after him until his last day. There was an old *jyapu* gardener, too, who would not have been allowed to be near the general in his heyday, but was his greatest help later on.

We heard from the gardener that the general did not have a *paisa* even to buy his meals. Every morning the gardener would go out in search of food with his *kharpan* (a *Jyapu* basket) for his master. It was so sad to watch the misery of a once wealthy man.

Our football team would collect a *pachanni* (a 20-paisa silver coin) or a *suki* (a 25-paisa silver coin) and give it to the gardener to buy some fine-grain rice and green vegetables (mostly cress) for the general and his wife. We did this to repay his generosity, helping JFC when we could not afford to buy even a football. How long could the school-going kids like us sustain him with our pocket money? We heard he died of tuberculosis. That was the end of what was once the richest man of Nepal.

The small bungalow house went to his widow. I do not know whether he had a child from her. The old *jyapu* gardener, we never saw again. Perhaps he went empty-handed? For a long time, we used to talk about the loyalty of the poor old *jyapu* gardener. He did not leave his master, even in the worst of his fate! The behavior of the *jyapu* gentleman was perhaps the most touching aspect of the whole tale for us to witness.

A day in the life of Vataspati Vaidya

The place is Bubahal, one of the fourteen Bahals of Patan, near Gabahal. One enters an old house, typical of the architecture of Lalitpur. On the third floor, a modest room without partition stretches from the narrow wooden staircase, in an east-west rectangle. The room has rice-straw mats, a few cupboards with medicines, and is well organized.

An imposing old Victorian wall clock is hanging behind his floor desk, almost a meter tall. Every fifteen minutes, it plays the Big Ben chimes, and at the hour it hits the gong, breaking the silence of the patients, warning of the time.

A tiny deity figure on one corner of the desk, a broom at one side and a floor cushion for him to sit, are adequate paraphernalia to start the day's duty of a dedicated man.

When the clock strikes 7am, he comes to sit behind the low, flat spiritual desk, which is black on top to scribble with *khari* (from Magnesite mines). For a while, he will scan the gathering of his clients intensely; looking upon the faces of women, men and children. All are squatting, leaning on both walls of the elongated room.

He scans the visitors with his large, piercing eyes, gazing sympathetically. He tries to identify the most miserable ones among the sufferers. He signals for the worst suffering ones to come to him first, leaving the other patients in the queue.

One by one he feels their pulse at the wrist. In fact, pulse is not the only thing Vaidya feels; there are other things on the wrists to feel too. He sweeps the patients with his Amriso broom (*Thysanalaena agrestis*) and shakes it slowly in rhythms in front of the patients' faces. Sometimes he hits their shoulders with it, trying to calm them. When the critical cases are examined, he comes to those with less immediate problems. So it goes, year in, year out for Vataspati. There is no change of season, no free days for him. Because sickness can strike at any time, there are no weekends.

The patients sitting on the straw mats wait for Vaidya Ba, hear the slamming of the metal Mortar pulverizing the herbs and minerals, on one floor up – the music of hope. A fine smell permeates the room, flowing down through the staircase. Outside in the courtyard, the pigeons rustle, fly out and fly home. They have wooden pigeonholes mounted on the wall of the house above the inner courtyard. It is calm and quietening for all. All throughout the five hours he gives for the sick and suffering, he remains cool, at peace and smiling, constantly and soothingly, exuding kindness to all, like Gautama the Buddha.

His day begins at 3am. Until 4, he goes for a walk and takes a bath in the Bagmati River at Sankhamul. By 5 he is home to take a medicinal tea (Tulshi leaves, *Ocimum basilicum*). He enters his spiritual room and meditates until 7. A few seconds after he is finished, he is on his seat to begin another day for his community. Some bring seasonal vegetables, fruits or cereals as a gift to Vaidya Ba. At noon he takes a bath, pouring water over his head, feeds his numerous pigeons as they hover lovingly over his head, sit on his shoulders and ask for more.

At 1pm he takes his lunch. Afterwards, he has a nap that may last an hour or more. His afternoon walk begins at 3pm. This takes him to the patients who appeared critical in the morning in his 'clinic'. He goes from house to house, and walks over the route where most of his regular clients live. He knows their houses. He knows not only their names but their family histories as well. Who of the allopathic doctors today tolerate a patient's visit without appointment, let alone visit patients in their homes without being requested to come over? Vaidyas do not live and do not work for money. Theirs is a service.

He carries little packs of digestive powdered herb(s)/minerals for distribution to children. When the kids see him walk by they shout, 'Vaidya Ba! Give us *pachak*!'

My whole family was a part of his community. I was brought up with his Aurvedic medicines and Vaidya Ba's calming voice. At ninety, he had better eyes than my Father at 50, his limbs sturdy like a soldier's and he could walk more than 3 km daily. Bataspati Vaidya Ba was a legendary man in his lifetime.

Years later, when I came back home from years of 'globetrotting', I went to look for him to thank him for helping me to grow up strong. I was never hospitalized – not even in the tropics where I spent years, working in drudgery. But he did not survive the hundredth year of his life. He died leaving behind only his two daughters and wife to tend to his clients. I do not know how long they carried on his legacy. He had no son.

In my memory, I have his picture engraved, with his piercing eyes and tender touch to sooth me well during all the (mostly minor) ailments I suffered like any other child. With the impression and inspirations he left behind in me, I can claim I am the product of his making.

Even today I follow his treatments. I seek Ayurveda anywhere: in Amchi's, Kunfen's, Menzikang's or Sano Vaidya's. I have been kept alive, in peace and good health by them. I follow Vataspati Vaidya's philosophy that a good life is the product of the balance between *ahar* (food habait), *bihar* (daily chores) and *syahar* (body/healthcare).

Of course, allopathic medicine does include some essentials, such as surgery, vaccines and antibiotics. But what Ayurveda has, allopathic medicine does not. They are complimentary partners in the service of the sick.

Vataspati challenges the traditional allopathic approach. His principle is that, if you want to serve the people in need of health care, doctors should go to the patients, not the other way around. The principle reflects the need of the people facing the geo-physical circumstances and living in the socio-economic conditions that we find in country like ours.

Increasing numbers of conventionally run hospitals, reference centers or pharmacies seem to function as a kind of 'business centers', taking advantage of poverty and ignorance of the people and are far from meeting the needs of our people. Doctors and health personnel, when mobile, may reach cases in their early stages and maintaining large hospitals and their ancillary services would become obsolete.

A gift for life

For women in Nepali culture, having a brother helps complete vital ceremonies at different points in her life. Usually, the brother develops a strong attachment to the children of his sister(s). He is called *mama* by the children. Mama's home is where *'heaven descends'*.

Mama is the one who loves his sister and stands by her side at any moment of difficulty. His role is that of a protector. She is shielded by him against an abusing husband or in-laws. And in the case of his sister's demise, it is his duty to raise, support and educate her children, as a tribute to her. Hence, the proverbial truth: *ama k*i or *mama*. Ama, the mother, carries the value of *maya* (motherly love), *mamata* (motherly care) and *matritwa*, (motherhood). Add 'M' to ama, it becomes, Mama, a proxy to the mother, an irreplaceable entity. Neither his looks nor his social status matters. We say, 'It is better to have a blind and dumb mama than to have none.'

Sharada, my better half (in the latter half of my life), felt a deep void in her life despite living among seven sisters. She did not have a male sibling. Nor did her mother have one. She often talked about it with certain regret.

We were planning for the Upanayan ceremony of Somi, my second son. At this profoundly important time in her life, Sharada needed a brother. In *Upanayan* the mama has an important role to play. In our culture one is free to look for a mama even outside of one's family, creed or community. The important point is that the mother must trust, or feel secure with the person who is going to be her brother, by culture and commitment. This is a lifelong commitment.

Sharada considered Ruedi (Dr. Rudolf Martin Hoegger, Switzerland), who has been a friend of mine for over four decades. We had many things in common, many moments of common experiences in Nepal and Switzerland. He was knowledgeable about our culture. She wondered whether she could ask Ruedi to be her brother.

That very thought impressed me a lot. It is not that she would not have found one in Nepal, had she looked around. But Ruedi was more important to her. This was a great moment also in Sharada's life.

She crossed all the barriers. She leaped over continents! It showed she had changed a lot. Since her visit to Switzerland in 2006, the assumed differences, in color, creed, costumes and race between the peoples had begun to change her thinking.

So looking at Ruedi, the best friend of her husband, and trying to win him as her brother sprang from her heart. Without a second thought, Ruedi accepted, knowing fully what it meant in value and moral obligations.

He and his brother Peter were the only siblings of a pastor's family, and they grew up in Baden, Canton Aargau, near Zurich. He had no sister. Was Ruedi looking for a sister, unknowingly? The credit for this transcontinental bond goes to Somi, our son. He became a special child with a different heritage to cherish. Ruedi now has a sister; Sharada has a brother and Somi has his mama. My friend was going to become a family member.

A Visit from the Pitri

Ruedi arrived in Kathmandu delayed by several hours, unfortunately missing an important part of the Upanayan ceremony.

That morning we had a ceremony to invoke our ancestors: generations of both parents held as the most important part of the ceremony preceding the Upanayan: *nanimukhi shrad-dha* (invoking ancestors).

Invoking ancestors is taken very seriously, and one believes the ancestors attend. An oil lamp was lighted for the next five days to guide the ancestors. But how do they manifest or indicate their presence? What indications did our ancestors give during the Upanayan ceremony for Somi or for my father's centennial ceremony?

When almost all aspects of the Upanayan ceremony were completed, a strong gust of wind swept through the courtyard. The gust ripped the tent's rope from its anchor, the five bamboo poles of the *jagya* swerved, and the holy *jagya* fire was almost extinguished, the *chanduwa* fluttered and everybody took shelter.

It happened on the 1st of April 2010, when the sky was blue, the sun was shining, and the weather was relatively cool for the season. The day could not have shone more brightly or appeared more pleasant. They say this is how the *pitri* enters your place of invitation: unexpectedly, in a guise never imagined.

Everybody was happy that the *pitri* came by and departed after being present in the ceremony to bless Somi. Although much of the ritual was new and unfamiliar to him, Ruedi remained enthusiastic, and patiently noted the happenings from a corner with inquisitive glances in between pauses of his pen.

*   *   *

Similar rituals are performed during the *Saptah* ceremony, when one vows or pledges pious work in the name of ancestors. Sharada's third sister, Nima, vowed to hold the ceremony at an appropriate time, in the name of their mother who passed away on the New Moon of November, 1999.

On *Purbanga*, the commencement day, the *saptah* flag – a long bamboo pole with a secret pack in – *pitambar*, a yellow cloth specially used in rituals, with Garud's image painted was hoisted on the roof to invoke or summon the mother who became a *pitri*. When the *saptah* is completed it is believed that the above-mentioned pledge is redeemed.

During the Saptah, an oil lamp was lit for the next eight days, to guide the ancestors. But how could we read that Sharada's mother *pitri* made a visit during the *Saptah*? What happened that last night in the *Saptah* house, at Putalisadak, Kathmandu?

The ceremony was held in the house where they had all lived with their mother. Three of Sharada's sisters— Bimala, Lajana and relative Durgadidi—were sleeping in the kitchen on the third floor, on a makeshift bed. The Saptah ceremony was taking place on the second floor, where their mother used to sleep. The other three—Liza, Sabitri and Nima—were sleeping in the first floor room. At around midnight, Bimala woke up hearing a noise: somebody opening the cupboard with the *puja* altar and closing it again, and the rustle of somebody sitting on the floor.

The cupboard with puja altar where her mother used to do her daily puja and offer prayers remained normally shut. It was pitch-dark in the room. The other two were alerted. They remained close to each other, spellbound. They could not gather enough courage to go and switch on the light. Then Bimala shouted, which alarmed the others on the first floor. In one go all three stood up and opened the door and in haste, and went downstairs to Sabitri, Liza and Nima.

Finding the door locked from inside, they knocked hard. Nima opened the door to let them in. Nima said in a fearful voice that they too heard familiar footsteps:

It sounded like Mother's. Mother went to the Saptah room too. We heard some rumbles of pots and puja materials.

Liza was fearful and covered her head with the quilt. A chill ran down their spines. They all talked at the same time. Sabitri wished,

If only mother would come! She should come alone, but what would happen if she came with all her Pitri friends?

One of them went and shut the door. For a while, all six sat on the bed huddled together under the quilt, with fearful feelings and the sense of another presence in the room. Then they all went down to the ground floor to wake up the priests, only to find them still chanting the mantra of the occasion. The priests told them,

We too heard somebody walking up the stairs. Such things have happened in other places too during Saptah. You all should feel content that Mother Pitri visited you.

They went back to their first floor room and passed the rest of the night without sleep. It was an awful moment of drama in the middle of the night. The businessman, Mr. Mulchand, from the adjoining house came in to ask,

I heard doors banging and footsteps. Who entered your house so late at night?

The noise of the footsteps first came from the *kausi*, the terrace where the *saptah* flag was hoisted. As the sun rose, the fear was replaced by the feeling that their mother did indeed visit, and she gave everybody the feeling that she was present. They found that what they were doing for their mother was worthwhile, even after 10 years of her passing away. She accepted the gestures of her daughters. It was also an occasion when all seven sisters were together for the last time. Soon, the eldest left for Heaven.

Somebody to turn to – New Era

There is one place that I visit as often as possible. It is over 35 years since I started frequenting it. It is Shyam Dai's, a second son of uncle Gopal Thulobuba, at Lajimpat, Kathmandu. My Father went almost every Saturday to Gopal Thulobuba. Many years later, his wife would tell me,

> *You know your father found the meat dish I cooked, a Panday family recipe, so tasty, that he would not miss it, especially on Saturdays.*

In a way I am inspired by Shyam Dai. He is a very practical and realistic person. I fail to see any disparity or contradictions between his thought and his actions. He is busy in a very sensitive, service-oriented business as an hotelier, which demands intensive input of mental concentration and also one's physical presence and time.

He had to forego personal pleasures and bear curtailment to his family life, to devote himself fully to the business during the initial years of the venture. That was a sacrifice that would keep him away from his children at home. But he was adequately rewarded with satisfaction. I remember him once saying,

I made it and I have all I ever needed. I have lived through sweats and joys. I think I could now take a retreat.

That is a philosophical commitment you will find very seldom. I gave him my opinion that,

All the greats have done this. Command over one's own cravings is the greatest achievement of one's life. This is the right attitude and the right moment for contemplating doing something in philanthropy, for posterity.

Very early on he was meticulous in planning, and artistic in designing things for his home or for the hotels. That was reflected in his creations, at home or in business. After 30 years of diligence and sacrifice, he was able to build two of the best hotels in Nepal, the Shangri-La Hotels in Kathmandu and Pokhara. Each one of them seems to have been dedicated to the cultural and natural heritage of the area they were located.

His children have a less strenuous challenge to face. They have opportunities availed by their father to make a flying start, while Shyam Dai alone had started from the bottom rung. In fact, pains and pleasures start early for a striving man.

The pains of struggle and sense of achievement felt might elude our children. Because there is a tendency today that those who get a start from the top do not see calamitous falls ahead, remaining at the top is not always guaranteed. Although the boys are groomed to do their best, if they acknowledge the legacy and gift they are entrusted with, nothing can stop them from becoming as successful, if not more successful than their father's generation.

Like him, incidentally, I had also to be the most struggling of my parents' offspring. Destiny forced us to play the role of the senior members in the family. In my case, I did not inherit any piece of physical property. After years of toil and sweat on my part, the efforts paid off. I could share much with my brother and Father and bear responsibility for the education, supporting their farming and the weddings of scores of my siblings and nephews. They all are doing fine in their struggle to survive in this challenging time.

Unlike in academia by default and in politics by necessity, in the business community, giving credit, acknowledging support and appreciating contributions are rarely practiced. There is a tendency to compete negatively. Conflicts tend to percolate into the home. Kinship does not prevent conflicts; rather it may augment them.

It is hard to believe that people in the situation of our Shyam Dai would not go through recurrent bouts of stress. I envy the inner calm that he exudes. One would always find him in a state of peace with himself, and in a cheerful mood, taking time to ponder issues and strategies to tackle in time. Such things come to people with positive attitudes. He is ready to lend his support and to cooperate in any justifiable social programs presented to him. Politeness, contact with people and generosity matter most to him.

Just after the first election for the Constituent Assembly, a gathering of eminent private businessmen, including our Shyam Dai, none of them directly or openly engaged in politics ever before, was called by Communist Party of Nepal (UML). It wanted to explore who could represent the business sector in the assembly. The party would offer a ticket for candidacy. The catch was, *'Stand on the communist line and follow party instructions, a kind of signing on the dotted line. No soul searching will be required in the House: follow the whip of the party in the Assembly.'*

One's conscience, truth and integrity had no place in the politics of the communists. When communists need capitalists, there will surely be strings attached. But the plan was most probably to procure funding from the capitalists, to a party that abhors freedom. It is obvious to us that a communist party would never fully support private entrepreneurship. Yet, surprisingly, some of the successful businessmen, contrary to conventional business education, trusted and felt honored by the gestures of the communists. They accepted the offer to be nominated by the communist parties without a second thought, without shame.

Did they have other conditions? Would they ever be able to represent the private business sector? For Shyam Dai, he needed time to think it over. The next morning I also gave him my opinion which was,

You need not be branded a leftist or be perceived as a communist party member.

Our Panday clan always stood its ground for the greater interests of the nation. We were the nation-builders. He would be judged differently in the future if he accepted the offer. His life would be scrutinized as a public figure. Life would not be the same anymore. But that is only one part of the story.

Being a self-made man, too proud to be associated with murky politics, the communists' platform was not for him. Politics, for him was for development: the social and economic uplifting of the masses and to seek Nepal's dignity in the global community. That was not the point the communists seemed to have on their agenda, so his declining of the offer was a natural decision.

All indications pointed to the fact that the communists wanted 'their' constitution (if they wanted one at all), but did not want to help chart a democratic constitution, which would undermine their political objectives. So it was going to be more drama, emptying the state coffers, and a loss of time and effort for development. There would not be a *quid pro quo* for the situation of freedom, but a jamboree without result. So why go for it? He was right pursuing his conscience.

As expected, after four years of the CA drama, no constitution was charted. The four years of their playtime was sufficient for the political parties, communists and ethnicity-based interest groups of all hues to lose credibility, undermining their own political base. They and they alone brought the country to the brink of economic bankruptcy, political misery and communal upheaval. As a matter of fact the country's sovereignty was never before so much challenged, stressed and weakened than during the leftists' drama and turmoil within the legitimacy of the Constituent Assembly.

My children are as much at home in Shyam Dai's home as in mine. As one gets older, nothing can replace exchanges and social bonds in fending off senility. Of course, geographically we are living very much apart, and as we grow older and the visits become sparser, each intermittent visit becomes more valuable.

The physical distance does not matter, as the closeness in the heart means so much. We share so many areas of life that we have in common – Shyam Dai too, despite being a *mahila*, the second son, had to be a crusader for the greater wellbeing of the family. He dedicated his share of the parental property (land and house, legally his) to his elder brother, who had twice the number of sons to look after.

I must say we were lucky. We were blessed to do all that we did. We feel satisfied with what we have become. We are at peace with ourselves. So these are the common meeting points between us cousins. That helps us to be at peace with ourselves.

If someone asks me about the personality of Shyam Dai, what quality of him I appreciated much, I would be at a loss to pinpoint an answer. Could it be because he valued tolerance, was always calm and accommodating with all people, his sense of *Basudhaiva Kutumbakam*? I respected these qualities in people from the depth of my heart, and that brought me closer to him.

Prestige pinned

We were looking for a good primary school for our two children. We found none around Jawalakhel that satisfied our criteria of a 'good' school. The prevailing evaluation of a school being good was that kids learnt in English, later to dream of a life in America. I have seen kids in the so-called 'best' English-speaking schools, and how they spoke and behaved. I thought: I have to help create a school to satisfy the needs of my children.

It was a big challenge to start the first Grade One class, but we made it in 1981. The school had boys and girls from the surrounding areas, of all socio-economic backgrounds, castes and ethnicities. The teaching staff were all-female. The maximum number of students per class was fixed to 25, to give each child a chance of individual learning.

This was the second time in my life I had an opportunity to help establish a school. In 1955, twenty six years earlier, I had helped establish a school, the Mahendroday Primary School, in the Jawalakhel cattle sheds, with the sole objective of catering to the needs of the poorest in the community. The newest school would retain these original objectives.

Renu Shrestha, daughter of martyr Dharma Bhakta Mathema, who had worked for many years as a teacher in a government school in Lalitpur, became the Head Miss of our new school. We named the school after the martyr, who sacrificed his life for democracy. Only in a democracy can schools be opened for all. Renu brought the experience of teaching in Nepal and of dealing with the district education authorities. Her colleague, Rosmarie Panday-Schaffner, the mother of our two children, brought the experiences of the Swiss schooling with practical learning and of training teachers in Dolakha. She worked on volunteer basis, introduced the Cuisenaire rod system for the mathematics education and developed educational materials for other subjects, which helped the students to sharpen their thinking.

Without their constant efforts for quality education it would not have been possible to impart excellent learning opportunities for the students. The success of the school reflected also on our own two kids who excelled in other schools too.

After four years, we had our school with its own property. We had donated towards the purchase of the land, and asked each of our closest friends to spare Rs.20,000 which enabled us to buy over 2250m² of land at Rs. 115 /m² across the Nakhukhola. Design of the classrooms, buildings and master-plan for the school area were to be my responsibility. I took over the responsibility of chairing the school management committee, with Mr. Biswakanta Mainali and Badrinarsingh Rajbhandari (both lawyers), and educationist Mr. Kedar Bhakta Mathema (cousin of the martyr) as members.

We went from door to door in the Nakhu and Chovar areas, contacted friends in Bungamati, asking them to look for kids who had never been to school. Parents would tell us their problems getting money. We mobilized friends in

Nepal and Switzerland to cough up some contributions to cover kids' tuition fees. It would cost less than Rs.500 per annum, which was the lowest in the area for sending a kid to a school. Over 50% of the kids in our school thus came to enjoy learning through sponsorship. They were the ones who needed support merely to attend the school. It began well.

We had kids from the so-called lower castes, as well as Brahmin, Newar and Chhetri; from laboring and working class households to academics, like Dr. Badri Dev Pande. Some were very poor, while a few came from upper middle class families. To give them the semblance of equality, we introduced a simple blue and red uniform, color of the dress was chosen by the students themselves.

In the beginning, most of the pupils were from the surrounding areas, so almost all of them could walk to the school. It was a big departure from the conventions of private schools in the valley.

Some families found the children from lower castes, backward and poor families in the classes, and deemed this as not up to their status, standard and expectations. Some families found the students from lower castes and Brahmin families mixing amicably to be against their social mores. One can understand the prevailing thinking.

We convinced committee members –mostly Brahmin, Newar and Chhetri – to bring their school going kids too to the school. Otherwise, it may have appeared that we were practicing a double standard, and over time we would not be able to convince parents to enroll their kids in our 'inclusive' school. Many years later we still received positive echo from our students about their happy time in the Shahid Dharma Bhakta School.

We knew many popular schools with lofty names, teaching in English and charging hefty fees that compromised on quality. They were burdened by their initial success, yet were still able to attract pupils from the rich sections of the community. It was a matter of social prestige for many with money made without sweating.

When I was taking a ride in the government vehicle of a friend with whom I had good personal rapport, he was curious to know where I had enrolled my own children. I told him the story of Sahid Dharma Bhakta Primary School, at Nakhu, Lalitpur. The mention of Nakhu was enough for him to turn his nose up, and he was no longer eager to question me. He did not want to know about the teachers and teaching methods being applied that made the school different. He did not buy it, but I wanted to tell him. He said,

I could never afford that school, in such a setting. I'm a high ranking government officer; I could never place my kids in a school of that category, in a backward rural area.

But why can't you afford a good but less expensive and more convenient school for the sake of your children?

I could never convince my class of people that my children would be getting a good education in a poor rural area, with local kids, from lower caste, poor and dirty communities!

But your children would get, I believe, good education, just as my own children are. I am convinced of this. After all, it is my responsibility to ensure that.

Your tuition fees are too low for me to believe that it is a good school. It is against my prestige anyway.

Of course, one cannot get diamonds cheap. But for whom is a diamond worth their money? Diamonds are for prestige, if not for industry. Poor people do not need anything for prestige's sake. The word – prestige – disturbed me. He had not finished speaking when my tirade started upsetting him so profusely that he had saliva flowing from his mouth, right and left of his lips. He was surprised to hear me talk in such a hard manner. In essence, what I said to him was:

What is important for you, the education of your children or maintaining your short-run job bound prestige bestowed by the government post? Suppose you choose a school by its cost and name, but without a good teaching system. Someday your children will be leaving that school. They will be looking for a job in the market, or going on to higher education. You won't be in your so-called prestigious government job all your life, to influence their future. Your job-bound prestige will be gone. How will your kid cope with his or her life?

Both my children were in Sahid Dharma Bhakta Primary School from its founding days. Very soon we needed to look for a secondary school for them to continue. We tried for a better-known international school in Kathmandu, for which my office would sponsor their tuition fees.

One beautiful day, a big surprise drew the attention of my colleagues. Our two kids had taken the basic entrance exams of the international school. Although they were halfway through in their classes at Sahid Dharma Bhakta Primary School, each one of them was placed one grade higher, to Grades 5 and 6. We were satisfied that the teaching of the lady teachers Rosmarie, Renu and Ms Devkota, Mrs Rai in our primary school was a good! That was a foundation well laid. As a parent and the founding chair of the school, I was deeply satisfied with the outcome.

But that had an impact on our kids. They had to work harder, especially in the English language subjects, but they got support from the school to attend extra classes. Both of my kids topped their classes from the beginning to Grade 12, and became Valedictorians of the school. That opened the door to the prestigious schools of the US, such as Mt. Holyoke, Mills, Harvard, Madison, and MIT. But they came back to Nepal for good, something I am proud of. They still cherish the opportunity they had in the Sahid Dharma Bhakta Primary School, which helped them make friends with kids with diverse social, economic, caste and ethnic backgrounds.

Looking back, I would regret only one little omission on my part. Due partly to their long stays in the US for further education, and my own failure, I could not inculcate in my children spiritual and cultural values, essential more than ever for life today, especially in Nepal.

Having perhaps been blinded by my own scientific education, the value of spirituality dawned on me late. That omission nags me profoundly. But it also gives them the freedom to be selective about the religious and cultural practices that satisfy them.

I can sense indirectly their irritations and insecurities about what they missed. But I know that, given a learning mindset, one can develop the habit of following the best of cultural and spiritual values needed to cope with life in this challenging land and time. At any point of time in life, that only can enrich them.

A turn in the new millennium

I was alone in managing my fate for some years. Time, I could manipulate to do whatever came into my mind. But I preferred company of those I respected and valued. One of my friends, older than me, lived on the other side of the district. As I had time, and he too cherished my company, I made a point of visiting him often. It was an expensive journey because of my age and my state of retirement. But I did not care about it as long as I could afford it. Social contact was worth it.

On many occasions my visits coincided with those of his married daughters and sons, who would sit quietly for a while and leave, a routine borne of compulsive visits. Without any niceties and respect expressed towards the ageing father, they would come, sit, and leave the house until next weekend. It was a strange feeling, every time I got to witness the frozen event, the so-called family gathering. In normal relationships, even in the presence of a stranger, the respectful bowing to one's parents would not be subdued. That is what we expected in Nepali culture.

I used to ask myself whether it was me who was the odd one to be there, but I am sure I was not. If my presence was not the reason for them to be cold to their father, then I could only assume that the relationship was strained long ago. I was unwelcome, especially to the girls, although I had always taken them as my own people, and yet they would stare at me. One fine day one of the four sons said to me, fairly loudly,

We do not understand why you come so often to see my father?

I wondered whether they were just jealous of me, or feared I would exploit their father, just like the 'shadow in captivity' of the previous story. If so, they did not know me, and they did not trust their own father. What they did not know was how much we two enjoyed each other's company. We had no selfish interest for our meetings, and I had no ulterior motives. My friend knew this well.

Soon they began to intrude laterally, interrupting our discussions and making cynical remarks to my points, which were not at all directed at them. On another occasion a few weeks later, one of the sons-in-law came along. He behaved the same way as the sons, and criticized my democratic values and credentials. My brief responses pushed him to spill his royalist leanings. At that moment, he had forgotten that I was the friend of his father-in-law.

That was around the year 2002. In 2006, the king was compelled to abdicate, and Nepal was declared a republic. The son-in-law lost his socio-political orientation and was devastated. Maybe he respects my viewpoint now, and understands that democracy cannot be defeated.

His children didn't know that I needed nothing from other people. I was a proud self-made man, standing on my own two feet. I had what I needed and was content with what little I had, and I was not craving for more.

I fell into a dilemma over whether or not I should reduce my visits to their father. It would be unfair to him, but nonetheless, we lost a little of what was valuable in our contact. Of course, my visits became less frequent.

Eluding give and take

Dasain, an annual family festive occasion, would come and go. We kids would be pulling around a castrated goat that the family purchased for the occasion, would parade it around to the neighbors to proudly show them what a prized animal we had for Dasain.

But then sadness would follow the next day. When the goat was slaughtered, we were witnessing a cold-blooded murder, yet rejoiced in the occasion because that was perhaps the only (or one of the few) occasions we got meat to eat in a year. Dasain is celebrated to mark the triumph of good over evil. The elders would say the goat is sacrificed in the name of evil.

In fact, human society always has to face evil that emerges from within, and mostly from within the family, the community and beyond – not from animals. The struggle is to be good towards fellow human beings (a difficult proposition for a human), towards nature and the Earth. I was unaware of this until late in my boyhood.

I would ask many a times why an animal as cute as a goat would have to represent the evil that has to be sacrificed. Why did animals need a tragic role to play as human beings' proxy enemy? Such thinking often made me sad, early on: it was unfair towards the animals with which we share this Earth. As we grew up, we realized there was another unfair thing about the Dasain celebration that affected my family. We could barely afford a goat of the size to feed the hordes of guests pouring into our house and crowding our kitchen, on the *Vijaya Dasami*, the day of triumph.

The guests brought along their offspring, naturally. Of course, we had a nice time together as children. We looked forward to Dasain because we could play with many more children, all of them relatives. But the fun was not to last. We grew up rapidly, and found ourselves witnesses to happenings that no longer made us rejoice at Dasain. Not that any feeling of shame or unease was to be noticed by the guests. Some who came over on this day were fairly affluent, when compared to our family. They all should have been obliged to share the cost and participate, but they would come to us empty handed.

The reason they came over to us was my grandmother. She was the magnet. She deserved a little gift from the guests, in exchange for the Dasain blessings and *tika* they all expected from her.

Even their helping hands and servants came along, taking it for granted they could loiter around, giggling, hands tied, without even a few words of courtesy. To lend a hand in the preparation of these festive dishes for the four-dozen or so mouths present, or in the cleaning chores afterwards was too much to expect from our guests, even those uninvited. Mother had also to make sure that the cows and goats were not forgotten. It was not their Dasain, after all, but a normal day in their lives.

It would be late afternoon by the time the guests would have had eaten, and the time consuming series of *tikas* and blessings were bestowed from the seniors to the juniors. At times not much was left for my mother to eat. With so much work behind her and all her energy sapped, she would not cook for herself.

By the evening, before the guests left us alone, the large goat was gone. The largest rice pot, the *khandkulo,* was emptied, and a mountain of dirty pots, pans and plates were waiting for my mother before going into bed. We have a tradition of not leaving soiled (*jutho*) utensils dirty overnight, beyond the next ray of sun. Neither my father nor we kids helped her, but that was only because we were not allowed. We were not good at washing utensils clean, and we children would not know of the hardships our mother faced until we were big enough to question them. Over time, I developed such bad feelings before falling asleep on these nights. The next morning I remember asking my Mother:

Couldn't we do it differently, so you could suffer less?

I cannot recall any of these guests coming back to celebrate Dasain with us after Grandmother died. Neither were we invited by any of them in return, during festivities. I felt Mother had been used, and never became a person to be visited by the same group who had enjoyed her hospitality for decades. We knew my family had no one senior to them anymore, and we were not affluent either. This and other instances of exploitation should have hardened my Mother. That was one of the reasons also for me to protest against animal slaughter during Dasain, and it became a new tradition in our household. We did not kill animals at home or sacrifice for the deity anymore.

A Day for the Pandays at Singha Durbar

It must have been sometime in 1949 or 1950 and I must have been around 6-7 years old. It was Dasain time, a day of the Pandays in Singh Durbar. Pandays were supposed to go to Singh Durbar to receive *tika* from the Rana Premier. During one of the 5 appointed Tika Days, holding Mother's hand, I accompanied her to Singha Durbar. All the Panday ladies and children under 10 or so were to enter the first inner courtyard, Mulchowk of the Singh Durbar.

There was a large rectangular high tent, a *samiyana* erected with mats on the floor for us. The eldest son of late Prime Minister Chandra, Mohan the Premier, came out smoking a *hookah*. The puff had to come all the way through almost 3 meters long rubber pipe joined to the silver *hookah* and earthen *chilim* carried by a servant. I said to Mother,

Mohan must be very strong to suck smoke from the hookah so far from him.

But was he actually puffing? There was no smoke blown out. He only held the pipe so that he did not have to talk to us. We were ordered to come for his *tika*.

His servants were carrying *tika* on a large silver *kisti* (plates), on one hand yellow for the *viduwa* (widows} and on the other red for the *saduwa* (married women). Another carried a plate full of *jamara*. There was another servant carrying silver coins of double Mohars (1 Rupee).

Premier Mohan would put *Tika* on the palm of the Panday ladies without touching them and threw Jamara on their heads. Children got red *tika* on their foreheads, and some *jamara* placed on their heads, one by one. That must have been the tradition. My Mother and aunties were together in the crowd. Ladies I saw got 5 coins. I got 3 coins as a kid. They were made out of pure silver. I had never had so much money in my hands.

Suddenly, I heard of a quarrel like discussion taking place between PM Mohan and my aunty, Mahili-ama, wife of the Uncle Tripur Bikram, our Mahila-buba. It sounded to me awkward that a lady from our clan had the courage to argue with a ruler, a virtual dictator. Our clan had faced the wrath of the rulers for generations. It seemed she was not afraid of him, because her voice was loud. The whole discussion sounded like,

You can't keep him in jail. You have no right. Set him free or else.

She had hardly uttered these words when she saw from his staring eyes behind his glasses that he was looking angry. At this moment the assistants started telling us to move on and leave the place; there were many queuing up for the *tika*.

When we came out of the inner *chowk* after the *tika*, I saw all the men folk, among them also Father, assembled like the soldiers, rows after rows, and some most probably seniors stood away from the rows prominently in front of the others, outside on the road under the Lion terrace.

Soon after the *tika*, I heard that Mahilabuba was a free man again, after years of incarceration. I had no clue how long he was behind the bars. For me it was the first time I remember seeing him. It was my aunty who launched the drive to get him out of jail. She was from a Mahat family from Kabre, married to Mahila-buba after first aunty had died leaving three children behind.

I heard that Mahili-ama was politically active even under the Rana regime. She was the founding member of the Nepal Mahila Sangathan (Nepal Women's Organization), an organ of the Nepali Congress working underground, chaired by Mangala Devi Singh, wife of Supremo Ganesh Man Singh.

The reason why Mahila-buba was jailed came to my knowledge years later. We were living next to Badri Rana. Badri was Premier Chandra's first son, but illegitimate. Mohan was legally the first son of Chandra, so he became

Prime Minister rather than Badri. A palace was built for Badri between Jawalakhel and Pulchowk in Patan. He had a son called '*Prahlad*'.

A towering figure with his lean body, Prahlad was known as the hardest of all womanizers among the Ranas of the time. He was married to a beautiful lady but his attention was on many others, so much so that he brought home to Jawalakhel a Muslim lady from India, a rare incidence then and spread rumors that he was now to be looked as a Sahenshaha.

Prahlad must have abandoned his wedded wife who shifted to a new bungalow specially built for her refuge in the north-east corner of the large compound. She looked on other persons for her sexual satisfaction. So it is to do with the wife of Prahlad that was the cause of Mahilabuba's traumatic life in Bhadragol jail of Kathmandu during the Rana rule.

Para-Normal Death – early 1950s

Kanchha Rimal, respectfully called *Subbabaje*, was living in an old, L-shaped building in Taphalonha. All the wooden windows and terraces were beautifully carved. Taphalonha was the exact name of the place, where the large boulder depicting Bhairab is located on the crossing of the road that leads to Purnachandi to the North and Kumaripati to the East.

He was a devout follower of the Hanuman deity. He had a large, fierce-looking Hanuman painted red and mounted on the North wall of his *puja* room in the attic, located in the Eastern wing of the house. His clan deity resided in the garden on the North side of the house. The shrine and its idols were very small. There were a few tall trees around it. I have the feeling that the shrine was not receiving regular ritual offerings. Traditionally, the Rimals would gather there to pay homage to their clan deity, once a year.

Subbabaje had a young village girl to help the family in the household chores. On the Dasain festival of 1952 she was not allowed to visit her parents who lived outside the valley. No one from her family came to fetch her. She felt very sad. On the Tika Day she was home alone, but she looked for solace playing nearby the Rimal shrine. Not knowing that it was taboo, she put up a swing between the trees and played, putting her feet on the shrine every time she descended from the swing. When the Rimals came home and saw her mischief they were horrified and angry. It was tantamount to a great sin – unpardonable, and likely to incur the wrath of the clan deity. Nobody in the house knew, in what form, or how the wrath or curse would visit them.

The little terrace in the attic kitchen Subbabaje used for washing utensils faced towards the shrine in the garden. Not long after the Dasain swing incident, strange things began happening in the four-storied house. From the terrace door, the Rimals would find bucketful of burning charcoal, stones and even pot full of human feces hurled into the house. By the next day, this became known to all those in the neighborhood, and others beyond. Word spread quickly, and many onlookers came over to hear, if not to see, what was happening!

Not believing the story, the then-Inspector General of Police, Nar Samsher Jung Bahadur Rana, father of the hotelier Prabhakar Rana, came to investigate. To test the story, the general took the mischievous girl and climbed up to the third floor. He was hit by feces, which fell down the ladder he was clinging to with the girl. Scared, both came hurtling down.

Subbabaje consulted the family astrologer in Patan. The astrologer prescribed certain rituals (*tsema puja*) to be performed to appease the deity. He performed the *puja* as told, and the strange incidents ceased, with calm returning to the house until the Tihar festival, two weeks later. My father, then about 39 years old and Sambhu who had just passed his 21st birthday, the second son of Subbabaje, were inseparable friends. Two weeks after the curse on the house, on the night of Gai Puja, they both visited a friend a stone's throw away and gambled with *kauda* until midnight.

The night is pitch-dark during Tihar, as the new moon falls right in the middle of the Tihar festival. Returning just after midnight, Sambhu went to his house and my father came home alone to our house, about two hundred meters from the Rimal house. Sambhu's wife had gone with her baby son, Deepak, to visit her brother for the *Bhaitika* due to take place two days later. Feeling sleepy, Sambhu entered his room and locked the door from inside. Early next morning, on the day of *Gobardhanpuja*, Subbabaje went to wake him up. Many bangs on the door failed to illicit a response. Subbabaje was alarmed. Soon, others came to help him. They had to break the door forcibly.

Early that morning, a boy from the neighborhood came to tell my father that his friend Sambhu was dead. My father was distraught! I followed him to Sambhu's house at a pace I had never imagined he was capable of running. For me as a boy of 9, relatively small I had hard time keeping pace with him. In the room lay Sambhu on the floor, in the same clothes he had worn the evening before, in the pool of blood streaming out of his mouth. The body faced north, towards the clan-shrine. The North-side window of his room was wide open.

Neither my Father nor Sambhu ever drank alcohol. It was a taboo in our families, in those days, so the cause of his death had to be found in something else. Sambhu's parents were expecting the deity's wrath, and finding him in such a tragic condition confirmed their beliefs. Did Sambhu die from supernatural causes?

Sambhu's body was brought down to the ground floor outside the house door, to the *dalan*. Subbabaje limped close to the corpse, put his head on the chest of Sambhu and tried to listen to the heartbeat, which had stopped perhaps hours earlier. He was banging the floor with his fist, lamenting in deep sorrow. I could not hold back my tears: this was also the first occasion in my life to see a dead body so close up. The body had been Father's friend until yesterday! He was the person who introduced to me my first *Devnagari* letters, on a wooden plank, the *pati*. He was no more, and it was frightening.

Years earlier, the family astrologer had warned Subbabaje that none of his sons would survive beyond 21 years of age, living in the particular home where they were born. Subbabaje did not want to believe it even after he lost his eldest son around that age, who had left behind a very young widow. The widow had shocked the family and the Brahmin community in the area by remarrying. A widow marrying or eloping with a man of her choice was a revolutionary act; taboo in a Brahmin family. She became an outcast, but had a loving husband for life.

Father told me that Sambhu too had just crossed that age. His fate was sealed. He too left behind a son and a beautiful young wife. Subbabaje blamed himself:

If only I had heeded the astrologer's advice! It is me and only me, to be blamed, the astrologer was right and I am wrong.

As a consequence, this time the family sent the third son, away to the Terai in southern Nepal. He survived the threshold of 21 years, and lives in Taphalonha to this day with his family.

Greed unquenched

One morning, feeling unable to stand the pressure, Father—now a pensioner over seventy-five years old—came to tell me that somebody was coming to visit him too often. According to Father it was a lady, but he didn't disclose her identity, lest I become furious and confront her directly. He only said it was a relatively rich and close relative. He told me,

We need to do something to thwart her attempt!

At first I didn't follow him. What attempt, from whom? Why? A severe chill went through my body. Who was putting pressure on my father at his advanced age? In a way, I expected something awful. Then, finally, the whole purpose of her frequent visits and the secrecy spilled open. The lady had proposed that Father, should sell his house to her. He could rent a cheap flat for himself and live more comfortably with the money thereafter.

She must have thought Father was economically vulnerable, and that he could be exploited. For a man of his age it was almost a marching order, a deceitful act by our own close relative. It was a nasty attempt, intolerable and worthy of a strong response. She had forgotten the very essence of our society, that of respecting elders – not only your own but also strangers. Father was right: it was an attempt to rip him off. He was deeply hurt.

The lady in question did not know that I was supporting Father, behind the scenes. All his extra needs (for which his pension was grossly inadequate) were well taken care of. He was doing fine. I asked him to put her off in the strongest possible terms. Soon he came over to me to tell me that he did it as we had discussed. After that, even though she was a close relative, she stopped visiting him.

Land and Luck

Our land at the side of the ring road at Jawalakhel was walled and its main gate locked. Almost every morning I used to go and look around to check that everything was ok. There were goats being dropped down over the wall for grazing and little annoyances were happening very often.

One morning I saw a Marwari gentleman, with a dark *Serwani* (long Indian jacket), taking measurement of my walls on the road side. He did not see me. I watched it from a distance. Next morning a Jyapu adult came around looking for me,

Oh Kaji, Will you sell this land?

No, you cannot buy it.

My answer was crisp and straight. He left without a second question. That two sentence dialogue continued every morning for the next seven days, as I recollect. The same question and the same clear cut answer. Then on the eighth he came with a voice a little shaken and angry, and put his final question.

How much do you want for it? How many Lakhs?

But my answer did not change a bit. On the ninth day, morning he came more angry and put his last offer,

My boss, Sahuji, is ready to give you any amount you ask for. How much do you want, ten, twenty million?

But my answer remained unchanged. I was shocked and felt something awful was going to happen, I had to end the dialogue. It was clear that the Marwari taking measurement of my land was his boss. Though they are Nepali citizens, the Marwaris are fairly recent immigrants from Rajasthan, and are known as cut-throat businessmen.

Some Marwaris have the notion there is nothing they cannot buy from a Nepali. I think I hurt his ego and arrogance. I explained to the *jyapu* lad, once for all,

> *Look this land is not for sale. How can you buy my land if it is not for sale? It does not have a value in money. Is that clear?*

> *Why did you not tell me right on the first day?* He murmured: *I've had such trouble from both sides.*

His anger subsided in a while. He explained in detail what the Marwari; the Indian businessman was up to. He had already bought 2000m^2 of land around mine. My land, about 600m^2 blocked his access to the east with the main road to Jawalakhel. He had planned for a hotel; my *ok* would have helped him realize his ambition, but that did not happen. So in a fit of anger, soon thereafter he sold his land to another person, a lady.

Her long time day dream: As I learned, the lady was none other than the richest property holder in the Pulchok area and the mother of many girls and a son. Perhaps I had played football with her son in youth. Now she started to frequent my place. She started to talk in sympathetic tone,

> *Son, you don't have enough land to expand your business at Bakena Batika. Isn't it so?*

> *Perhaps so, but I have no ability to buy land adjoining my property.*

Don't' you worry, you have your mother. Meaning herself.

I was surprised. How could a person I did not know be ready to assist me? Perhaps she had something else in mind!

Whatever area you need I can transfer my land to you officially. You can pay me in future. I have a man who can get it done in no time for you.

No, mother I cannot take anything on loan, from a mother.

No, you really can have. Take it.

She insisted I was to get it. I thought of the odd piece of land, a triangular piece in front of Bakena Batika that would enhance the property value. No one should build anything in that land otherwise it would block the front of the house. I said,

I will take about 50m² in front of the house to begin with. Is that ok?

But I did not have the means at hand. I tried to sound out my friends, it was difficult but I got it in the end. The required amount was ready and I informed her of my readiness to go to the land registry office.

She was there before me. The papers were ready and within an hour I had a piece of land in my name, without paying a paisa to her. On our way back home, she invited me for tea. I thought it was the best opportunity to pay her due. At her home, we squatted on the floor and had tasty tiffin that we all seemed to enjoy. But I knew we shared a different interest and were creating a trap against each other.

After some food and some nice words, I pulled out the money from my pocket and placed it in front of her.

Did I not tell you that you could pay me in the future?

She got annoyed and pushed back the money towards me. I did the same and shoved the money back to her side. So it went. At the end the last one to push the money was me. I told her,

I cannot take a loan from mother.

From that day on, at every meeting she became angrier. But I got one by one three crucial pieces of land within the matter of two months totaling 250m^2 on three sides of my land giving it a good shape at last. Then I drew a full stop to the transactions. She could not have been angrier. She seemed to have realized her tactics not working in my case.

Then she became softer in tone and friendlier than before. She changed her strategy. She began to open up. She thought of extracting things I liked, for example my jeep,

Oh that is the thing I was looking for my trip to Bardiya mauja. Can you give it to me?

That was not for me to go into. She tried to sell me another 500m^2 with the same conditions as before, buy now and pay indefinitely later.

I became cautious and started to smell a rat. I told her,

Shall we stop talking about land? I am not interested in more land, even if you were to give it to me. Am I clear, mother?

She did not say a word more, that day. It seemed her game plan turned foul. The following morning she came to me with tears in her eyes, and said,

Look son, my dreams got shattered!

But she did not blame me for that. Her dream and the dream of the Marwari were identical. They even thought of a joint investment in a hotel, at the place. A big game was on the anvil. She wanted to lump loans on me that I in no case would be able to pay back. That would give her right to take over my property. The same old game, for which I looked naïve and she had thought I could be trapped easily.

In fact I realized that it was not my prudence. But I played naïve, and it paid. I did not have to act naïve. But what divine power protected me from the traps laid by the greedy '*female-canine?*' I am grateful to Him even today, long after I had left Bakena Batika.

Moments with Friends

Because friendship does influence one directly, some of the time and indirectly all of the time, that justifies talking about friends most of the time. Some became friends very quickly and remained in friendship that I cherished, while with many it took a long time to nurture lasting friendship.

It is pretty uncertain with whom you might strike a friendship or from whom you get severed. It all depends upon the cultures among the friends. There were friends great and small, equal to me at home and abroad who left lasting impressions on me.

With the closeness we overlook their heights or with attachment we undervalue their strength or weakness. Of all things, writing about friends is thus difficult. In any case, I cannot be right all the time, nor can I err in most of the cases I mention about my friends here. It is not intended to make judgment on friends. For sure, one does not write all about a friend even if one knows a great deal and intimate details. Still, I know I should expect retaliation of this or that sort once they read what I have written. I had to be choosy about whom to write and I have to justify what I write about them.

A Democrat in Disguise

In the lobby of the Royal Nepal Academy Hall, Kamaladi, Member of Parliament Mr. Man Mohan Adhikary, President of Communist Party of Nepal and Agriculture Minister Ramchandra Poudel of Nepali Congress and I were sipping tea and chatting during the break of a meeting. The first point of our discussions centered on the delay in the delivery of chemical fertilizers to the farmers. In answer to my query Mr. Ramchandra Poudel said,

Well, the process has begun. It will soon be settled and farmers can have their fertilizer on time.

I did not buy his excuse. In fact the govt. had not even called for a tender. That often happened in the past, very often. There was nothing new in the delay in the process of procurement. The farmers were being denied the fertilizer at the time they needed most. The whole story of increasing productivity through the application of chemical fertilizers was a farce.

But Mr. Adhikary was more vocal and differed with him outright. Mr. Adhikary, with his mouth gaping wide, seemingly putting his right hand, into his mouth, indicated that the ministry wanted 'a mouthful'!

The corruption was omnipresent. The delay in the procurement was only a tactical strategy to come to bigger bait.

Mr. Adhikary's Party and Social Democratic Values: Taking advantage of the presence of a respectable leader, I asked Mr. Man Mohan Adhikary, why his party still fluttered a flag with a hammer and sickle. For the political layman like me, by all indications his party seemed more and more to represent social democratic norms and values. Yet his party flag betrayed the true objectives of the party. Was I right?

He was surprised a while, gathered his breath and said,

You seem to be a little naïve about our situation, Dr. Panday. The flag we carry is a rallying symbol of discipline for the more left or extreme leftists among our party cadres, especially the youth. If we changed the symbol they would jump to the other side.

He did not elaborate, but what I gathered from his words was that there were left extremists lurking to lure the youth on the so called 'other side' which carried similar symbol of bait on their party flag.

So your party and your flag are two different entities!'

He hemmed,

Well, yes and no!

But the symbol on the flag is not enough to convince the new generation.

Mr. Adhikary nodded in the affirmative. I asked,

What is hindering you from engaging your young cadres in productive activities? They need income, whoever promises that will have them. But for the extreme leftists, their bare promise was good enough as bait. You don't even promise.

His reply was left on hold, as we needed to enter the hall to resume our participation.

Within a few years, early in 1996, the Maoists began their revolt. Many youths, economically poor, socially deprived and geo-physically disadvantaged, joined the murderous foray of the left extremists. Perhaps many of them came also from Mr. Adhikary's party. Was it out of desperation and hope of change in their lot, or were they brainwashed to join the enemies of democracy and development?

The left extremists had not the ability, the vision nor the plan of action to help the poor, deprived and disadvantaged section of the population. They proved it. After a decade of bloodshed, society seemed to descend below even the pre-conflict era's state of economy.

It was a partial educative process for the common folk. People would never again allow the extremists to raise their heads to allure youth and disoriented people to shatter their dreams and the loss of the precious lives of their beloved. People should by now be convinced that the extremism of any color or creed hinders the advance of civilization.

Another occasion, on which I spoke with Premier Man Mohan Adhikary, was when King Mahendra Trust for Nature Conservation was celebrating its 10th anniversary in the Megha hall at Hotel Soaltee, Kalimati. We were guests of Chairman of the Trust, Prince Gyanendra. Even in the secure atmosphere of the hotel a military guard-- with his sharp eyes scanning the room–was following Premier Adhikary at close proximity.

I started a conversation with Mr. Adhikary, talking about the growing problem of pollution in the Kathmandu Valley. The Prime Minister was the ex-officio chairman of the Environment Protection Council (EPC) and I was a member. The council was supposed to meet at least four times a year, but Premier Adhikary had yet to call a meeting. The omission was not intended. Perhaps the priority of the government lay elsewhere. I asked him,

Whether we could hold the meetings of the EPC regularly?

He gave the impression that he was unaware of the fact that he was chairman of any such thing. I enlightened him.

During the last 3 months there has been no meeting held, and in fact, none at all so far under your chairmanship since your premiership began.

His surprise and my inner dissatisfaction collided, and at one moment my finger was directed towards his chest to stress the point I was homing in on.

At that very moment the army guard acted swiftly to hinder me from injuring him by mere touch. I appreciated his alert posture and friendly gesture.

I had just assumed chairmanship of the South Asia Partnership. We had an international meeting taking place in Kathmandu. Participants from B'desh, Pakistan, India, Sri Lanka, Canada and Nepal were attending the inaugural ceremony.

Out of courtesy, and in honor of the international community, we invited the Premier to inaugurate the 1995 meet that was taking place in Hotel Malla, Lainchaur.

The inaugural time was set for 11 am. Most of the international participants were already seated but our fellow countrymen were outside the north hall or below in the lobby, or were just making it into the hotel, dillydallying. Very few Nepali colleagues were seated when Premier Man Mohan Adhikary entered the hotel with his deputy, Madhab Kumar Nepal following. I was waiting to receive him at the door to the hall on the first floor. It was exactly 11 when the Premier sat on the dais. Feeling a little embarrassed I went close to his ear to seek apology. Before I could do it he asked me to start the function and not wait for the others to come in. The Premier said he did not have much time, but would like to make few remarks and leave the venue.

Suddenly other participants started pouring in. In my mind I was juggling with the feeling, why do we in Nepal, where the sun rises on our mountain tips before the rest of Asia gets a ray; and we put our clock 15 minutes ahead of the rest of the Himalayan subcontinent, behave the way we do, thinking it is still dark and not yet the time?

The five minutes of time he took for his 'few words from the Chief Guest', Premier Adhikary used lecturing us on the value of punctuality, its relevance to human development and the importance of it in such an august gathering. The message was clear. Yet in my later experience the message remained irrelevant.

As for me, I come from a school of thought that has time as the most important factor influencing the results and quality of productivity in research or in development efforts. For me a delay was a loss and I would get a headache when I could not maintain time. Even at home most of the time it is a constant fight for enough time and punctuality in things we do.

A Single Deed that made someone unforgettable

It was in the evening, at Malhar Hall at Soaltee Hotel, amid a large gathering for a party. I saw from a distance, former Premier Kirti Nidhi Bist (Kirtinidhibabu) and former Principal Private Secretary to HM and ex-Ambassador Mr. Iswori Man Shrestha (IMS) sitting on a couch, holding glasses in their hands.

Seeing me from a distance, Kirtinidhibabu gestured me to come closer and join them. I approached them. They were both in a festive mood. As expected, Kirtinidhibabu had already emptied his first glass with some pegs of whiskey, stood up and tried to introduce me to IMS.

Mr. Shrestha, do you know Dr. Panday?

Of course I do.

He was surprised and asked how we came to be acquainted. Both IMS and I related him how we got to know each other back in the '70s. Then Kirtinidhibabu turned to me and told me,

So you know each other. But there is one thing about us you do not know, and about just what IMS is. It was he made me the Prime Minister, you know. IMS confirmed it.

I was so surprised to hear that. I asked if he was joking.

How could the secretary to His Majesty make you the Premier of Nepal?

He just recommended it to HM the King.

I was asking to myself if it was so simple to become Premier in Nepal. They were not kidding. In fact they were good old friends from very early on, and had studied political science together in India.

I have known IMS only as an Ambassador to the Federal Republic of Germany and Switzerland, and he was our guest in Zurich. But Kirtinidhibabu was the person I really wanted to know.

After 1990, thinking he was a true Pancha, a relic of the *'Partyless Panchayat System'* he confined himself in his house. He was more or less out of sight out of mind and was living as a recluse. He had started to feel that he was just history, outdated at best. But I had not forgotten him. I had noted his role in the politics of the sixties at a critical moment of Nepal's history.

In particular, his great contribution related to the threat to Nepal's sovereignty should not be undervalued by Nepalese. After the 1962 Sino-Indian border war, politicians came to realize that the Himalayas could not be regarded as a reliable buffer zone anymore.

The Indians in close alliance with USA placed border posts on the Nepal Tibet borders and Nepal let the Indian Army personnel to dig in. After the war they lost their importance. But Indians hesitated to pull out from the posts. It was of utmost importance that India pulled out from the Nepali-Tibet border and respected Nepal's sovereignty. It was Premier Kirtinidhibabu, with the backing of King Mahendra, who made India to withdraw their military posts from the soil of Nepal.

Sometime before our meeting at Hotel Soaltee, I had invited Kirtinidhibabu to participate in the *Jara Juri* Workshop. It was the occasion in which the book on *Jara Juri* was launched, the Nepali edition by former Chief Justice Biswa Nath Upadhyaya and the English edition by Ms. Carol Lang, UN Resident Representative in Nepal.

I wanted to introduce him to environmentalist men and women participants from 26 districts of Nepal who had gathered in Kathmandu to take part in the *Jara Juri* Trust's workshop. In Jara Juri he was reintegrated into the current wave, as a tribute to his contribution to the nation. One can do the sort of thing he did for Nepal once in a lifetime.

Present on the occasions were former PM Girija Prasad Koirala together with his daughter Sujata, former ICIMOD Chairman Dr. Rudolf Hoegger and many others friends of the people engaged in environmental protection activities.

I offered Kirtinidhibabu the floor as he deserved. The remarks he made were touching. From that day on, I gathered he was back in the open and no more considered a Pancha Pariah.

Did He or Didn't He?

Sitting at Bakena Batika: It was not a special day for any reason. We just wanted to be together. I had extended an invitation to former Prime Minister Kirti Nidhi Bist and his spouse. The same invitation was extended to former Premier Lokendra Bahadur Chand. LB Chand had earlier called me to inform me that his spouse would not be accompanying him. LB Chand came but did not stay for dinner. It was a very informal moment. When LB Chand was leaving we even joked, how he would not like to miss his dinner at home cooked by his 1st or 2nd wife. He just threw a smile of his brand, with lips tight and slanting a little!

But the evening became more interesting between us three. Mrs. Bist had a pleasing personality, and I am grateful that they came. I do not know if she was bored, but she seemed to enjoy the chitchat. She must have been used to and lived through many such moments in life when the discussions are thrown around un-aimed. She remained in a pleasant mood throughout our discourse.

Beside the Indian army involvement in Nepal and how they were evicted, I wanted another point raised for Kirtinidhibabu to spill. That was about King Mahendra's last moments. Kirtinidhibabu was the Premier during a critical time of Nepal's history. I asked Kirtinidhibabu to write a memoir. He asked,

'*Who would read my book?*'

I felt if he only could do that the future generation of students might appreciate the insights he had of the country.

First, I related the story I had gathered over time, the circumstances, the last meal offered to the staff of Kasara Durbar, Chitwan, by the royal couple. How the King ordered that his face was to be covered after his death, and not allowed to be seen even by his sons.

Were they just rumors? I asked him outright,
What was the reason for all that? Was it a suicide? Did King Mahendra suffer from depression? Did he regret his actions against the democrats?

King Mahendra seemed to have trusted Kirtinidhibabu more than anyone else, even his family members. Coming back to my point, yes, I put too many questions, but I was seeking only one answer. Whether King Mahendra wanted to die so soon as per his own wish? If yes then what was the reason for it?

Although there was no clear answer from Kirtinidhibabu, and he seemed more elusive and tried to divert the point, I insisted upon his answer. He did not speak even to deny it. His silence was indicative of what I feared, so I did not press on.

I still suspect King Mahendra did in fact die of his own will. Sometime later, I asked Sirdar Yadu Nath Khanal about the issue. He was more poignant.

Yes, I also heard people saying that.

Associated for Friendship

Back in the late seventies, I was interested in establishing the Nepal Switzerland Friendship Association (NSFA). As was normal, a draft of the association's constitution was prepared. In 1969/70 I had been one of the founding members of Swiss Nepal Friendship Association in Switzerland. We were thinking of a similar association in Nepal.

Some of the founding members of NSFA had one or the other kind of contacts with the Swiss working in Nepal. Renu Shrestha, the daughter of Martyr Sahid Dharma Bhakta Mathema, was a friend of Ursula Meier; Mrs. Jamuna Kayastha who was teaching Nepali to the new comers in SATA and others joined with me to register the association in the Kathmandu district administration.

When, everything was going well, an unexpected hitch cropped up. Our friend Dr. Narain Khadka came forward saying his group wanted to register the association under his initiative. I told him that after all the work we had done to bring the association so far; he had no right to intervene. If he wanted he could join hands with us. He had one Swiss friend, Walter Jutzi who played Sitar almost with perfection, and who had stayed in Nepal for many years. Walter Jutzi, a Swiss teacher was also a friend of fellow teacher Dr. Ram Sharan Mahat while in Nuwakot then. Dr. Khadka agreed to our suggestions but I do not remember him joining the association. He later became an NC leader and MP from Udaypur district.

As the founding president I continued to work for the association for some years. I tried to highlight the salient points of Swiss efforts in Nepal to Nepali audiences through diverse programs. But the little conflict right at the inception was a bad omen for the Association's future.

After three years of tenure I called a general assembly meeting of the association. The venue was offered by Naraini Hotel, Pulchowk. The owner Mr. Bacchu Gyawali was also a member of the association.

An election was to take place to renew the executive committee. From the beginning it appeared that the hall was divided into three panels, Hari Raj Joshi from the offices associated with the SATA/SDC/Helvetas administrations, the panel of musical friends of the Swiss, Tyagi (violinist), Tabla Vadak duo Hari P. Upadhyay and Tamrakar and the Mainali panel with people like Biswa Kant Mainali not a known friend of any Swiss, his wife, his brother Bharat Mainali and the vice-president Mrs. Renu Shrestha.

The plenum failed to propose a candidate for the president. My request that a new president be elected was met with silence. No person wanted to be the president of NSFA; hence, no balloting was needed for the president. There was no other option available except for me to agree to stay for another term to keep the association going and they elected me without a single opposition voice. In a way I was sad at the outcome. For me it was undemocratic to 'elect' somebody as the office bearer simply because there was no opposition candidate. I always make it a point of staying at a responsible post for no more than a single tenure. More sadness was to follow that evening.

For the vice president, two candidates were proposed by the plenum. Hari Raj Joshi from the large panel from Swiss administration and Mrs. Renu Shrestha incumbent vice president from the Mainali panel. The Joshi-panel would not budge one step back. The Mainali-panel was for Renu Shrestha to continue as vice president. So an election by balloting procedure was agreed upon.

Mrs. Mainali, a teacher of Padma Kanya College and wife of the lawyer Biswa Kant was requested to be the election officer. Balloting was undertaken. But a dispute erupted when the votes were counted. Joshi's panel voiced anger; saying it voted in unity and claimed victory.

I did not want any controversy in the association, over vote rigging etc. But soon the opposite was unfolding. I suggested the panels accept a recount of the votes.

Before the recounting procedure was agreed upon, Mrs. Mainali packed all the ballot papers cast and hastily stuffed them in her handbag and left the hall in haste, followed by the Mainali brothers. They were running fast away from the hall, towards the staircase.

I became very suspicious, asked all to stay put in the hall and rushed out to bring the Mainalis back. Outside the hotel entrance there was a little car waiting for them. Before I could get hold of them and say a word they entered the car and whizzed away.

I was left standing there like a fool after a joke; neither could I laugh, nor cry. Saddened, I came back to the hall to tell, the plenum, that I was helpless. The ballots were hijacked by the election officer, a teacher of the famous women's campus, wife of the much talked about leftist advocate and his accomplice brother. How would I believe that they would deceive this mini democratic game so devastatingly?

I wrote my resignation from the post of the president of the association on a piece of paper right then and there and handed it over to the vice president Mrs. Renu Shrestha telling her that since I could not be part of the fraudulent practice, I had no place in the NSFA.

Photos Making a Big Difference

Over a period of four months in the winter of 1979, I started giving the finishing touches to my book on *Fodder Trees and Tree Fodders in Nepal*. I was invited to use the basement room of our family friend Rolf Knapp, a man with a creative mind in the printing sector of the time, in the beautiful hill top village of Bremgarten, near the city of Zurich. I had the required ambience and hospitality to concentrate on my work.

When the draft was ready, I showed it to my friend Andreas Speich (forestry engineer). He was trained in ETH, and was the forest officer of the City of Zurich. With his experience in Third World problems, some also on fuel and fodder, through his work with the FAO and his experience in Nepal on short missions, I thought he would be the right person to get my draft perused in a critical way.

After what he had seen in my draft, he suggested that I meet Dr. Bosshard, the Director of the Swiss Federal Forestry Research Institute, Birmensdorf. We met and I showed him the draft. The discussion with him was fruitful and he showed interest in publishing it. The cost of publication would be borne by his institute. He recognized the work to be unique from the side of his institution. This was going to be the first book treating the subject comprehensively in recent times, and this would bring his institution out of its narrow focus to the outside world. Dr. Bosshard said he would do his best to mobilize resources and we should sit down again for its finalization.

As I was going to my University, the ETH-Zurich that day, and the November weather was as unfriendly as ever, Andreas Speich gave me a lift, since his office was just 2 tram stations ahead of my institute. After all the niceties to warm up, Andreas Speich opened his heart while driving downhill. He suggested that I agree to include some of his beautiful photographs, even if they were not necessarily relevant to the subject of my book.

That surprised me. I had all the relevant photographs ready. Those I had taken during the course of years of my work on the subject had been included in the relevant sections of the draft. I was not keen to change or to swap some of them with irrelevant photographs no matter how beautiful they were. It would create technical problems and acknowledgement would be a little clumsy and misleading. Few would doubt I had taken the rest of the photographs.

I appreciated his support but not his intrusion in my work. I responded politely that his suggestion was not acceptable. The whole work should be in my authorship, which is right, or I would forego its publication in Switzerland. That seemed to have turned the table.

In the next sitting with Dr. Bosshard and Andreas Speich, a few days later, the front they had built against me was hard to crack and penetrate. Although no part of the book had been worked out in or with Dr. Bosshard's institute, he said he wanted the book to be published with a grey soft cover as an occasional publication. His name would appear as editor and mine in the inside page as contributor. That was the only way they could publish it and finance its cost in full.

I knew through my search in the Palo Alto data bank and diverse libraries that my book was to be the first of its kind and quality of materials to be published. Letting it appear in a grey cover would turn it into a kind of regular occasional paper of Bosshard's little known institute of forestry research. That would not only keep the book from being taken seriously but also reduce the importance of the subject.

I rejected the proposal. The repercussion was immediate and blunt. The original offer of 100% financing of the publication was withdrawn. Dr. Bosshard would cough up perhaps 10% of the cost. It was slightly disappointing to me.

My effort to mobilize the goodwill of friends in Bern paid off. 90% of the cost of publication was to be borne by the federal office in Bern. Federal Institute of Forestry Research at Birmensdorf, near Zurich, would be allowed to cover the rest provided they took the administrative responsibility for getting it published. It would come out as per my draft and in a colorful book format.

The language editing was done by an English lady married to a Swiss working in the research institute. I was given the liberty to mobilize the help of a Swiss for 6 months to look into matters related to copyright etc. I found a former colleague Thomas Gruenenfelder, a forestry engineer of ETH who could use the time waiting for his next job in Switzerland to devote on the book.

In All Respects a Nepali

Dr. Tsuyoshi Kadota came to Nepal initially as a Japanese volunteer. He assimilated to a high degree with Nepalese society, mastered spoken Nepali and was extremely happy to be in Nepal.

The first time I met him was in 1992 at the International Christian University, Tokyo, in a seminar on Environmental Conservation and Development Cooperation in the Himalayas. I was attending the meetings together with Dr. Harka Gurung, the renowned geographer and Dr. Chandra Gurung who had worked for the King Mahendra Trust for Nature Conservation, Nepal Government Secretaries, Mr. Baban Prasad Kayastha, Forest, Dr. Heramba Bahadur Rajbhandary, Agriculture, Dr. EF Tacke, Director General of International Centre for Mountain Development (ICIMOD), Pasang Khambache Sherpa, who had worked over two decades in the horticultural development of Mustang, Dr. Jiro Kawakita, Chairman of Japan Chapter of KMTNC.

At a tea break a sturdy man approached me and started talking to me. His light brown complexion made me ask him,

Where in Nepal you come from?

He replied that he was Japanese. I was so surprised that Japanese could appear so much like a Magar and also speak like a Magar from Myagdi Mustang area! He was talking to me in mountain Nepali slang words, so I had mistaken him for a Nepali. That was the time we became good friends.

Kadota San was a graduate from Kyoto University. As a 35-year-old expert in watershed management, he was working for the JICA project in the Pokhara area after his tenure with the Shivapuri project north of Kathmandu.

Later, back in Nepal, he wanted to accompany me and be of assistance in a work-related week long trip starting from Kristi-Nachne Chaur in Kaski, over to Tribeni and Falebas to Kusma in Parbat. He was extraordinarily helpful and went out of his way to make my travel pleasant and successful in my work. I appreciated his presence.

At one point of time during the trip, he started to tell me his sad tale: JICA wanted him to be repatriated to Japan. He told me he felt completely Nepali and could not face the prospect of returning to Japan.

Besides his own fondness for Nepal and Nepali people, whom he found friendly and loving, he had a special reason to stay put in Nepal. Some years back he had met a girl in Tukuche, in a Thakali house where he was staying in the course of his work, and he fell in love. The girl had her own history to tell, at once both sad and pleasant.

She must have been around 6 or 7 years old from an unknown place in India when she had accompanied a Jogin on pilgrimage to Muktinath. On their way back the Jogin requested the host Thakali family to accept the girl as their daughter. The family readily accepted her as a gift of Muktinath. She grew up in that house as a member of the Thakali family at Tukuche.

She stood out among the Thakali girls because of her different beauty. Her appearance betrayed her origins and aroused curiosity, yet she grew up in Thakali culture, fully assimilated. Kadota San and she got married and he became the son-in-law of the Thakali family. The family later shifted to Pokhara and ran the Mona Lisa Hotel at Pardi.

Both of them were at home in Nepal and wanted to settle here. Their request either to extend his tenure or let him stay in Nepal was rejected by his boss Katsura San. Kadota San had learned that I was on good terms with Katsura San. During the trip in Parbat district, he wanted that I talk to Katsura Watanabe for him.

I had met the duo Katsura Watanabe and Andreas Speich in Nepal, for the first time when they were on a whirlwind mission for community forestry. I got to know Katsura San better when he was in Nepal for the community forestry project under JICA support. He was very fair and friendly towards us. I got along well with him. He was clear in his head and his decision was final. He was JICA head for the Pokhara project too.

But when I tried to talk this over to Katsura San, he did not want to hear about Kadota San. He said that the matter was final, and that Kadota San should first go to Japan.

I still cannot get it why Kadota San could not go to Japan, then come back to settle in Nepal. Although they did not have a child, they were happy with each other. On several occasions I was their guest at the Hotel Mona Lisa.

At another meeting in Pokhara, I heard that, Kadota San had driven a jeep over the Seti cliff near Pokhara airport. So they said or was it something else, somewhere else? He had died instantly.

But behind the suicide I felt there must have been strong motive. I am still convinced that the one man who could have saved the precious life of Kadota San, a good husband, expert in his field and a friend of Nepal, was Katsura Watanabe.

I cannot blame Watanabe San alone for Kadota San's death. With him I lost a friend.

The Loss of a Nepali Legacy

Of the people frequently visiting my family in the 1950s and 1960s, were the family of Toni Hagen from Switzerland and the engineer Peter Aufschneiter, an Austrian-born Nepali citizen.

Like Kadota San, Peter Aufschneiter (1899-1973) liked Nepal. After eight years in Tibetan life, having escaped there from a British-Indian internment camp in north India along with Heinrich Harrer during World War 2, he did not go back home to his birthplace Kitzbuehl, Austria when he had to leave Tibet during the uprising of the early fifties. Instead, he came to Nepal, the place closest to Tibet sharing a common culture, settled here in 1956, and became a citizen of Nepal. He joined His Majesty's Government of Nepal's irrigation service, and travelled around with his Nepali passport #0666/2027.9.3.6. His last years of life were spent from his last home, a room rented from the Swiss Association for Technical Assistance (SATA), Ekantakuna, the house used for SATA administration at Jawalakhel, and was happy, but in 1973 he died a lonely man while on a visit to his sister in Austria.

His room at Jawalakhel was like a museum. It was crammed with a collection of bronze figures from Tibet and Nepal. Plans of construction schemes, maps, drawings and books lay everywhere scattered around.

My visits to his room were moments of discovery for me. That one could collect so many valuables! One had to literally jump from one little free space on the floor to another over the stacks of papers, idols and books. It was amazing how he found his peace in that room. In a way the items in his collection were his friends. His room had high ceilings, tall windows. Although facing west the room was cold and dark. But that was his heaven and recluse. He shaped it to his liking. He did not have to share the space with any mortal being.

I did not see him much in interactions with others in Ekantakuna. He was quiet and with very few words. On government holidays I would see him take a back-pack, a picnic and his 'little trek' boots and disappear in the then peaceful, wide open fields and patches of forests of Nepal Valley.

The only way he could not meld into the Nepali crowd was his physical size. He was slim, very tall and with a whitebeard. He would stand out among the crowds. We used to joke about his height, like the Naga who came to Bhoto Jatra Matchhendra festival in search of his wife.

We were his neighbors at Shanti Chowk. Through my contacts in Ekanta Kuna I came to know him and found moments to talk and observe him. Way back in the fifties and sixties, Peter Aufschneiter used to come to visit us. He liked to eat what my mother cooked, simple farmers' recipes.

In one of the last visits to us, one moonlit evening, Peter Aufschneiter came to have dinner at our home. As usual he would smile and listen and talk little but he would share his experience of Tibet and Nepal, captivating our attention. We did not go into his pre-Tibet life. That was ok. I had only heard he had a sister surviving in Austria. At about 10 that night he said he wanted to go to bed in his room at Ekantakuna. I said I would accompany him as far as his gate, but he insisted on going alone.

Off he walked. In the light and shadow of the moon lit night, he did not notice that I was following him. I was walking without making noise choosing the shadow of the wall on the right and left of the street. I had rubber slippers on. Just when he arrived on the main road he started going towards Narain Bhawan, a different direction. Perhaps in the relatively dark unlit road he missed the direction. I had to rush to get hold of him. He was somewhat scared by somebody being so close to him and pulling his arm, and was surprised to see me following him. I said,

See, it was good that I came along.

Then together we trekked back to the main road and started marching towards Ekantakuna. He was walking and I was running to keep pace with him. He felt uncomfortable that I had come along to see him enter Ekantakuna. I knew he was used to being alone, but he had missed his way home, and I was a bit worried. Now I did not want him to go alone.

The two meter tall large iron gate of Ekantakuna was locked from inside. We were too late for the watchman to be expecting us. Nor did he have any information that Aufschneiter was out.

Let's not disturb the poor guy. I can climb up the metal gate.

I could not believe him; neither would I let a man of his age do that. I started shouting at the gate keeper who was fast asleep in the guard house. That was it. I walked home feeling good.

Sometime in 1973, Peter Aufschneiter left Nepal to visit his sister. That was his last trip. He did not make it back to his Nepal Home. I do recall that his large room, full of artifacts and valuables mostly cultural goods and documents, was emptied. The materials were packed and shipped in haste to Austria? What happened with his 'assets'? Who could forget that he was a Nepali citizen and Nepal was his last home that he loved? Peter Aufschneiter died a Nepali citizen, and his collections of valuable cultural goods should not just have been shipped away. We have not come across the inventory of the valuable goods and documents taken away from his room after his death. We failed to preserve his legacy for the future generations to come.

What was he to us?

When he came as an expert in the early fifties, many could not guess then who he was to be for us. For me Toni Hagen was the first white man I saw and my first contact with a European. Later his family members: Gertrud, Christoph, Kathrin and Monica came to Nepal. Werner Schulthess, Peter Aufschneiter, and Peter Arbenz followed. Over time I had scores of European acquaintances also through Christoph, Toni Hagen's only son, at my birthplace at Jawalakhel. We were of similar age, became playmates and I frequented his house, Ekantakuna.

Who Toni Hagen was and what he was to us are two questions I have tried to answer. Being close to his family from my early childhood, and over time, becoming professional friends in our own rights to interact in good or worse times with him, gives me extra insight to be fair in writing about him.

For many Toni Hagen became a legend in his life time. That is what many of us in the Valley thought and believed. Many were mystified by him. Many capitalized on his presence as a PR stunt in Nepal by the royals and tourism entrepreneurs and in Switzerland by the gnomes of Zurich.

Over time I could begin drawing a clearer picture of him. I was the student of Prof. Del Vasco of ETH in his classes on petrography and mineralogy in the early seventies. He said he was as a student colleague of Toni Hagen in the late thirties and early forties. He told me Toni always needed a position in the center and relished being in the limelight. That quality and drive for prominence that took him into contacts with high profile people in many countries might not have always been his weakness. But Prof. Del Vasco's brief remark was apt to characterize him. Toni remained unchanged throughout, and my knowledge of him also remained static.

Who was he in Nepal?

I could not answer this particular question of Prof. Del Vasco.

Many believe he left behind a legacy of contributions and controversies for posterity. He was sharp, hard and straight in his remarks and expressions. Whether they were untimely, unwarranted, impertinent, irrational, impolite or even inhumane, it was not his habit to have them tested or reviewed or appraised by critics, which he would not have tolerated. Anyway, it had to be as he wanted it to be. One particular description, I quote from his travel notes,

> "My porters (Nepali) were 'bottomless pits'. They gobbled down everything, including innards and even bones. The crunching they did was what dogs do when going at a bone. Heads seemed to be a special delicacy:

they cut them up with their sharp Khukuri into thin slices, along with everything in them. These slices were divided among everyone. Everything was consumed, with the customary canine crunching."

He was not telling this jokingly. One can brush it off or pardon him for it as his usual weakness in his perception of poor Nepalese by a man infatuated with Nepal. Much controversy and confusion was created by his actions and words at home or abroad. I will come to them later in this write up.

I had known him and his family since I was about 7 or 8 years old when I came into contact with Christoph and spent my after-school times playing with him and his slightly younger sister Kathrin in Ekantakuna garden. I taught Christoph to fly paper kites; he was fascinated and I was mad about flying kites myself. Kathrin had a tri-cycle. I had never seen one before; such a machine that one could ride and pedal around in comfort. She would not let me try it.

Madhukarraja, Rajesorimaisab and Bimalamaisab, children of Maheswor Rana, would also join in our games when they were home from their schools in Darjeeling. We especially enjoyed playing football together on the large grassy front garden of Ekantakuna. We continued playing football even after the Hagen children had long left Nepal. Rajesori Diju proudly introduced me to her friends, in my presence, some 50 years later in Kathmandu by saying what football partners we two had been then.

My family was a place the Hagen's would walk over and say hello and talk to us. They were fond of the flower garden maintained by my father, especially his collection of varieties of geranium flowers and mother's vegetable garden. On many occasions they relished our vegetables and I think they praised Mother in Swiss language. Sometimes, while passing by our red house they would stand and lean on the garden wall for some time there looking at the plants in the garden.

The Saga of Toni Hagen Foundation: On 21st November 1989, in a Panel discussion on Environment and Development of Nepal in the 1940s and 1950s, between Sirdar Bhim Bahadur Panday, Prof. Yadu Nath Khanal and Toni Hagen, I had put to discussion a proposal to establish an Institute of Toni Hagen Studies, focusing its attention particularly to the remote rural areas, which need special attention in our planning efforts.

My cousin, Mr. Shyam Bahadur Panday, the Chairman of Hotel Shangri-La, and I discussed how we could preserve Toni Hagen's contributions for posterity, especially his findings on Nepal's natural potential. Toni had claimed how he had been instrumental in bringing tourism to Nepal, thanks to his pictorial book, *Nepal*. He was a favored guest at Hotel Shangri-La, Lajimpat and sought privileged attention. He got it and appreciated it.

Later on Shyam Dai and I were the profounder of the idea and initiated steps to realize a Toni Hagen Foundation. From our end we would come up with some land and build a house to house his research materials, artifacts, the photographs and Thanka paintings and bronze figures, and we expected Toni Hagen's commitment to repatriate to Nepal all his scientific and cultural artifacts collected in Nepal, in original form and format. We communicated this to Toni Hagen. We had a tripartite gentlemanly, but verbal, agreement.

He put a condition to be fulfilled from Nepal's side before handing over the materials,

> *Firstly, I be permitted to hold an exhibition prior to handing over of the materials to you and,*
> *Secondly, the exhibition is to be inaugurated by His Majesty King Birendra.*

The first condition was reasonable to us as we could then see what he could bring and show us in their original form and state, and the second condition was positive and doable. We started to sound out the idea and negotiate with the palace. My acquaintances and HM's Secretaries, Mr. Narendra Raj Panday and Mr. Narain Prasad Shrestha were my contacts in the palace. His Majesty agreed and so we launched first the activity for the exhibition.

I often heard him talk over the money supposedly flushed out of the country into the Swiss Banks by the Palace. Surely others would have heard it too. So while he was not technically *'persona non grata'*, he simply was not so welcome in Nepal for some time. Rumors were circulating that Toni was involved in smuggling of weapons to Khampa fighters fighting for their homeland occupied by China, collected religious relics and idols from the Tibetan Refugees pouring into Khumbu area etc. They were serious matter in those days and Nepal was in a difficult position to accord him again easy access to Nepal

Entry into Nepal was very important for him. Somehow, here in Nepal he found what he needed for his life, a purpose. In fact it was Nepal which produced a Toni Hagen. In an effort to get rid of the virtual status of *'Persona non grata'* that he felt tarnished his image, he thought it worth trying everything permissible. He had told me how after he heard of Crown Prince Birendra touring Ethiopia, he rushed from Switzerland to see him, to request him to annul his status of unofficial *'persona non grata'*. What happened after that was clear. I am not saying he was a *'persona non grata'* for me. Nepali Palace had reason to keep Toni Hagen happy.

Negotiations were undertaken with Bal-Mandir where the Art Gallery and the orphanage were located. My relative Mr. Krishnabahadur Panday was the Secretary of Children's Organization in Bal-Mandir there. Bal Mandir agreed to host the exhibition; Toni Hagen would come with the materials to Nepal. In November 1993, he did come along with nails, clips and display panels, photo frames and what not, for the exhibition, with the Director of St. Gallen Museum of Ethnology, the bespectacled friendly Roland Steffan, a German to help set up exhibits in a technically correct way. The materials were first stored in Bakena Batika my house at Jawalakhel where Roland stayed before the exhibition and for a few days more before leaving for Switzerland.

His Majesty the King inaugurated the exhibition in the morning of 16th of November 1993, at Bal-Mandir, Naxal.

Toni Hagen was conscious of his art of maintaining an image of him. For the first time I saw Toni well donned in festive attire, with formal western suit and tie and not in his usual brand of a Khaki safari polo shirt and a tie that did not go together. But he was conscious of the opportunity made available that day.

Just before the arrival of the Royal guests, when we were making sure that everything was in place, there was a big commotion in the exhibition hall. Toni wanted to know what had happened to an exhibit. There was only a sheet of paper with a caption pinned on the display wall. It was the curator from St. Gallen, who handled all these materials, from hitting a nail to hanging artifacts, and no stranger was allowed to enter the room or let alone touch any exhibits.

The police dogs had done their security checks. Perhaps either Roland or Toni forgot to bring along the particular exhibit from Switzerland, now supposedly lost. Toni cried foul and insisted that it was stolen here in Nepal. I argued with him, that it could not be lost in Nepal. He would not track back to the point in time when they were packing things for the exhibition in Switzerland. That was the way he was. I can for sure tell that no exhibit was lost or stolen in Bal-Mandir, prior to or after the exhibition. Now, the question was how to cover the space with the caption without the item.

In the meantime HM arrived. We had to rush down the stairs and out to receive him. There was a lady who Toni introduced to me, clad in high-mini frock and a large hat, her tall thin figure with her extra-long legs, exposed indecently. I was taken aback by her appearance in front of our royal family. I do not know whether Toni, as a Nepal expert, had not informed her of protocol at such times. I do not know whether HM noticed what we were doing.

She had followed Toni Hagen because of the materials he had brought to Nepal. Only much later would I know that they were to be '*hers*'?

Supreme Leader of Nepali Congress Party, Ganeshman Singh with his secretary Krishnabahadur Panday and Prince Gyanendra and Toni's Japanese friend Mr. Masada were present. Toni took the occasion to hand over the *draft copy* of his memoir in English to King Birendra. I always wondered why he did it. Did he fear that the palace might protest in case something unacceptable appeared in the book, so that he still would have time to modify it before publication? After I had read the German version, I suggested to Toni to have it published also in an English edition. He had it done by Mr. Philip Pierce, and the book was released in 1994. I noticed the error only on the published book.

So the exhibition was not held at Kamaladi in the Royal Nepal Academy premises. RNA had not organized it, nor had the KMTNC, to be acknowledged as Toni has done in his 'memoirs' for the exhibition.

After the exhibition, without any discussion with us (Shyam Dai and me), Toni repatriated all the materials, as I came to know later, not necessarily to Switzerland. Toni had spread the news that Nepal wanted 'all his materials exhibited in Nepal, in original'. Surely there were others who were aroused by his ad strategy to make him lucrative offers.

Not long after the exhibition at Bal-Mandir, Susan Van der Heide called me by phone for a chat. She had just arrived in Kathmandu and we met at the Annapurna café. The whole purpose of her coming to Nepal this time was to meet me and tell me she had all the original materials from Hagen for Germany. Did he sell his Nepal research materials to her in Germany? To avoid unwanted attention, the dialogue ensued in German language. She bluntly told me,

> If you in Nepal want Toni's material I could give it to you. For Nepal the copies I make would suffice. If you want I can have them sent to you. The photographs would just look like the originals.

My curt and brief reply was not to be a diplomatic one.

> So you have come all the way from Germany to bring us the bad news. We are not such fools as to accept your offer. Toni had promised us to deliver the originals to us. Why is somebody hijacking his intellectual property and collected artifacts for which Nepal can lay claim? I better forget about the Toni Hagen Foundation. Thanks for your effort. Good bye! And good luck!

I felt deceived, disappointed and dismayed by what I heard from her. I communicated this to my cousin Mr. Shyam Bahadur Panday. He too found it hard to understand. We let fall the idea of establishing a Toni Hagen Foundation.

I later heard from a German friend in Bonn that Van der Heide ran a museum of her private collections. Surely, Toni was not the one to make free gifts. He did the same to St.Gallen Museum, Switzerland, just like Heinrich Harrer did. How much money Hagen made I could not ascertain then. Heinrich Harrer was not in Nepal but he also made a million of Swiss Francs by selling his Tibet collections to St. Gallen Museum.

This reminds me of a story from Mustang. Time and again a certain *gompa* went up in flames. We know a *gompa* is not a simple prayer hall; it is also a library of Buddhist Holy books. It needed to have at least 108 books to be taken as a respected *gompa*. So after the burning down of the *gompa* the books vanished. That did not happen only once. A short, sturdy man from Sikkim had first arrived wearing Lama Garb, and was instrumental in leaking the books out of Thakkhola. How authentic was the story time will tell and only Mustang people would know its details, and what they lost of their heritage.

According to Tulachan, as soon as the Thakalis had evidence of his involvement, he was declared *'persona non grata'* by the Thakali, but he stayed in Pokhara for some time. Soon also Pokhara became a hot seat for him.

Whom he was working for? Was he only person acting as bait?

Years later we could see the 'same' man who had been in Lama Garb floating around Kathmandu in western dress, but he had kept his goatee and long hair, and was thus easily recognizable. A very tall western lady introduced him to us as her husband. Not long after I heard he died.

This led me to remember the story of Melina Mercouri, the culture minister of Greece in the seventies. She launched an international campaign and moved UNESCO to help her country in particular and all the culturally rich countries in general get their artifacts and cultural goods repatriated from rich countries. That alarmed the artifacts-mafia and promptly somebody from Germany joined UNESCO to try to hinder that move, unsuccessfully.

UNESCO ratified the Mercouri's proposal. That was also the end of the German person's mission, albeit unsuccessful, in UNESCO. We had our man at Paris, my friend Ambassador Keshab Raj Jha, who was also instrumental in trying to make the campaign to repatriate cultural goods a success.

'Birendra Pragya-Alangkar' (King Birendra Academic Decoration) and Toni Hagen: I was home for a month's rest before my exam to defend my PhD (Technical Science) in ETH-Zurich on 30th of April 1984. Sometime late in March 1984, Artist Lain Singh Bangdel, VC of Royal Nepal Academy called me to come over to him. I met him at his home in Sanepa. He gave me a letter from the RNA to deliver it to Toni Hagen on my return to Switzerland. He told me that HM wanted to bestow Birendra Pragya-Alankar to Toni Hagen in the near future.

I was to brief Toni Hagen on the ins and outs of protocol during the ceremony and the importance, perks, prestige and favor the Alangkar carried, and especially, what it meant for him. The date for the ceremony was set for June the 5th, 1984. VC Lain Singh Bangdel regarded Toni under different light. He had even painted a farewell portrait of Toni in July 1962 two days before he left Nepal after his prolonged stay.

On my return to Zurich, I met Toni at Federal Institute of Technology (Post Graduate Course for the Developing Countries), where I too was acting as a resource person for a subject one day. I informed him I had something important to talk to him about and a gift to hand over. He called his wife at Lenzerheide, in Graubünden to come over to their boathouse in Staefa, by the right bank of the Lake of Zurich.

That day I had the last session and Toni waited for me. Then we went by tram to the train station Stadelhofen, at Bellevue Platz. He bought me the train ticket saying I was his guest that day. I was surprised by his gesture. Had Toni changed?

On the train to Staefa, where the boat house was located, he started to spit out, loud and clear, his not so new criticism of projects, particularly, the Lamosangu Jiri road (LJRP) and Integrated Hill Development Project (IHDP) where I had toiled for three years in Sindhupalchok district of Nepal.

The train ride to Staefa continued that evening, and reached the boat house in time, before dark. Meanwhile Toni continued to talk about how everything had gone wrong with the two projects, IHDP and LJRP. All eyes and ears of the fellow passengers in the Rapperswiler train were directed towards us. It was embarrassing for me.

Let's drop this when we get to the boathouse. Others in the house will be bored and annoyed. I want to see Gertrud and your children and enjoy the evening with them.

Toni stopped and we were back to normalcy. Actually, we did not have much else to talk about during the rest of the train journey.

In the boathouse present to receive us warmly, were Gertrud (Toni's wife), daughter Monica and her friend. His eldest daughter Katrin did not turn up. Gertrud told me how badly she wanted to have Christoph, who was working in the heritage office of the City of Zurich and lived nearby with his family, for the evening as well. I missed him that evening. Despite his mother's request to come over for the evening, he declined.

When Toni had stepped out for a moment Gertrud gave me the explanation for Christoph's absence. 'Father Toni and the only son Christoph had age-old tension. Toni never sanctioned him marrying a German girl, the 'Schwabe' for him.' According to her, Christoph held the view that his father dominated him, bluffed too much so he never felt free at home.

So Christoph did not come to see me, his childhood friend, and we could have seen each other after over 30 years! That was not his fault. We both had become ETH engineers and active in our professions.

Yet it was a very enjoyable evening and I relished the good meal prepared by Gertrud. We giggled and reminisced about our time at Jawalakhel and how we had changed and so on.

Gertrud made a point that I meet Christoph; she called him to arrange for me to meet him. Next day we met after over 30 years and he invited me for a good lunch in a small restaurant near the Stadt Haus. It was good that we met and I could hear from him about his contacts with his parents and siblings, about his profession etc. and reminisced about our childhood time at Jawalakhel. I was happy to meet him after so long and hear about his work and mission but I was also sad to get confirmation of what Gertrud had hinted to me evening before.

Back in the Boat House: I handed over the letter from VC Mr. Lain Singh Bangdel to Toni. I could see a glow on his face. As Mr. Bangdel instructed, I informed Toni that with the decorum came with certain perks, privileges and preferences he would acquire from Nepal. Most important, since his reinstatement, he was to get a free visa every time and all the time. He could ask for an audience with the King at every visit. He would enjoy unrestricted movements within Nepal. That would be one side of the coin.

I also whispered him as I was hinted to do by Mr. Bangdel, that the decorum obliged him to be responsible for what he would be talking about and representing to the world from now on about the Palace and people of Nepal. I could not quite read his mind, immediately he got a large grin and exclaimed,

I have it!

His long coveted wish was to be. But who would stop him doing what he wanted? Isn't a habit difficult to tame? Hagen's would be no exception.

On June 5, 1984, at Kamaladi Hall, there were about 25 persons attending the low key ceremony, among them Prince Dhirendra, Dr. Mohan Man Sainju and Vice-Chancellor Artist Mr. Lain Singh Bangdel and I. Toni was earlier asked to address and talk freely to the audience in the presence of the King. He did but concentrated on the banal subject 'farm gate price of farmers' products', out of context of the Royal Nepal Academy, for *his day.*

He had a private audience with the King at the far end of the lobby of the Royal Nepal Academy building while all of us got a cup of tea. I had not seen him that happy for ages. My impression is that Toni became less critical of the Palace from that moment. Was that the sole objective of the Palace? He would not take it that way and thought he deserved it as his reward.

The issue of money put in Swiss Banks could have been dug up during President Koller's visit to Nepal in 1997, but Toni was silent about his favorite issue. The Palace was quick to make the dignitaries comfortable in the fold of the Royal Family. But did I raise eyebrows with an article in *The Kathmandu Post of 14 December 1997*: 'What Nepal Can Learn from Switzerland, in which I had tried to raise the issue of Nepal's money in Switzerland?' Certainly not! *It* published the article without feathers and plumes, the all colorful points about the money in Swiss banks, it just did not fly. Chief Editor Mr. Shyam Bahadur KC should have killed my bird rather than to have maimed it with his censor knife.

Kishunji and Hagen: In 1993, with only about 4-5 days of breaks, Toni Hagen stayed for 42 days in Bakena Batika, my house. One evening he wanted me to invite the founding member of Nepali Congress Party and the current Nepali Congress Party leader Mr. Krishna Prasad Bhattarai, Kishunji. He told me that Kishunji was his good friend. I did manage to bring Kishunji as the guest of Toni.

I gave them a cozy corner to be together. Sometimes I joined them. They had a good time with drinks and dinner. Dr. Narain Khadka, Nepali Congress Party stalwart, came along. Hagen wanted me to offer them a bottle of Johnny Walker Whiskey. I complied. When he wanted another full bottle of the same, I had to restrain them. I pulled Hagen out and told him in whispers,

You invited them. I don't see why I have to offer the expensive whiskey.

The second one was ordered by Toni and went to his account. Kishunji started to murmur, was boozed up. At around 10pm I asked Dr. Narain Khadka and Toni to stop the spree and call it a night. Narain Khadka understood the situation.

I on one side and Narain Khadka on the other, holding his arms, we two pulled Kishunji, brought out of Bakena Batika and placed him in the car. But the amazing thing was that Toni served most of the whiskey to Kishunji while remaining sober himself.

Tenzing, Hillary and Hagen

Ekantakuna in 1953, where the Hagen family was staying; One day late in the afternoon, we kids heard that Tenzing and Hillary, two of our heroes, were coming to visit the Family Hagen.

Father had brought a Murphy radio that we had to place on the window so the neighbors could listen. We were proud that ours was then the only house with a radio in the locality. Radio Nepal had been announcing the feats of Tenzing and Hillary. The reception began from Banepa, on horse drawn buggies taking them first around the Bhaktapur city, to be greeted by hundreds of thousands of people. The jubilant reception continued in Kathmandu and Patan. Nepal was becoming more famous because of their deeds. The radio was blaring Dharma Raj Thapa's song, *'Hamro Tenzing Sherpa le Chadhyo Himal Chuchura'* (our Tenzing Sherpa climbed the tallest Himal). The patriotic song was on every body's lips. Tenzing our hero was to come. We had a song about him and now we would see him in person. I was bouncing with expectation.

We all gathered near the front portico of Ekantakuna. Toni Hagen and Gertrud were waiting to receive them. Hillary and Tenzing, if I have not forgotten it, came by jeep.

If at the age of ten I could not have understood everything, I could at least discern meaning of tears flowing out of people's eyes. I saw Toni's eyes were wet. His tears moved me too. The bearded and imposing man,

Toni Hagen, was weeping silently! That was new to me, that a grown up man and a Swiss at that, could weep.

I had begun to speak some English with the Hagens. At least I could follow most of their conversations.

Why didn't you wait for me? I wanted to go with you. Now you have conquered Everest! I knew every step of Everest, and I wanted to be the 'first man' on top!

That was not the moment to joke. So Hagen had met Hillary and Tenzing before they had left for the Hunt's Everest expedition! I did not need to understand much of the English words they were exchanging.

In the beginning I thought he was joking with the two great guests and his tears reflected his joy. Not so; his somber mood, with tears in the eyes, was there in his eyes while he was taking them into his house.

Tenzing Norge and Jamling Sherpa

Nepal was proud that Tenzing had made history, but not for long. Soon after, Nepal's pride was stolen by India. Lured by perks and paisa, Tenzing disappeared from Nepal, for good.

I have no idea whether Tenzing ever came back for a visit. King Tribhuwan did nothing more than bestow the highest Nepali honor 'Nepal Tara' and decorate the mountaineers, when Tenzing could have been rewarded with a decent life in Nepal where he could have led generations of Nepali mountaineers. We failed at a historic moment to sustain our pride.

The people's reception, immortalization by Dharma Raj Thapa in his epic song and the decoration and prestige that came with Nepal Tara medals were too little and too worthless for Tenzing. The shrewd Nehru knew how to deceive the innocent Nepalese. Tenzing was a Sardar working for money.

In 1965 when I visited Darjeeling, I met Tenzing in his institute. I shall also be talking about the encounter with Tenzing in Darjeeling in a book on reminiscences of my travels.

I think, King Tribhuwan's successor King Mahendra was upset by the episode. He started to lure the best of Darjeeling Nepalese back to Nepal. One of them was the Artist Lain Singh Bangdel who contributed immensely to Nepal's pride. Many others followed.

The trend continues. Some who made names but were rejected by their homeland, like the Indian Idol Prashant Tamang, look to Nepal for recognition. The tide has turned.

Years later I met Tensing's son, Jamling, at the Soaltee Hotel, in Kathmandu for the premier of the IMAX film on his tragic Everest Expedition with Hillary's son, Peter. Over the tea I had the opportunity to talk with him. He had become a naturalized Indian citizen. In answer to my queries he said,

> *My father harbored a grudge against the Nepali government. Being a Nepali he had the right to have an honorable place for the glory he brought to his country. Nepal did not give him the place he deserved.*

How much Tensing was right is questionable. A good son does not abandon his mother simply because she fails to bestow enough attention to him, which can be subject to so many factors. Did Tenzing Norge become the 'Kaji Lhendup' of 1st ever Everest Vijay? Did he fall prey to Nehru, who lured him and gave him the Mountaineering Institute and a comfortable life in Darjeeling?

'The Sun Rises from the North'

That was the title of a poem submitted by my colleague Siddhi Lal Singh at the literary symposium being organized in our Patan Degree College **to celebrate** Reunion Day, in December 1966. As the cultural secretary of the students union I was collecting stories and poems from colleagues for presentation..

There were to be awards and medals given to the best poem recited or best story told. A group led by Siddhi Lal Singh, my senior student colleague, was opposing everything I was doing. The reason for that was my rejection of Siddhi Lal's poem for presentation. It was entitled *'The Sun Rises from the North'*.

It was the time of Mao Zedong in China and Siddhi Lal Singh (*son of Paicha, the messenger of the school*) became ardently impressed by Mao's dogma. There was a moment in Patan High School of which I am a witness and a player when events pushed him towards a political path.

Ours was an institution of learning. The Principal of the College was Dr. Mangal Raj Joshi, a renowned astrologer, astronomer and geographer of Nepal. We could not make mockery of his leadership, tarnish the college as a 'red fort' and contradict the universal truth that the '*Sun Rises from the East*'.

Because of disagreements with Siddhi Lal Singh, he made it sure that my story submitted for the occasion was taken out of the contest. The compromise of the students was that Siddhi Lal would not read out his poem to the audience either and I was to be barred from competition. But I would be allowed to read out my story to the audience.

So my story and Siddhi Lal's poem did not go under the hammer of the jury. I gave in as long as he, Siddhi Lal, did not recite his poem. So I read out not only the story 'Pasaro' (helplessness of a girl who lost her love through orthodoxy of her parents), but also I recited the poem 'Nyasro' (solitude/melancholy, a love lost in death) too.

There was applause after they heard the first page. I could read the face of my friend Siddhi Lal Singh. The audience regretted taking my presentations out of the contest.

But Secretary General of our Union and senior student, Madhav Rana, from Kopundole, proposed to the audience that he would award me with what I deserved, at least a silver medal. I appreciated the friendly gesture more than the jury's decision. Madhav Rana showed his courage at a moment when the students were slowly drifting apart to their respective political camps, which I learned about only later.

Siddhi Lal's opposition to me was not limited to the controversy over his poem and my story. He was against all cultural programs being organized. It became an issue. There was a dance and singing event being planned. At the college venue he said he would dismantle the stage, cut the curtains and destroy musical instruments, should I continue organizing the cultural program.

He was hell bent on making the whole college's Reunion program a failure. My colleagues were not impressed by his behavior either. We did not let him discourage us. We sought a new venue. We found one, at Narain Bhawan, Jawalakhel; a Rana era theater hall with a raised podium and even a little balcony, just the best of its kind we could have close to the college and my home.

But we feared Siddhi Lal would come over to Jawalakhel too and disturb us. What he was doing was pure hooliganism. We thought of some muscular musicians from Sundhara, and contacted one Tabalchi (drummer) and one harmonium player in Patan who were known for their muscle and physical appearance, besides their musical skill. We did not really mean them to be our vanguard in the eventuality. It was just a 'show of force'.

That evening the cultural event started without a hitch. The hall was packed with students. Everybody was enjoying the dance and songs. Suddenly somebody hinted to me that Siddhi Lal Singh's entourage was at the entrance, looking at us menacingly. I said we would continue the event.

But after seeing the 'heavy weights' from Sundhara, it seems Siddhi Lal's group from Chyasal in Patan was scared from undertaking anything unpleasant. They were there for quite a while. I think they too enjoyed the event.

Our performers, mainly our colleagues, boys and girls, gave their best. The next day we appeared to present a better face in the college than Siddhi Lal's group. Our Principal Dr. Mangal Raj Joshi congratulated us, for our peaceful encounters.

Struggling and Revolting Character

Historically they say that Panday and Bista never got along well, yet I have not come across any Bista who clashed with a Panday. Nepalese history is silent about it. Sometimes Dor Bahadur Bista (whom I usually called as Dor Dai) and I took it as an issue, jokingly. We were serious about our historical enmity. But none of us could prove it. We were at peace again. There were many funny encounters between us. We did it more for fun.

Both Dor Dai and I grew up in the vicinity of urban and rural areas of Kathmandu Valley, seeing things as given and the social orders unquestioned. Yet what we found later in life left in us tremendously meaningful imprints through caste system prevalent in our societies.

After the publication of his book: *Fatalism*, in 1991 AD Dor Dai was openly opposed by the traditionalists for his thinking. Who were they? In the end two groups of people would come to our mind: the Brahmin priests and the ruling Royals. I remember two of his prominent questions:

Do we have to continue to believe forever that the ***priests*** *(whether as shamans, Fedangvas, Nokchoes,*

Bajracharya, incarnate Lamas or Brahmans) hold their position by **birth***?*

Is it absolutely necessary to continue to accept the totally untrained **priests** *once they are born with certain caste or religious* **backgrounds***?*

I was inclined to believe that Dor Dai did not leave Monarchy outside that question.

The book on *Fatalism* is the pinnacle of Dor Dai's achievements. The conclusions drawn by his analytical brain are not based only on his scholarly studies. He was born in, lived within and came out to rise above the caste, creed and color of skin like my illiterate mother did; like the ones of the history Siddhartha Gautama Buddha, Mahatma Mohandas Karamchand Gandhi or Martin Luther King, who helped overcome hatreds, oppression and segregation between the children of god, in their respective time and societies. They questioned the evils and created a new legacy of hope.

It is perhaps the 'struggling and revolting' character of Dor Dai that rightfully questioned through the medium of the book, *Fatalism*, the culprits and sustainers of the caste system, exposed to its basics and made the perpetrators insecure. Perhaps the advocates and highest beneficiaries of the caste system felt, and still feel, threatened and found in him the crusading spirit that ultimately cost Dor Dai's 'visibility' physically. He disappeared!

There were many rumors in circulation about his disappearance. He was working for small households of the remote district of Jumla helping them build toilettes and improve lives. It is said and till now held as authentic, he vanished after he alighted from a bus in West Terai while on his way to or back from Jumla.

If we conclude that he 'disappeared', it would grossly negate his contributions even when he is not around. In fact he is going to be reborn, come with an incarnation to help create a new social order without castes, creed and cultural bias, in the new democratic constitution of Nepal that is to come.

I hope we already have settings created within the last decade towards that stage where many more Dor Bahadurs will emerge and there will be no need of 'disappearance' of them. Monarchy was replaced by Republic. Brahmans do not hold birthright to priesthood. Dalitism is illegal. Neither, the shape of nose or cheeks, nor will the degree of slanting of eyes matter in the new Nepal. To say equality, equity and freedom of all are the fundamentals of our age, now written in the heads of all Nepalese in Nepal.

As against the reign of crusaders trying to change minds and belief through violence, Dor Dai has many students to follow his peaceful beacon. Because he chose the educational, intellectual and non-violent way to eliminate the injustice of the Caste System, he will be successful.

We would do justice if we could go a little distance towards the pre-*Fatalism* period in which Dor Dai lived, the social and scholarly life he lived and see what had made him come to the point we find in *Fatalism*. The book alone would be grossly insufficient to make any judgment on him. We know one has to travel a long and arduous route to come to such convictions and determinations as those of Dor Dai who did not fear the consequences or was shy of the cost.

The Bista duo, Mustang Raja Jigme Parbal and Dor Dai were to talk to an audience of young minds at the Russian Cultural Centre, Kathmandu. It was a time when Mustang was the pet issue of Berkeley students, so far the inclusiveness in politics and ethnic rights, and the rights of the people living in remote areas while *Fatalism* of Dor Dai was feeding arguments for equality at home.

The organizers had wanted the Mustang Raja to come in his full regalia, rather heavy and warm, topped up with the Highland Hat, in the sweltering heat of the auditorium without air conditioning and in the summer heat of the Kathmandu Valley. After the Raja's turn there was a tea break. Dor Dai and I stood in one corner of the lobby outside the hall and sipped our tea and munched some biscuits, undisturbed. No one came near us. That was pretty ominous. I thought we needed to be prepared.

Do you smell it; why they wanted you to give a talk about Fatalism? I see the audience in a strategic mood, what are they up to?

I know the conspiracy behind this. They disagree with my thesis. I know I am right in my analysis in the book. They feel hurt.

Who are 'they'?

Well mainly the Guru Khalak (the priests/Brahmins) and other (the royals) of course!

What are you going to do?

They need me to talk, that I will do and use up the allotted time not saying anything either to please or to anger them.

Can you do that?

Just wait. You will hear me in the hall.

Dor Dai was to be on the podium/dais after the break. I sat in the front row. Dor Dai started to talk. The talk spread over lot of time and echoed in the void of the hall's space above the heads of the audience. The audience seemed to have been mesmerized by his talk, most probably trying to fathom the contents and context.

I said to myself, well Dor Dai did what he said he was going to do. I was smiling at him and he replied with the same grin. We marched out of the hall into the lobby. I knew he said nothing his opponents could use as a stick against him, nor did he hurt anyone through his ramblings. That was good. But I had hard time understanding the context of letting the Bista Duo who represented 'two worlds', give talks from the same podium to the same audience!

From that day on I thought he was a man of mystery. When he disappeared from public view and knowledge, there were many theories about what had happened. Some came up with bizarre and tragic thoughts. I saw his action as typical of his brand. He just vaporized like many great sages we had read about.

When he was doing simple but important social work, such as help people to build cheap and clean hygienic toilets etc., in Jumla he had even invited me to come over and see for myself. I regret not having been able to respond to the call.

One story he told me has always remained in my head. It comes from Dor Dai's journey to Jumla. One morning he coincidentally was walking towards the village of his Khas porters. Arriving not yet close to the porters' mountain village, he found himself stranded and abandoned by his porters, who looked every bit and every way poor, needing an income.

Dor Dai did not know what to do. He was alone with loads of materials. He had no choice but to wait, standing on the path side. Soon he found some passersby who were ready to help him carry his loads.

Continuing the journey with new porters and further ahead, the owner of the house where Dor Dai wanted to take some rest and stay overnight declined to let the porters cook their evening meal inside the house. The porters supposedly came from the same area and were familiar to the house owner. Dor Dai learnt that the porters were none other than the so called low caste tailors, the Damai from the same village.

A few days later, Dor Dai met his former Khas porters high up in a village, on his route to Jumla. They called themselves, Thakuri. They were in their own village and were from the *high caste* families having higher social prestige. Their acquaintances and relatives were living all around. To their community the carrying of loads for other people belonged rightfully to and dutifully done by a lower caste people and not by them.

The low caste people had come to terms with their fate. For the Khas it was the status offered to them by the system. Economically they were much in need of some earnings, yet menially working for others or strangers, was shunned.

It turned out that the Thakuri were ashamed to come to their village carrying a stranger's loads. It seemed clear that the Khas porters did not want to face the wrath of their class and caste for loosing 'dignity'.

I gathered that the caste system within one's own relatively intact society and circles was strongly practiced and securely maintained. It could be avoided outside one's own realm, where identity was not sought nor necessary to disclose. Far from one's own social circle or milieu the social status was either not recognized or carried no value. The double standard was pervasive, hindering the development.

I could see the potential of menace of such double standard. One could do anything (even commit crime or indulge in offence) or anything goes outside of his or her *ijjatko ilaka* (area of dignity respected). Now I get the point why the Maoists lured the youth to fight for them in faraway areas and not in their own home districts, where nobody could or would recognize them.

The boundary of shame or caste consciousness lay somewhere, where one's own people would not be seen doing menial work. The change in conventional identity and migration of the community to newer areas could address the issue to some extent.

For the Damai it was the sense of untouchability that made it difficult to live a normal life like the others, with all its shame and prestige. The shame and prestige was more of a psychological barrier. Where is the boundary of shame and prestige? No matter how much difficulty one may have, our society runs within a jealously guarded virtual social boundary defined by shame and prestige. That hindered development.

It is this tenet of double standard within the caste system that makes it weak, inhuman and illogical which Dor Dai courageously questioned and established scholarly precedence without overlooking some positive aspects without which it could not have been introduced at all in the first place, centuries ago. However, it lost its original meaning and continued to degrade humanity. That was probably not the original principle of caste division based on tasks.

A Tribute to a Buddhist Scholar

Somebody without a visiting card, he had left his home in Solu Nimar of Solukhumbu close to Salleri, to immerse himself in Buddhism and Tibetan cultures. That was in the forties and early fifties. He went to learn classical and colloquial Tibetan language at Shigatse, Tibet. He spent years studying the Bhutanese language and Kajuba Buddhism in Bhutan.

He was renowned as a Buddhist scholar and partnered with the famous professor of Buddhism, Dr. David Snellgrove (author of *Himalayan Pilgrimage* and *Buddhist Himalaya*), in the School of Oriental and African Studies at University of London for seven years from 1955 to 1962. He also underwent training in Viticulture *(wine making)*, in Montpellier, France for five years. All that exposure only made him do more for the country and its mountain people.

A soft spoken scholar, Pasang Dai, born in 1934, had a chequered life. For 22 years Pasang worked for Mustang's development. He lived in a modest way that reflected the life of a scholar. He became known both as Buddhist scholar and a development expert. He married a Magar lady from Ulleri village in Kaski district.

His passion for spreading the cultivation of apples, apricots and to some extent his trial with Saffron (Crocus *stigmas*) and cherry trees was unmatched. The apple, apricot and their alcoholic drinks marketed to major towns of Nepal have become the economic mainstay of Mustang. That was Pasang's contribution. He was so successful, he was promoted from a non-descript 'official' to Officer First Class (Technical) by command of King Birendra on his visit to Mustang. Pasang changed the face of Mustang and its image for good.

That seemed to have generated jealousy among some Thakali professionals, who were yet to do any notable development in their own area and for their community.

Pasang Khambache worked in their highland abodes continuously for over two decades while many of his contemporary Thakali friends opted to leave Thakkhola.

In 2012 while on a trek visit to Mustang area with my family, I happened to meet the retiring horticulturist Mr. Buddhi Ratna Sherchan of Kobang Debithan at Tukuche. He was visiting his ancestral home.

Late in his life, after retiring as horticulturist, Buddhi Ratna Sherchan came to Thakkhola on a visit. In 2012 I met him at Tukuche.

He looked like a visiting expert, with a bulging briefcase with questionable papers to convince me that it was he and not Pasang who brought about the change through apple plantings in Mustang. I was expected to believe him.

At that time Tukuche people had just completed the Bhupi Sherchan memorial house at Kobang, an ugly object to challenge the traditional houses of Tukuche. The great poet's intact ancestral and architecturally beautiful house was not considered for the purpose. That was pathetic to see and learn. What a shame!

Pasang and I were good friends. No hardship was too much for him. No modesty was modest enough. I still have with me his gift for me. Once, back in the 90s, when I was low in spirit, his gift to me of *Yarsagumba* and Nepali Ginseng in a bottle of apricot brandy from his farm in Marpha, put me firmly on my feet.

A Single Letter of the Alphabet Making a Difference

In 1997, the twin books (English and Nepali) on *Jara Juri* were released. They were welcomed by the *Jara Juri* scattered over the mountains of Nepal who appreciated reading about the committed likeminded people trying to protect environment.

The Nepali version landed in the lap of a well-known literary critic of Nepali language. It seems the language used in the book drew his attention. One early morning a phone call came from him. Luckily I was in a mood to listen, on an off day and had time to chat too. I was surprised to hear that he had read my book but was not sure whether he had read beyond the introductory chapter. Anyway, I felt grateful and thanked him. I knew the book was outside his area of interest.

He did take some interest in the Jara Juri Awards ceremonies and attended attentively. The award money, ranging from one to 500 rupees was the object of amusement to him. Even as award it was too little to impress him. He came more to see how we conducted such ceremonies for simple folks. He would see how we gave much importance to their work and respected them as they were great people for us.

That morning he drew my attention to the Preface I wrote in the book. He was pointing out the letter त (Ta) used 15 times in the first 9 pages of the book. It is one of the six single letter words very often used in Nepali language and it is important in the parlance; the word used to give emphasis on a word or sentence.[1] He commented on my writing style. I normally prefer writing in simple Nepali, where possible using *Thet* (typical words created and used by simple folks to communicate locally) words as much as possible. The book was targeted to the simple farmers, of course not the likes of him.

I was surprised for the second time in my life by the comments made on my style of writing. Back in high school Nepali was my weakest subject and I was the target of the Uddhab Duwadi of Mattar (*Imadol*). Even now I do not claim to be better. But the editing of the *Jara Juri* book was done by a specialist working for the Sajha Prakashan.

I expected from him a word of encouragement. In contrast, former chief Justice Mr. Biswa Nath Upadhyaya, my respected friend, wrote encouraging words to me in his own handwriting on my personal copy of the book. There was no comment on the use of words.

After the telephone discussions, I went to see Biswa Nath Upadhyaya to discuss about the issue of Nepali language today. He loved simple Nepali language. I asked him,

Who is the one who decides what and how the Nepali should be interpreted?
Mr. Upadhyay was clear,

---

[1] For example the word छ has multiple meaning, त a particle, न used as a particle, a term of negation and a link word giving emphasis to both words, म meaning I, a pronoun, र an adverb, a conjunction and ल a particle, a word to mean acceptance or request, grief or surprise.

It is the people. But it cannot be stationery, the language evolves over time. There is no fixed rule to it.

I was satisfied with the explanation. I forgot about debate on त (Ta).

Truanting with a Warm Heart

As serious as he may appear Harka Gurung was a jovial type. He could make jokes, and enjoy himself as well as being a serious thinker. His unique facial architecture, not to be found in others far and wide, made him a more interesting and attractive a person.

Apart from meeting and interacting with him in many meetings in Nepal, I had the opportunity to know him, my friend, better in a different way, mostly outside Nepal. I would like to write about our two joint trips to Europe and Japan. We were roommates, had enjoyed our meals together and took time to make jokes and to ponder about Nepal's development, with which both of us were deeply concerned and actively involved at different stages of our lives.

On our return trip from Japan we had to leave Tokyo city a day earlier because of congestion in the commuter trains, in order to reach the airport in time for our flight early next morning. We stayed in one of the airport hotels near Narita Airport.

We bought a bottle of Johnny Walker and lay on our beds. We did not need glasses. Like his earlier ego *Bhendigothalo, (the sheepherder)* we drank from the bottle directly. We were giggling and the bottle was almost empty, the time was about midnight, when he put on his reading glasses low on his nose, took a file and put on his lap, resting on the pillow and the bed head, he started to make notes and read a document. I asked him,

Harka, can you do that after so much Johnny?
Well somehow I become clearer in my head when I am a little boozed up.

You say 'a little' after sharing a liter?

For you, sure, you, Lure (frail)!

Funny that you can do that, but I am feeling sleepy, I had more than I wanted. I won't wait up for you. We have to get up early to be at the counter on time.

Good night Kk.

After the alarm sounded when I got up, Harka was in the same posture.

At another occasion in Tokyo's Mitaka-ku township, we were attending a workshop at the Christian University. This time we were a big group from Nepal and ICIMOD. Dr. F. Tacke, Dr. Heramba Bahadur Rajbhandary, Sec. of Agric., Mr. Pasang Khambache Sherpa, Dr. Harka Gurung and Mr. Baban Prasad. Kayastha, Secretary of Forest. Finding the hotel food a little dull, Harka and I decided to seek a cozy little Japanese restaurant in the town. It was late in the evening, and we were feeling hungry.

We two sneaked out hurriedly without telling our colleagues where we were heading to. Our search was rewarded. At one dark alley corner of Mitaka-ku we thought we found what we were looking for. There was a room, on the ground floor with a Japanese curtain half sized, leaving the bottom drawn up. We had to peep inside from the lower end. The room was very small hardly 2m wide by 4m. We saw gentleman and a lady who were watching their TV. Nepal Himalaya was on the tube. We became curious; letting our heads penetrate deeper into the room from under the curtain, we asked whether we could pop in. It was after all the restaurant that we were looking for, small, rustic and with smiling owners. We got it.

As none of us spoke Japanese, we introduced ourselves in English that we came from the mountains they were just looking at on their TV. They spoke good English. That was a great surprise for us too. They welcomed us as if we were their long lost friends. Harka could tell them about the mountains. That was his subject. That made him proud too.

We wanted food. The restaurateur asked whether we preferred fish. We could not have wished for a better dish. We both liked fish. We got some *shochu*, a Japanese drink like *raksi*. The fish was cooked in front of us. We were enjoying our food and drink, and were talking a lot. Time and again big laughter would help to change the theme. The door was kept open. We were asking the owner whether he expected more guests coming in at that hour. No! He would say. Soon, we saw many heads looking into our place from the lower part of the curtain. They all were almost kneeling down to peek through the low hanging curtain. Guess who they were?

All the colleagues from Nepal had come to join us, including Dr. Tacke. They had sensed that we two hatched a conspiracy to leave them out of the fun in the evening. They had gone on a rampage from one corner to another around our hotel trying to find us two. They heard our giggles so their heads were put together at the door of the restaurant. We had no choice but to ask them to come in and join us.

The partying went so well. It was the best evening we ever had in Mitaka-ku. But the restaurant was just too narrow to give each person a place to sit. We just squeezed touching and pushing each other's knees, sitting with our legs crossed (in Nepali *paleti*), on stools, benches and tables and on the floor.

In the Netherlands: There was an occasion once in Groningen. There too we were participating in a seminar. After the seminar and dinner we went in search of fun. This time we two were the only ones from Nepal. There was Casino running in a hotel. Unlike in Nepal, we as Nepalese were not barred from entering but we soon discovered our allowance was nowhere near enough to buy a second's pleasure. We went to a 'drink and food hole' nearby.

Back in hotel we read on the bed, and Harka had his Johnny for company. I could not see any difference in him even after some pegs of Johnny.

We took the best breakfast and enjoyed the Dutch butter and cheese. Naturally our discussions were always rounded up with our concern and ideas for the development of Nepal. We did not always agree. During the breakfast I was countering him against his proposal in a draft document he gave me to peruse, for a 25 administrative districts re-division of Nepal. I was for smaller districts, about 100, with more freedom for resource use and management and autonomous local governance. He was for bigger districts in order to minimize administrative costs. Even now many areas of larger districts are in administrative shadow, because some are very large and their administrative headquarters are located at one end while the other end of the districts cannot be accessed without much difficulty.

See for example, Lalitpur district headquarters was located at the wrong place of the district. It all depended where the HQ was located.

It did not impress Harka. I would agree,

The administrative costs for smaller districts do not come cheap, but we needed to raise incomes from manageable areas keeping the administrative units simple and small.

But our discussions were always done for a start and never meant to end, as is the development process of a country like Nepal.

Every time he came back from trips inland or abroad, he would drop in at my house, at Bakena Batika. If he did not find me there he would leave behind a piece of paper or his visiting card with his scribbling,

'Kk, tan thiinas, ma aeko thien, Hai!' (You were not at home, I came by)

Hate and Love with Computer

Both being the first professionals to join ICIMOD, Dr. Colin Rosser, as the first Director and I were to meet often for getting the center organized and to make it operational, before other professionals were contracted and the administration enlarged to cope.

It was mid-eighties, the representative in Kathmandu of Apple Macintosh computer came over to demonstrate their product in the Centre. It was the first of the Apple computers with a mouse, the baby Mac that had just been released. Colin was so impressed.

It is so simple and easy to use. It accepts my commands!

He did not wait to place an order for two for the director. I asked him,

What do you want with two sets? You are not even using one, and you won't even let others to use computers. You were the one who was always against the 'devil' computer.

He answered,

One I'll keep in the office for me to work at my desk. The other I will leave at home. I can take a floppy disk back and forth for work at home.

That was a big departure for Colin.

Before Apple Mac entered ICIMOD, sometime in 1985, after I had spent a year working at the Centre which I had joined on 1st of July 1984 as the coordinator of the watershed management division, I requested Colin to import computers. He was surprised and told me he had never touched a computer and had no intention of importing one for the office either, for any one. He cited the cost as well. But my secretary Renu Shrestha was using more expensive IBM-ball head typewriter than a Taiwanese computer available.

The discussion ended when one day soon after I had asked him again to import one from Taiwan at *my* cost. His nose and face turned red with anger. He shouted at me that I could have one if I wanted, then called David, the administrator, and told him to do as I said.

That was it; I soon had a cheap Syntax computer from Taiwan and started paying back in installments to the office. Colin would time and again pop into my room and watch how I was using my computer. It saved a lot of paper work and paper. The printouts needed no tedious editing as with the manual typewriter. My secretary, Renu was pleased to get her work eased and simplified.

Anyway that set the stage for him to wake up and develop an interest in computers. Soon the Apple representative was allowed to demonstrate the functioning of Apple's Macintosh computers. The computer age began in ICIMOD.

Colin and I had developed a very open friendship and he would accept my criticism without any problem. One day he asked me to join him and his wife Tessa for a dinner at his home, in Dhobighat. He had colleagues, Professor and Mrs. McFarlane, from his University of Oxford coming to visit him. Prof. McFarlane was an anthropologist and had done his PhD in the studies of the Gurung community of Kaski.

Colin soon found out that we were brandishing our tongues as weapons and exchanging fire with our opinions. We were not boozed, and Colin was amused at my English with a slight Swiss accent confronting an English professor. It sounded funny to him. But it did not deter me from starting to argue with the English gentleman professor.

Did you learn the Gurung language before you started to work with them? I asked.

No but it did not hinder my work. He answered complacently.

I tried another tack. 'Is anthropology based solely on observations?

Mostly so, it is about understanding their social and power structure, who exercises what sort of power how and so on. We observe.

So there was no communication with your Gurungs? Or were you just observing them as we do animals in a zoo, but then they are animals? Here you have the Gurung community, a cultured, highly developed social group of Nepal before you.

But we could still understand what they were doing and how they were doing it. Establishing intimate contacts and communication, something that comes with learning the language, could push us into a different situation. Bias would prevail. That is what we avoid in our studies.

But it looks like you are confirming my hypothesis that anthropology was developed as a tool the colonialists used to conquer other countries.

You can't say that, but it certainly helped them, particularly in Africa.

Is that the reason for example, that we from the 3rd world are 'perhaps not 'allowed' to study the Scottish or Welsh tribes: because it could pose a danger to your sovereignty?

There was no answer to my last question, so we drifted to another topic. The talk went towards, who was victorious in the Nepal-Britain war of 1814-16, full century before the WWI. The name Gurkhas is derived from the coining of Gurung and Khas communities now used for the ethnic Nepali soldiers in the British army.

My point started with the English troops defeated by the Nepali army in many battle fields. Butwal and Sindhuli are glaring examples of Nepali valor. Desperate to defeat Nepali morale, the water supply to the fort on the Nalapani ridge was cut off by the British. At Nalapani, Balbhadra Thapa was not defeated, although his troops were outnumbered. Because the supply line of water was cut off and the plight of the garrison was unbearable, he ordered all men, women and children to stop fighting and open the gate. They left the fort fully armed with honor intact.

Not a shot was fired by the English forces; they just stood there awed and gaping for a long time. So by the time they realized they were to go after the Nepali forces, it was too late.

Tradition says no epitaph will be erected admiring the valor of an enemy. What happened in Balbhadra Thapa's case in Nalapani, Dehradoon (now in India)? Perhaps, the British only wanted to say, indirectly, that they lost with grace by praising their enemy. There is a long history of the British Empire taking over the countries they defeated. How could Nepal remain outside the British Empire? 565 of Nepal's neighboring Kingdoms in the Himalayan subcontinent were subjugated and ruled under their suzerainty. Were those monarchs retained to make Queen Victoria, the Empress of India?

You had the pen and the writers who were eager to scribble before we even thought of writing about the history of the battles we won against the British. Many of our historical documents and war diaries ended up in the hands of British representatives. Have the British ever asked the Nepali version?

Prof. McFarlane was disturbed for a while but our parting words could not have been friendlier. Colin intervened to stop the debate, and we all went to the buffet placed by Tessa. Colin filled his plate with a great quantity and variety of food until Tessa, who was concerned about his weight, put a stop to it.

A Democrat Through and Through

My first contact with Mr. Biswa Nath Upadhyay, our Chief Justice, was when in the Environment Protection Council, I launched a campaign to get the working days reduced to five per week starting at 9 am instead of the traditional Nepali starting at 10 am. I had three major points of concern: the offices could save energy, the employees needed time for their families, friends, internal tourism etc. and at least one day a week there would be cleaner air to breath. The bureaucrats present as observers came to voice their protest against my proposal. They took the example of their peons who would have to come much earlier for the 0900 office start. Where would they be eating?

My answer was, even at present they were required to enter the offices earlier than any other staff members. Had we thought of their difficulties? They would have one extra day off to help in the household and the weekly Saturday they could retain for their usual activities. The Council was against it for its early introduction. It said it needed time to think it over.

Soon after, I met Chief Justice Biswa Nath Upadhyay at a party at Shambala Garden of Hotel Shangri-La. I talked to him about the negative attitude of the government. He said he liked my idea and would help to implement it starting with the courts in the Kathmandu Valley and gradually implement the plan all over other courts under his jurisdiction in the country.

Premier Girija Prasad Koirala was against the CJ's decision but he could not do anything against the decision of the judiciary. But Premier agreed to introduce the concept also in executive's offices from the 1st of the next household year. So we had a 5 day office hour for many years. It was the autocrat King Gyanendra who abolished when he came to power.

Once the Maoists had decided to end their so called 'People's War', Biswa Nath Upadhyay, both as former Chief Justice and the Chairman of the 1990 Constitution Drafting Committee, was one person who could not be left out in the peace process. Switzerland was showing interest in conflict resolution in Nepal. Many delegations came here from other western countries to sound out a way out of the political impasse in the post-Maoist era. They were coming nowhere close to understanding the current and historical background behind our conflicts. Missing here was the opportunity for a good dialogue between the parties.

The issue at stake was democracy or autocracy. There is no compromise solution to it. One party had to give in. Freedom could not be split. It did not work amidst the turmoil of Kathmandu. The Swiss later thought of a change of venue in a quieter place far away from home that would go a long way toward bringing about some rationale.

Several times Switzerland invited Nepali politicians and so called civil society members to get them in a dialogue away from Nepal. These were a kind of Klausur (a kind of closed door thrashing of issues to be settled) which the Swiss valued in times of fundamental differences of opinion or when parties were adamant, to sit around a table for official dialogues.

I remember Dr. Rudolf Martin Hoegger, a friend of mine coming to Nepal on behalf of the Swiss Government to seek actors and stake holders in the peace process for a Klausur in Switzerland. As a man who knew Nepal inside out, he was mandated to woe the participants.

Since the Maoists had landed and agreed to swap their weapons for a political role in the post-conflict time, the nature and extent of a new constitution was an important issue also for them. In any dialogue the issues have to be looked into seriously. The political conflicts could only be averted in the future when constitutional provisions were so charted that they reflected the people's wishes and accommodated political agendas of all stake holders, the parties, without splitting the universal definition of freedom.

I suggested Dr. Hoegger talk to Biswa Nath Upadhyay (BNU) once the Maoists had decided to lay down their arms and try to persuade him to participate in the meeting in Switzerland. At the same time the economist Dr. Devendra Raj Pande (DRP), a member of the so called civil society was also contacted and he showed keen interest in going along.

Thinking the participation of the two veterans would enhance the meetings; Dr. Hoegger extended an invitation to Dr. Pande and Mr. BN Upadhyaya. When the date of the meet neared, Dr. Pande told BNU that he had decided not to go to Switzerland after all. BNU answered that if friends like him were not going, then he would not go either.

But when the meetings started in Switzerland, the first to arrive there among others was DRP. When I met BNU later and asked him whether he knew of the DRP's participation, he showed ignorance and wondered why DRP behaved the way he did, unexpected from a friend!

I was inclined to seek motive for the behavior. Dr. Devendra Raj Pande tended to prefer a place in the center, needed to be looked at, listened to and appreciated!

Had BNU participated in the Swiss seminar, in which even a Maoists representative rubbed shoulders with others, the position of attention would have been taken over by the more senior, experienced intellectual, BNU. In fact I knew BNU was very upset after the episode.

Earlier, nine of us were active and played the role of watchdog for democracy. We had worked together in the 90s for the strengthening of democracy in Nepal. BNU coordinated the committee of nine diverse personalities like Mr. Kedar Koirala, *diplomat*, Dr. Madhu Ghimire (*Gastroenterologist*), Dr. Laxminarayan Prasad (*ENT Surgeon*), Dr. Devendra Raj Pande (DRP, economist), Dr. Mahesh Khakurel (*surgeon*), Mr. Kulsekhar Sharma (*veteran administrator*), Mr. Krishna Prasad Bhandari (*senior advocate*) and me (an *agronomist*).

Things were running smoothly. I was acting like a secretary too. There was one moment we needed to hit the streets to protest against a government decision, to table anti-terrorism bill in the House without prior discussions in the cabinet. The issue we were raising was that the bill would go against human rights and we wanted it to be hindered in the form it was being tabled and more time be taken for wider discussions. The government led by Premier Lokendra Bahadur Chand was showing apathy for our cause. It just did not listen to our argument. We, all nine members of the group decided to demonstrate in front of Singha Durbar, and all of us would be there, to draw public attention.

I knew that the attention of the government as much as that of the public would have been drawn by BNU's presence because of his credentials. Perhaps things would have taken a new turn. The evening before, DRP pulled out without plausible reason. Had we gone ahead without him it would have been obviously judged as division within our group by the Chand government? We would look weak and loose moral clout.

BNU saw the Panchayat system as an autocratic system. His court decisions had chipped off the King's power when he had even attempted to intervene in court decisions. In a landmark decision he quashed the army's right to prosecute civilians, so he was becoming highly unpopular with the army. But he could not be harmed by punitive measures, such as when the Palace tried weaken his moral by putting him 'on ice' for 12 years, and made Dhanendra Bahadur Singh CJ twice against the legal provision only to reduce chances of BNU's becoming CJ on his own right and turn. He was not to change his opinion, stand and position. He had immaculate credentials against which the Palace itself could not hold on its position. His credentials as a democrat eventually paid off.

After the 1990 revolution, despite its dislike, the palace wanted BNU to ask for an audience. In reply to a call from a secretary, BNU told him why he should have to ask for an audience.

King Birendra and BNU did meet however. I did not ask BNU whether the King had called him personally. It was obvious. The King asked him to lead the constitution recommendation commission. BNU was surprised by the King's gestures. He at first had difficulty believing him. BNU then asked him if he was aware of the kind of constitution that would result from his leadership. Would the King support a democratic constitution? King made an unexpected reply,

> *That is the reason why I'm asking you to lead the CDC team. I trust you.*

His team was composed of members, who were not interested in the rule of law, the leftists of all shades and the royalists. They found it hard to come to an agreement that would make them play fair and democratic politics. But he also had intellectuals like Immaculate Integer Person Pradumna Lal Rajbhandary, Justice Laxman Aryal and slightly left leaning Nilambar Acharya supporting him. Persons like Madhab Kumar Nepal, the Secretary General of the Communist Party would argue vehemently against some of the most fundamental of democratic politics, but would submit nothing on paper. BNU kept the record in a file.

Soon after the promulgation of the new constitution, BNU became the Chief Justice, a crown almost denied by the Palace. Crowning his tumultuous life, the decision of Bhadra 12 brought him face to face with the group that was against the rule of law from the beginning of the drafting of the constitution. Mr. Khadga Prasad Oli, from the Communist Party, was Home Minister; BNU was greeted by mob of the Oli's party pelting stones at his car while going to the Supreme Court.

That was happening in front of the very seat of the government and parliament, 200m away from Home Ministry, Singh durbar, under the pointing finger of King Prithwi Narayan Shah's statue. Out BNU came and told Oli, he should be ashamed of leading a mob. As the Home Minister it was his duty to control the mob and unruly crowd.

If I find one pane of CJ's car broken, I shall shut down all the courts of the Kingdom.

Oli was forced to make his party cadres retreat.

But he continued arguing with BNU. CJ Biswa Nath Upadhaya challenged him to face the court if his decision leading to the reinstatement of Parliament that Premier Man Mohan Adhikary wanted dissolved was illegal.

After 2008, when the Constituent Assembly was being set up, the parties had prerogatives to nominate personalities whom they thought could contribute in the drafting and bringing out a new constitution. When Premier Girija Prasad Koirala invited BNU there was no surprise. He would be a driving force provided the others, especially the Maoists, were serious about a new constitution. The next morning I had a telephone chat with BNU. He was still mulling over the proposal of GP Koirala.

I asked him if he felt he could dent the Maoist position and help chart a democratic constitution.

If there was any political party that is inherently committed to govern without the rule of law and the political system, it was the Maoists. If there was any party that would go alone to govern the country totally under their hegemony it was the Maoists, the extreme leftists, not much different than Pol Pot's party or the Kims' of North Korea.

There would be only a drama being played. In the end when the drafts did not turn out for a one party rule under the Maoists, they would hinder a new democratic constitution. The Maoists thought they were in the majority. They used all methods possible to have the election result in their favour. The international community remained in tacit agreement with the Maoists for their violation of election codes of conduct and rules.

In such a circumstance BNU could become only an onlooker of the communists' *game of deception*. I begged him not to go.

I think he heard his heart and decided to decline the offer made by PM Girija Prasad Koirala to have him nominated to the CA. We were right. The CA was made to fail by the extremists. Now we are back to square one and have come up with a CA-2 to draft a constitution. BNU did not survive to witness another drama unfolding in the CA-2 with the people's verdict having no meaning.

The Cost of Believing in Democracy

Two helicopters hovered over Dandapakhar, Sindhupalchok. It was a government holiday. The project offices were shut and the senior staff members were away engaged in their usual pastime, playing cards, the Paploo.

I looked up on the sky and noticed that the helicopters were seeking to land. We had put up an improvised big **H** on a piece of flat ground within perimeter of the project's service center, near the health post. The ground was just large enough for parking two helicopters at most. It was earlier meant for the King's visits. They found it.

They were flying in from east Nepal after the inspection tours, I learnt. I happened to be free and was never having been a card player, hurriedly approached the army aircrafts. Out came officers. I greeted the one alighting first,

> *Permit me to introduce myself to you. I am Kk Panday, agronomist.*

> *Aditya Sumsher Rana, Adjutant General!*

> *It is my pleasure to receive you. Do you have any official purpose landing here?*

> *Not at all! We wanted to take a break. It looked attractive here and we wanted to have a look.*

With thatched-roofed stone houses and green all around, it might have looked attractive from the sky. But for us it was an improvised settlement, with bare necessities appropriate for the kind of work we were doing.

After offering tea from my abode, I introduced the officers to the workings of IHDP. That was the beginning of our years of friendship. I got a standing invitation to come over to General Rana's house and be his guest anytime I came down to the Nepal Valley.

Over time and with each visit to his home at Babar Mahal compound I came close enough for him to open up.

I am brother of Bharat Sumsher, the politician, previously of the Gorkhadal Party which agitated violently in the early fifties to prevent ousting of the Rana regime by the Nepali Congress. Later he joined the Nepali Congress Party. Have you heard of him?

Of course, I have.

But that has not been an asset to me. I have remained the adjutant general and I would not be allowed to be promoted. A new man will become CnC but I will again be second in command, perhaps, if not retired out.

How come? Who is punishing you?

Well the Durbar never wanted me to become the CnC, simply because of Bharat Sumsher, my brother.

Out came a bitter tone from his mouth and a sarcastic grimace around his lips. What could I say but,

That is unfair!

In our subsequent meetings, he opened up further. In one visit he showed me around his former cattle sheds and horse stables. These were used as his factory, employing craftsmen from Patan. He was producing cultural artifacts with impressive precision and an artistic touch, bronze casting of Buddha statues (*Murti*) for export. The Murti factories have given way to the present day Babar Mahal Revisited. He continued.

> I have placed the best cows and pigs in the army barracks. They get quality fresh products and I get money. The soldiers look after the animals. Having been denied the highest job I deserved, with prestige being in the army, I make it up with money.

Years later, when he retired, he was in charge of the construction of Social Services Building at Kantipath. With this assignment allotted to him the Durbar showed him he was under its fold and would not be left outside its periphery of control. Being a brother of Bharat Sumsher cost him his pride.

A Highest Intellectual Mind

It was purely out of curiosity and to utilize some leisure time, while at Nepal National College, at Kathmandu, I too attended the law classes, especially, those given by Mr. Pradumna Lal Rajbhandary. They were attractive to a beginner, like me. The number of students attending the class was very small; perhaps not many were interested in studying law. It was then that we became familiar. Mr. Rajbhandary later became the Secretary of the Ministry of

Education and some years later the Ambassador to the Federal Republic of Germany and Switzerland.

It was early 1968AD and I was just 24 years old when I went to see the Secretary of Education. There was no hindrance, I could just tell his PA and pop in. I related my wishes to Secretary Pradumna Lal Rajbhandary: my first law school teacher was the man I was talking to.

He put some questions, about my subjects in SLC and the division I passed in, IA etc.

Your ambition to study agriculture or architecture, both technical subjects, needed you to be coming from a science background. You are not qualified as you did not study science, so you are not eligible for any scholarship.

That was pretty disheartening. Fortunately I did not tell him I was trying for a scholarship to study in Switzerland through the Swiss Federal Government (Bund) and the Federal Institute of Technology (ETH-Zurich). I only wanted to get a hint from the Secretary of Education whether the government would encourage me or hinder me from getting a scholarship from Switzerland.

I left Singha Durbar saying to myself that I would not return to that office again. I feared the worst. Should they find out my short cut to university study, might they simply pull me out, just because I did not fulfill their criteria and not consider my commitment? They would not believe that I could make myself eligible for the study, of course given opportunity to do. They themselves would also not be sending any one on that offer from Switzerland. I wanted that scholarship.

In the meantime I had already contacted the Swiss Association for Technical Assistance, and I would most probably get a chance to apply for a scholarship.

It was the Dasain of 1970 AD, we were invited for the Dasain by Mr. Pradyumna Lal Rajbhandary, now the Ambassador of Nepal to Germany, and living in Bad Godesberg near Bonn, a four hour train journey from Switzerland. On that day, Ambassador Rajbhandary had received a call from Frankfurt Airport. It was Minister Gehendra Bahadur Rajbhandary, from Patan, his relative, calling him to inform him that he was on his way to Bonn and he should receive him at the Bonn train station, for his drive to Bad Godesburg where a building in the form of a luxury boat was our Embassy.

Mrs. Rajbhandary served us lunch. We were enjoying the meal when the second call came telling him that the Minister had arrived at Bonn station. The Embassy's car was sent to pick him up. Just before the minister's entry into the house, to my surprise, we were asked to vacate the dining room and were placed in the top floor, in the bedroom of the Ambassador couple, to continue our Dasain meal. At first I was a little sad and thought, we were being pushed into oblivion and taken as unwelcome guests in an inopportune moment. Or were we just there when the big shot surprised our host with his unannounced visit? Even the Dasain atmosphere of the Embassy would be spoiled by the 'high guest'.

The minister Rajbhandary had enjoyed the 2nd position after the King as the chairman of the Council of Ministers put up on 12th April 1970. He was too important to Ambassador Rajbhandary to not render his highest attention. We thought we were peanuts! But it was not to be so.

Every few minutes, either Mrs. Rajbhandary or Mr. Pradumna Lal Rajbhandary, the Ambassador, would pop into their bed room turn by turn to be with us, spend a few minutes and bring some additional servings of different dishes to try. We were asked to take our time and enjoy our meal.

But they seemed to manage. I found their gestures the greatest thing in my life. They were so humane! They treated us not less than their boss the Minister, also a kin to them who was also the minister for palace affairs. The Rajbhandary couple was my real intellectual ideal.

Unsolicited Friendship

On 6th of March 1982, after reaching western border township in Nepal, Mahendranagar, a day earlier, Mr. Sundar Lal Bahuguna wrote me to tell he would be on his way to Dhangadi the next day, on foot. I felt a little disappointed by his insensitivity.

After a four days walk he reached Dhangadi, and gave a press release there. I was surprised he indeed did not heed my suggestion, that he drop the idea of including the Kingdom of Nepal in his 'Kashmir-Kohima Chipko Foot March, itinerary. He needed to be handled differently. The whole story of the Chipko movement was started by Gauradevi of Reni, Utterakhand. The village women hugged around trees to prevent contractors from cutting the trees. Over time this became a movement called Chipko. Bahuguna, a journalist of Tehri Garhwal, India, had only capitalized the movemnt pushing the women who started it into oblivion. It seemed he would not listen to others.

It started all in the meeting room, Sitzungszimmer of Kaefigsturm, Bern on Friday the 28th of August 1981. I was in ETH-Zurich when I got an invitation to come over to meet and listen to Bahuguna. Member of Parliament (SPD) Mrs. Ursula Mauch (wife of my friend Dr. Samuel Mauch), Mr. Omkar Singh, 1st Secretary of the Embassy of India, Andreas Speich and others from Swissaid, NADEL-ETH-Zurich, WWF *et cetera* we sat for two hours to see, to read and hear Bahuguna.

He told us, he created a so called 'sensation' by carrying a load of firewood on his head into the plenums UNEP Hall at Nairobi. Bahuguna told me this with pride. As we all know such is a 'fodder' to the media. There was no surprise when Bahuguna was invited off the UNEP Seminar in Nairobi by BBC and WWF to visit the UK. On his way home he dropped into Switzerland. There were Swiss foresters who needed him too. In the Kaefigsturm Hall of the city of Bern at the end of the meet, Bahuguna asked me,

'*To arrange an audience with the HM the King of Nepal*', so that he could present Holy Water from Gomukh, Gangotri Jal to the King,

Coordinate his planned Kashmir-Kohima Foot march through Nepal.

It smelled a little foul of undeserved self-aggrandizement and I had to tell him, in front of Mr. Omkar Singh, the first secretary of Indian Embassy,

Arranging an audience with our King was beyond my reach. You could better try through your Embassy (with Indian Ambassador Mr.NP Jain, Ambassador) in Kathmandu.

As far as the Kashmir-Kohima Foot march is concerned, I suggest you better take Nepal out of your itinerary. It is your unilateral decision to include Nepal that will be questioned.

As I see it, your good mission, 'The Foot march' is obviously directed towards the Indian villagers, especially, the mountain farmers within India, particularly in the Utterakhand area. It is a sensitive matter and I am sure all of us in Nepal would not support you, because it lacks our consent and participation, when you go ahead with it as you wish.

As far as your objective of making villagers aware of the importance of trees is concerned, you have a lot to learn from Nepal. People in the Nepali villages do more than the government. We did not have the kind of forestry management that you inherited from the British Raj. So even if you had requested us we would have given second thoughts as whether the 'Foot march' was at all relevant in Nepal's case to make it an international campaign.

As for your visit to Nepal you are more than welcome, as all our Indian friends are, anytime as tourists. For that the border is always open.

I could read the change of mood in the faces of Mr. Omkar and Mr. Bahuguna. Some of my colleagues in the room found my reaction stark but justified. The Swiss know as much as we Nepalese do how sensitive it becomes when the bigger neighbors decide for us over our shoulders.

Since the Bern meet Bahuguna misused my good will and my postal address. I became a 'dumping ground' at my own home at Jawalakhel in Patan for his x-posts, papers and books. Not only that, first he redirected his mails and book posts to me and they reached me in heaps. Later he instructed me through the Tinao Watershed Project to forward all his mail to Dhoom Singh Negi in Siliguri, India. I was not impressed. He did not seem to care how much this would cost me. I did not do it. I waited for him to collect them from my house.

He wanted to use me as his contact person in Nepal without my permission. He wanted me to write about him to officials introducing him to facilitate his '*Foot march*'. I did not agree and did not do it. In fact I had not known him much except seeing and talking to him briefly during the two hours meeting in Bern participated in by about a dozen Swiss.

He did continue his Kashmir-Kohima Foot march from Mahendranagar, passed through Dhangadi to Birendranagar (222km) and reached Tansen. He was writing letters instructing me for further favors from Mahendranagar, Dhangadi, Birendranagar, Tansen, and Pokhara. A Nepali youth Mr. Prabhakar Bhandari called me from somewhere *en route*. He was impressed by Bahuguna and had accompanied him all the way from Surkhet. I told him that he was too naïve to understand the implication of his participation. Did he want it? He abandoned Bahuguna. On 1st April, 1982 I had written him,

> *Your Embassy in Kathmandu knows about your travels, I presume!*

A certain Mr. Joshi and Mr. Gupta of the Embassy had earlier called me informing of his arrival at Mahendranagar. My letter should have reached Bahuguna at Tansen when he arrived there on the 8th of April, in that letter I asked him to,

> *Write or send a telegram from any district headquarters to your Embassy for further program so that they can arrange lodging for you and for your entourage. You are travelling through the holy country of Nepal. While walking on the country paths through villages and fields, through forests and rivers across hills and plains you will certainly experience our eternal desire of living in peace, living in harmony with nature and in friendship with our neighbors. You will certainly be inspired by the atmosphere on your route to write to politicians and journalists of your home country, India, of the desire and rationality of Nepal to declare itself Zone of Peace.*

*Only a peaceful Nepal will be able to check or (help)
control the floods which sometimes bring tears (also) to
our neighbors in the South. Floods cannot be controlled
by constructing dams on the border. Only people who
manage the headwaters can do so.*

His '*Kashmir-Kohima Foot March*' seemed to have
aroused interest of the donor community too in Nepal who
had no stake in it and were unaware of its implications.
Rolf Sulzer at Tansen and German Volunteer leader
Herman Warth at Kathmandu received him well,
encouraged by Gerard Pfister (Assistant Coordinator of
Swiss DC/India) in Delhi.

Early January 1982, I had briefed Heinz Joss, SATA
Coordinator about the Foot March of the Indians. He
wrote to Pfister on 27th January 1982, telling him of his
concern. He questioned him:

*Is the Plan supported and approved by the Nepali
authorities?*

Heinz sent him a photocopy of my letter to Bahuguna
telling him that the Nepali officials rejected the idea. Prior
to that on 17th Jan 1982, I had written to Mr. Bahuguna,

*As for the Chipko Foot March Kashmir to Kohima to be
continued through Nepalese territory we are of the
opinion that a proper request has to be made through
proper diplomatic channel, especially to the Ministry of
Forest and Soil Conservation of Nepal. I think I voiced
the same to you in Bern. It is our time for efforts and
less for political movements. Nepal has quite a different
historical development base. We do not have*

commercial exploitation of trees in the hilly and mountainous regions. Of course, we have problems even without such.

As he had requested me earlier to help him find a place to stay in Kathmandu the first night 21ˢᵗ or 22ⁿᵈ April 1982, I had in mind the Tribhuwan University hostel. He found a niche within the Indian Embassy for the further duration of his stay in Kathmandu.

I took it seriously because Bahuguna was pressing hard to make it, despite many of us doubting his intentions. The press was briefed through reporters Krishnamurari Timilsina and Basu Rimal Yatree of RSS, four days ahead of Bahuguna's arrival at Kathmandu.

A gathering was organized at the Nepal Bharat Sanskritic Kendra for an open house meeting with the press. I had to get my colleagues ready for the friendly confrontation. I gave an adequate briefing to the students in the TU hostel on Bahuguna's purpose and plans. They were prepared to give him a treat he deserved. Students were to grill him at the TU hostel right on the first day of his arrival.

A day before he was to leave the Kathmandu Valley, German Volunteers chief Herman Warth organized a get together at his home in Dillibazaar to interact with Bahuguna. It seems Herman was unaware of my 'being involved' with him when he invited me. Bahuguna had changed. He had a 'surprise' to tell me; how he was treated by the students at the hostel the very first night of his arrival, as well as the Press being hostile to him, which he had not expected.

A Day at Osho Restaurant

Prof. Dr. Jack Ives of Boulder, originally from England, migrated to Canada, worked in UC Davis and Boulder, Colorado USA, now retired. He became known for his commitment to establishing understanding on the process of mountain hazards and the wellbeing of the mountain people.

Together, we were part of the efforts leading to the establishment of the International Mountain Society at an international meet in Mohonk, upper NY State in Dec. 1982.

I remember our participation in an international joint 'expedition' to remote upper Yunnan at the behest of the Chinese Government. We worked in many venues together, including in ICIMOD.

Jack Ives and I met again in Nepal when he was on a private visit, and he called me to have a day only for us two. We took a day out, and we went to the Kakani area, had a stretched out vegetarian lunch at the Osho restaurant *en route*. There we sat almost the whole day, reminiscing, doing catching ups and debating on issues that had kept us apart in the later period. As I remained silent about the issue of Arun III, Jack became curious to know what I had thought of the issue.

> *Krishnakumar, I have not heard about you taking sides on the Arun III issue. What was your position?*

I had expected my friends to raise the fundamental part of the issue before the whole hue and cry. Jack, you should have put this question before you 'guys' were successful in derailing it.

But what do you think of it? Was justice done?

No, Jack, we did not expect such activism from our learned friends, like you. Looking back I feel happy about one aspect of the turmoil.

What is that? I'm curious to know!

Well, now we too feel free to oppose any project that you plan in Canada or the USA, if we simply see it, subjectively of course, as not good.

Why?

Because we are just as much concerned, about any damage there, as you were concerned over our problems here. The world is getting smaller, solidarity knows no boundary. After all, we all have only one blue planet, our common home to share. We all need to protect it.

Well, we never thought of that!

There was an occasion in which the issue of Arun III Hydro Power Project dominated the thoughts of many friends of Nepal in the wider world. It was also a time which created division between the realist of Nepal's development and those dreamers who were against power generation through bigger investments. Among them were also the naive *'Jet Set'* youths, the pendulum generation of, supposedly, who could not write a page without a computer, work in a room without a fan or heater or an air conditioner or move around without burning fossil fuel, now the electric vehicle.

The time was very challenging to take sides. Even among Nepal's friends in the international community, there were hard nuts that opposed Arun III and took it as a triumph when it came down prematurely with the World Bank pulling out of the process, arbitrarily. The likes of Prof. Bruno Messerli, Swiss, and Mr. Herman Warth, German and Prof. Jack Ives of the USA, to name a few in the international arena, were actively sharing similar sentiments.

It was not only the World Bank and the Germans who became misled, the Nepali people particularly in the site districts in particular and the power needs of the Nepali people in general became the victims of misunderstanding, misinformation and propaganda. Even the political parties, especially the communists in the minority government of 1995 undermined the aspiration of the mountain people. The people of Sankhuwasabha, as Mr. Gauli, the local politician articulated, felt let down by their own politicians and the foreign-educated youths of the capital.

Beside the so called high cost per KW of electricity generated they thought Nepal did not need the mega-project, Arun III and thus Arun III was opposed. I wonder what they would be thinking after hearing the news that after all Arun III is now being constructed and does not come cheaper!

'Ahead by Four Days'

The Pandays have a historic family relation with Lamjung. Our ancestor Ganesh Panday, who reached Gorkha from the Sinja valley, married a girl from a Khas Chhetry, Pantha family from the then Kingdom of Lamjung and celebrated his first Diwali clan festival in Gorkha, in 1579 AD. Almost 410 years after the historic year, I had reached Lamjung for the first time back in 1989.

There was an opportunity again to make a four day-trek in Jita and Samibhanjyang of Lamjung district. With me were my son Arnico, my longtime friend Rudolf Hoegger and his son Michael and friend of Michael, Mr. Pfaff, from Switzerland. We had accompanied Lekhnath Adhikary from Kathmandu to Sundarbajaar in Lamjung. With his familiarity and political prowess he quickly arranged for a gathering of the local youths at the agriculture school at Sundarbajaar and made us, *say 'something to the young generation'* who supported him.

It was Samibhanjyang, the home village of Lekhnath Adhikary, which was awarded the *Jara Juri* Prize for environmental protection in 1988 AD when I met him in Kathmandu. With Lekhnath Adhikary, it was a meaningful contact from the beginning.

With his long mustache, smiling face and very communicative personality Lekhnath Adhikary exuded confidence and warmth. As we developed our friendship I was more impressed by his articulation and political leaning. He was a democrat through and through. At the award ceremony he said,

If the rest of Nepal emulated the example of Kathmandu, we would be doomed.

I could not have agreed with him more. He was right. What I saw in Kathmandu, was all pervasive abuse of plan, power, prosperity and pampering of Kathmandu's citizenry. Almost all the changes of 'modernity' in Nepal that have taken place over the last 50 years, concentrated to a large extent in Nepal's political, economic and transportation hub, the Kathmandu Valley.

Kathmandu was behaving like an introvert and spoiled addict. The Kathmandu Valley forgot its heritage and its historic role of showing the path to the rest of the country. That did not escape the eyes of people like Lekhnath. He was running for the election from his district. He had been the district chairman for over two decades even under the Panchayat system, with the urging from his party, the Nepali Congress.

When I met Lekhnath Adhikary, I saw him too visiting the villages with simple gestures and smiles all over his face, his extraordinarily shaped moustache moving up and down. He was four days ahead of his opponents visiting villages. Everywhere Lekhnath talked to people, asking them personal matters, enquiring about their relatives by name, eating in their homes. At the end of a visit to the houses he would ask if they had promised the votes to anyone. If the answer was negative, he would ask them to vote for him. Many answered,

We have not promised to anyone yet, so feel assured of our votes.

Most of the villagers responding in that manner were the famous Gurungs.

It was in the midst of political agitations of 2005-6, when he used to visit me at Jawalakhel to discuss the political situation. Being a non-political person myself, any comments I was making he would question me for justification. I would tell him, that for the plants we grow there are essential elements necessary for their growth and to fruition. As soon as any one of the most important of all elements of life such as water, oxygen, sunlight and nutrients is missing, the plants collapse.

Such may be compared with the 'reigning authority' for which the army, the administration, public support and resources are the four pillars of power as its basis of survival. I had told him that the 'reigning authority' was being undermined by its own making and losing its grip of the situation and power.

In spring of 2006 AD, one morning he came, unannounced, along with Shivlal Joshi, the local politician of Samibhanjyang in Lamjung district to talk about *'politics'*. I was in a hurry and was about to depart. So all of us three stood outside the gate and were talking about the political situation of the country. That showed how worried Lekhnath was. The King was becoming ruthless. They looked a bit worried about the future. What would happen if the King became too cruel? They were interested to get my opinion on whether the King would prevail.

I had already deliberated about it for some time now and had come to the conclusion that,

He must go and he will go.

Both of them were surprised to know such 'conspiratorial' opinion from a lay person like me in political matters. They then wanted to know what would make him go. I said,

Even if he were to become benevolent, a trait which he did not inherit, he has lost all four bases of power to stay put.

Then in March of that year I was interviewed by the Tages-Anzeiger, a popular daily newspaper in Zurich, Switzerland. My long interview had one conclusion:

He will go sooner than expected.

The paper waited to publish the interview. They must have found it too sensitive to publish, a priori. That would have raised political fury in the tiny politically balanced land. They waited for the right moment. Perhaps they could not wait further, as the journalist who interviewed me was pressing hard and was in contact with me assuring me that it would be published soon. And suddenly on the fateful Monday of 24th April 2006, in the morning it was published, before anyone could have known that the following night the King would put down his crown. In our subsequent meetings, I was a 'political expert' for Lekh Nath Adhikary to come and interact with, pretty often. What an irony!

After all, it was the Palace!

Some of the intrigues, conspiracies and reprisals by the palaces of Nepal did not leave us common folk alone. There are accounts of happenings transmitted by family members; my own intimate, direct and at times indirect contacts with the gnomes of the royal palace, the moments of thoughts shared with me by close relatives and friends affected. I find myself very blessed to get to the present point of time when I can communicate them. Times have changed and we can now reveal things we had put on hold for fear of acrimony.

Forbidden to smile

Our college, the Patan Degree College had organized a picnic party. It was a chilly morning of December 1966, and we reached Gokarna very early. Colleagues started to prepare food. It looked a tedious job. Cauliflower cut into pieces, meat chopped, utensils cleaned, plates arrayed; all the tedious jobs that had to be done. Peeling potatoes was a job I hated. My kind of picnic was to take food prepared at home, and enjoy the time and place of the outing.

Prince Gyanendra arrived. He was in our class. We were told to talk in English with him by our Principal Dr. Mangal Raj Joshi. We were not supposed to call him by his first name, but were to call him just, Prince. He was not one to sit in the picnic kitchen and help, because he was a prince. This gave me an opening to justify my own absence from the picnic kitchen. I suggested to the Prince that we go for a walk. In no time Sishir Sthapit, in the habit of seeking center stage, joined us. One of the girls from our class called me from behind asking us to wait for her.

She blurted to me that she found Prince Gyanendra a most handsome guy. She wanted me to introduce her to him. I knew she was infatuated with him, and I said to her in a voice loud enough the Prince Gyanendra would also hear that she could join us in our walk and introduce herself.

I could not help her more. Prince Gyanendra just nodded a bit. On our loitering, passing time or waiting for a call to come for food, we walked through a grassy area of Gokarna, albeit not far from the food spot. The sun was not to show its glow, it was getting a bit cold and we started feeling hungry. Prince Gyanendra was wearing a tweed coat, with leather patches on the elbows. A new fashion I thought. You could not find another guy so smartly dressed in our group of picnicking boys. How could they even afford such *haute couture*?

Prince Gyanendra was serious as usual, mostly tight lipped most of the time. He would not share much. The response from his side was boredom. We were joking and talking. He walked in silence and displaying an outwardly serious mood. He would only murmur and reply in serious tones. Somebody trying to assert his personality, was it? I lost my patience and asked him,

Don't you see that we're all joking? Can't you smile or laugh?

What he then said shocked me, and I never forgot it.

In the palace it is forbidden to smile or laugh outside the family circle with the commoners.

I asked him why. He replied the people would find it easy to discover his weak points and not take him seriously.

My reaction was,

What a pity. You are not allowed to smile?

He fell into serious mood again.

Princes Princep was one of the daughters of Gen. Nar Shum Sher Rana and wife of the Himalaya Shah. As the Chairperson of Nepal Red Cross Society, she once invited her colleagues of the Red Cross Society for a dinner at Hotel *de la* Annapurna. It took place sometime in 1966.

I was wearing *Daurasural*, the Nepali national dress, a red scarf as my waist band and a red/blue Tartan vest. Being the youngest in the congregation, I seemed to draw attention. Their gaze was more like jealousy than admiration.

I was already familiar with the princess. Long before working for the Red Cross, for a year or so we were classmates in evening classes at the Nepal National College at Durbar High School premises.

Sometimes, we talked about the Fohora Durbar just at a few hundred meters away. The price of the Fohora Durbar land was almost 475xs higher than at Jawalakhel. That was beyond my imagination. I was biting my tongue when I heard of it. The times were different.

The student union, the literary programs and taking stock of the health condition of great Poet and writer Laxmi Prasad Devkota were the common points of curiosity among us. One of the class colleagues was a close relative of the poet. We had daily briefings on his health condition through him. Laxmi Prasad Devkota was in our hearts very early on.

Almost 7 years later, I could chat freely with the Princess Princep Shah at Hotel *de la* Annapurna. There were only a few people present, and she was in a friendly mood.

The Nepal Red Cross was small then. The General Secretary was Ramesh Kumar Sharma who later chaired NRC for decades and developed his Sahayogi press.

When the Princess was turning to me and asking me about my work in the Red Cross, a lady, perhaps her chaperone intervened in our discussion. She sounded a bit rude as she told me,

The way you are behaving and talking to the Princess, is incorrect. Your language is too 'rough, rural, and impolite,' towards Her Royal Highness.

I replied to the chaperone, in the presence of the Princess, that being a common man, I knew nothing of such so-called politeness.

I don't know and I don't want to learn your fancy language.

The Princess was friendly enough to tell the lady she should not worry about her and told her to leave us alone. I was telling the Princess about the difficulty of getting a Dakota to land at Bhairhawa's grassy airstrip. We needed to bring food to Pokhara for the Tibetan refugees who were demonstrating against our handling of the food donated by the USA. But the airport was closed to other flights and was incurring big loses while the hungry refugees demonstrated in Pokhara.

The princess died mysteriously in a foreign land.

A Royal Intellectual

The year 1993: Kumar Khadga Bikram Shah (Kumar Khadga), son of the Sallyani Raja from West Nepal, was a man of letters. He was married to Princess Sharada, late King Mahendra's second daughter and elder sister of King Birendra.

We were going to hold the *Jara Juri* workshop in Kathmandu at the Shangri-la Hotel with the participants from 23 districts of Nepal, many of them farmers and teachers.

Sirdar Bhim Bahadur Panday, *Jara Juri* Trustee, suggested we invite Kumar Khadga to chair. Since Kumar Khadga was a man of letters, it was a good suggestion. I contacted Kumar Khadga by phone and briefed him about the program and he agreed to participate and would be there on time, at 11 am sharp. He told me he would only have one hour free, and if that was ok he would be happy to participate. I told him that was OK.

The status of 'royalty' that even Kumar Khadga carried meant all the participants were supposed to be seated beforehand and wait for the prominent guest to enter the hall. The clock was ticking. It struck 11, but our chief guest was nowhere to be seen. We opted to wait, but Sirdar Bhim Bahadur Panday insisted that delaying the session would be a bad precedent.

We waited five minutes for him. Then I requested my friend Dr. Harka Gurung, who had come on time, if he could Chair the Inaugural Session. He agreed. It started as usual, with the *Jara Juri* tradition of lighting an oil lamp. The session was on.

The hall was well attended. From the corner of my eyes, I saw Kumar Khadga enter into the hall from the far end of the banquet hall of Hotel Shangri-La. He sat in the last rows of chairs by the entrance. I said to myself that I would not be the one to go and usher him to the podium! I pretended not to have noticed his arrival and continued the program of introduction.

The inaugural session was concluded at noon. We all went to the Shambala Garden for the lunch break. I said to myself, I would not request him to come along, but he came along to the garden. He did not show any embarrassment. All seemed to be ok. He had lunch with us and looked relaxed. An hour later we were back in the hall. Kumar Khadga followed us and participated in full. The first day's program concluded at around 4 pm, and he attended the workshop the whole day, *'unusual for a member of the royal'*.

We must assume that he did it to save his dignity and show us his intellectual face. May be others took it for granted that Kumar Khadga stayed. They did not know that Kumar Khadga wanted to be with us only for an hour in the workshop. Only we two, Sirdar Bhim Bahadur Panday and I knew about it and it was not worth telling the participants about the embarrassment.

I wanted to talk to him about the Annapurna Conservation Project (ACAP) note that I had written during my trip to the ACAP area of Kaski, Myagdi and Mustang districts, so Kumar Khadga invited me to come over to his home. I had never visited home of anyone related to the Palace until then, except on official occasion on invitations.

We met at his Kamaladi house. Kumar Khadga was walking around towing a little boy in the garden.

I asked him, who the little boy was.

My grandson! Who else?

Well, did I miss the wedding of your son?

No. Not at all! I will tell you, but let us go to my room first.

It was a room on the ground floor, with a direct entry from the garden, glass doors, sound proof with aluminum partition and air conditioning; a cozy place for a small gathering.

On the table there were sweets, homemade *rasbari,* elongated, instead of a ball as usual such I had never seen before and many other good things in fairly large quantities already placed before our entry. His household was prepared to receive this 'commoner'. Maybe this was the first time in their house. I asked him if he was expecting anyone else.

No! Not at all! We too need to enjoy, don't you think?

It looked he was playing truant. Because of his tendency towards obesity his wife, Princess Sharada, was rationing and controlling what he ate. I knew this because he had mentioned it when he had come to my home. He really enjoyed eating.

So my presence was the perfect *alibi* for his appetite. Yet it was just too much for us two to finish up. Coming back to his grandson, Kumar Khadga told me,

You know how I came to this little gift, my first grandchild?

I will tell you in brief what had happened.

After hearing the story from him, we can imagine the dilemma and the tussle in the family. I have great praise for my friend Kumar Khadga.

That was a big departure within the family of the King. My thoughts went to the story of father of Kumar Khadga's wife Princes Sharada, Mahendra then the Crown Prince and his mischief at the age of 13. In a similar way he took advantage of the situation and weakness of a beautiful lady named Gita in the palace service. Mahendra could not deny his responsibility. The best evidence was the boy Rabindra, who looked a carbon copy of his father. Not only that, much like his father, he also became a poet and lyricist, a creative diversion for the mind of a boy who could not get the crown. He was allowed to be called a prince, was the first son from his first love and de facto wife, Gita. Prince Rabindra had to live and grow up outside the palace. Then, Crown Prince Mahendra had to marry the eldest daughter of Hari Shum Sher Rana, Indra Rajya Laxmi Rana as his official wife.

Crown Prince Mahendra had no courage to marry Gita and make her the future queen. Because she was denied the royal and nuptial solemnization, Rabindra could not get the title of the Crown Prince. We might have had Rabindra as the future King of Nepal instead of Birendra, and the history of Nepal would have taken a different turn.

Status of the Royals: A Tea Party was given by PM Girija Prasad Koirala to celebrate the Democracy Day, in the front garden of Singha Durbar. I left the jeep at the compound of the Foreign Ministry. Marching over in front of Singh Durbar towards the north, I met Kumar Khadga. We chatted and decided we would go together. It surprised me that he was alone.

There were two entrances for the invitees; the one close to the Singha Durbar was for the Royal Family members and the highest dignitaries. The one further down towards the main gate, south side of the Home Ministry was for the, others.

As we marched down Kumar Khadga turned towards the first entrance and was almost through, when he was sent back by the guard to use the next entrance. Even though he had married the senior sister of the King he was denied the dignity of being the member of the royal family. That was how I understood why he had come alone. But why did he try to take the first entrance? He had no need to impress me even if he had succeeded.

He came back to the place where I was standing watching the situation. We marched together and entered the arena using the entrance for the 'others and the commoners'. He did not look embarrassed.

I think he got used to frequent loss of personal dignity. That was the greatness of an intellectual but had to pay dignity to be attached to royalty. We had tea and snacks together.

Annoyed by Truth

On return from the Rio-92 Summit on Environment and Development, the Premier, Mr. Girija Prasad Koirala established the Environment Protection Council; a high level body to oversee issues, policy and programs on environment protection in Nepal. I had the privilege of becoming one of the founding members of the EPC chaired by the PM himself.

Since I put my hand and heart into the issue of environmental protection since the time of my engagement in the rural development works in the seventies, the world I looked at was much more interesting. It was a mixture of despair and hope.

With the garbage pile ups and the docile and indifferent denizens, despair was to be felt in the urban areas. But hope was profound and persistent in the rural areas. It was like energizing yourself while visiting the countryside which I often did.

Back around 1994 while trekking in the lower Mustang areas I started to monitor the activities of the Annapurna Conservation Area Project (ACAP) out of sheer interests. Activities presented at the site offices of the ACAP at Kagbeni, Jomosom, Ghorepani and Ghandruk were not convincing, to me at least.

By the time I was back in Kathmandu I had seven pages of file notes.

The man ultimately responsible also for ACAP was Prince Gyanendra. I printed out a copy of my field notes. Although I had known Prince Gyanendra during our college days, I was not sure of whether he would recognize me after more than 2 decades, and I did not want to show him the notes, personally.

I did not have opportunity either, even if I had wanted to. Thinking, it would be a worthless piece of paper unless the right person would get to see it, I called Kumar Khadga Bikram Shah, husband of second sister of Prince Gyanendra, with whom I had an academic friendship, and asked him if he had contact with Mahila Dai (Prince Gyanendra). He answered that he had only a nodding acquaintance with him, but that was enough for my purpose.

I have a memorandum on the ACAP that he should read. Can you help me?

He promised to read the notes and bring them to Prince Gyanendra's attention as soon as possible.

In January 1995, the King Mahendra Trust for Nature Conservation was celebrating its 10th anniversary. One day earlier I got a telephone call from friends Mr. Karna Sakya and Dr. Ram Prakas Yadav members of the Trust, telling me that I was being given an award by the Trust, chaired by no other person than the Prince. There was to be a citation and a purse to me.

I wondered why I was getting an award! I could not claim to have done much. Then I remembered the notes I had sent to 'him' through Kumar Khadga in which I had subtly criticized his work. Did the Trust believe that I could be silenced by an award? Was that it?

By evening there was a call from a person who seemed to exercise much clout in the Trust. Anyway he started to give me instructions. I did not know who he was.

Tomorrow, at Soaltee Hotel hall you will be honored by his Majesty with the KMTNC Award.
The ceremony will take place in the morning.
HMs will be arriving at 10 30 and you are supposed to be seated in the hall by 10.00.
You should wear white daura suruwal official dress, a black jacket and a Nepali cap.

I became a little bit annoyed. I told the man on the other end of the line that I saw no reason to arrive at 10, but that I would be there punctually at 10:25. I also told him that never having been an administrative officer, I did not possess the funny-looking black and white outfit he mentioned, but that I would wear the Nepali dress that I had and was proud of wearing.

Then the protests began. Neither of my points was agreeable and they went against protocol. I gladly told him that he could look for someone else for the so-called award.

He was not accustomed to hearing such words from a '*commoner*.' Eventually he said,

> Do *what you want but make sure you are there tomorrow*.

My attendance obviously mattered to him,

I calculated the time that would take for me to reach the spot. I was at the Soaltee Hall exactly at 10:25. The hall was packed with national and international dignitaries of the time. All were seated. When I walked down the aisle, people right and left looked at me, obviously in mistrust. I was ushered in hastily and seated with Mr. Min Bahadur Gurung of Ghandruk and Mr. Ghimire of Baghmara, Chitwan, who had, I presumed, arrived long before. I took my seat 5 minutes ahead of the King's arrival. *Voila!*

We were the three people to be awarded. I was the last one to be called on to the podium where Their Majesties, the Crown Prince, Prince Gyanendra and Premier MM Adhikary, were standing.

When they called my name to go to the podium, Dr. Chandra Prasad Gurung started to tell a long story about me much of which I myself had forgotten, though I was grateful to him for reminding me. It was long and boring. I was standing in front of their Majesties. The long introduction full of praise was surely not aimed at me but was meant to impress HM the King and to justify the award before the audience. That was what I was feeling, standing before their Majesties.

All eyes were on me. Every minute was like an hour. I was ashamed to face the gazing stare of the Queen. I was asking myself, what did I do to deserve this awkward moment of injustice?

After the ceremony, when Their Majesties had left the Hall, the enforced silence was breaking into commotion as the selective crowd of invitees, poured out of the hall. One of the invitees was my senior cousin Shyam Bahadur Panday, Chairman of Hotel Shangrila. He was surprised about all this. Apparently pleased over the award, he invited me to celebrate it with a lunch at the posh-restaurant of Soaltee Hotel, the venue that was once used to host the SAARC Summit dignitaries.

As we took a table by the north window, Prince Gyanendra entered followed by Prabhakar Rana, maternal uncle of Prince Gyanendra and took a table to the south west side. Only our two tables were occupied in that large room. It was an awkward, very funny moment. For a moment Shyamdai and I talked in gestures and hush. For the sake of politeness, I said I would walk over to Prince Gyanendra. I went to him and said thanks and told him I hardly deserved the honor. As usual, the tight lipped Prince muttered just,

That's OK Kk.

There was no further word or gesture from either of the two. While going back to my seat, at the other end of the room, trying to make myself comfortable, some points crowded my mind and pinched me,

'There are only four people in the whole of the restaurant, all four of us know each other, yet there is no sign or no word that we could go over and join them for the lunch. In fact, the restaurant belongs to the other two gentlemen. We are real paying guests they perhaps are not. They are the owners. It must not be a matter of cost. Protocol-wise on our part it would have been impolite to invite the Prince over to our table, but they could have invited us.'

I must have looked pretty perplexed, and Shyamdai signaled me to be at ease.

Let us enjoy our lunch. What would you like? It is your day! It was so nice of Shyamdai.

That evening Prince Gyanendra gave a reception dinner at Soaltee. Premier Adhikary and I were discussing about a meeting of the Environment Protection Council under his chairmanship. PM Adhikary's military guard was right behind him. Unconsciously, I was using my finger to elaborate a point. To the guard it posed a threat to his boss and he promptly intervened. I apologized. While discussion was going on, Prince Gyanendra joined us holding a glass containing, perhaps whiskey. He looked a bit boozed up, and was in a jovial mood. Amazingly, he started to chat,

Hi, Kk! So he did not pretend not to recognize me!
Why don't you call on me at home, when you get time?' He must have heard our discussion.

I shall, but how should I reach you?

This could be my chance to pin him down as chairperson about my report.

Well you can just give a call to my ADC.

Testing him about his opening up, I told him that I was sure I would have trouble getting through using that approach.

Then, do you have a piece of paper and a pen?

On a piece of paper torn from a pack of cigarettes, he wrote his private telephone number, all in the presence of Premier Man Mohan Adhikary and his military guard. Weeks and months went by. I had still not tried for an 'audience'.

At home, there was beginning to be a slight chill to our domestic discussions. My wife's opinion was summed up as,

Well he might not help you when you need him but this man can harm you, unexpectedly.
You need to respond. There was wisdom in her words.

I wanted to test the line of communication through the ADC before trying the ultimate *line* to the Prince. I started calling Nirmal Niwas, the prince's residence. The ADC asked me why I wanted to speak with HRH.

I just want to.

That did not impress the person I spoke with at all. However, I continued trying to reach the Prince. Over several calls he started to be annoyed and sounded angry at me. He spoke unpleasantly to me, yet I tried for days. But he would not let me get to the Prince. At perhaps the seventh time of my call to the ADC, I told him,

If you cannot arrange for an audience with him, I will try to call him directly.

He was surprised and said that it was not possible for me to call HRH directly. I read out the number and asked him. Whether I should try myself or if he would get the audience for me?

That is but HRH's private number.

I know I got it from him.

He was so surprised and shocked, and his manner changed completely as he now addressed me in *palace etiquette and palace language.*

Sir please, have some patience. I will bring the answer immediately.

Then he disappeared from the line, and I was kept on hold. Promptly he came back and said,

Please excuse me. HRH has graciously granted you an audience for 11:00 sharp tomorrow.

So that telephone number scribbled on a piece of paper by a boozed up man worked. Not a single digit was wrong.

The next day, I reached Nirmal Niwas five minutes early, as was my habit for appointments, dressed in a light beige Safari suite without a Nepali cap/topi on my head. My style seemed to be out of protocol. I did not care. Nobody pointed it out to me, not even the ADC.

I hesitated to park my jeep outside the 'palace'. At that time my jeep was the 3rd one to reach Kathmandu and the second white one and any of my acquaintances passing by would have recognized it, also because of slogan I put up on the spare wheel cover: *'Make Polluters Pay'*. I was wondering to myself if I should park outside of the 'palace' on the road side and risk being branded a *chakariwala*, a lowliest subservient person. I would have hated for that to happen to me.

I almost bumped into the gate, blew the horn. A soldier opened the gate. I asked him where I should park my vehicle. He was obliged to show me the parking lot on the right side of the gate. It seems that my voice sounded perfectly commanding and I even got a salute too from the soldier.

The ADC came out of his room and asked me, with *palace etiquette and palace language*, to wait a few moments. With equal obsequiousness, which I was not used to, he asked me be seated in the waiting room. He went into the main building, then came back to usher me into a large living room on the ground floor of the 'palace' building. There was nobody. The room did not reflect any warmth. It was so scary.

I took a seat on the single couch in front of another one. A coffee table separated the space between the couches. The whole thing was placed too close to the door through which I came in. Was that done intentionally?

In no time Prince Gyanendra came in with a glowing cigarette in hand. Standing, we shook hands. This was not the first time we had shaken hands.

After the initial polite exchanges, I started to talk about the seven page file note that I had sent for his perusal. He claimed he had not received the paper. That I could not buy. Every time my points hit home, he would light a new cigarette. So it went on. The exchanges began in an amicable atmosphere with coffee and some good biscuits served. The point I was hammering was that being the chairperson, he should have personally looked into how the things were functioning.

I saw the review reports, he countered.

They looked good.

I told him that while things might look good on paper, in reality the ACAP was functioning as a parallel government. People were not happy about the way things were managed over their heads. The behavior of the officials was far from friendly, and did not motivate the local people towards nature conservation and local development.

Is that what you found there? He asked.

Yes. KMTNC was mandated for 10 years to prove that the concept of conservation area management is good. We see the Makalu Barun area waiting for the outcome of ACAP. KMTNC is nowhere to it.
The documenting of experience was especially absent.

What should we avoid in new Conservation Areas, or what should be our strategy to make the CA concept more effective?

Irritated perhaps, Prince Gyanendra puffed more cigarettes. By one and half-hour's time we were on one-to-one discussion, many cigarettes as half burnt butts ended up prematurely on the ashtray, wasted.

I remembered Bhupi Sherchan's poem: *The Cold Ashtray*. The Prince looked tense; and I was of the impression that any loosening up at all was not to be expected from him. We were way apart in our views. It was of no use going further. I stood up and without protocol said that I would be leaving.

We shook hands and parted, perhaps both thinking never to come so close to each other again. But it was not to be so.

I had provoked him enough. I knew that this was a guy *forbidden to smile*. He would attack me in one way or another in the future. But I was an independent person. I could not simply be kicked around like the bureaucrats. A month later I heard that the guy was making the rounds of his programs. So the meeting helped.

Did he or did he not deserve a Congratulation?

Fast forward to the year 2001, we now had Prince Gyanendra as the new King in the wake of the Royal Massacre. Four of us--Dr. Tirtha Bahadur Shrestha, Dr. Harka Bahadur Gurung, Dr. Dayananda Bajracharya and I—were sitting on two sofas facing each other enjoying our drinks. Dayananda and Tirtha simultaneously suggested that,

> *We go together to congratulate the new King Gyanendra.*

I politely replied that they should go without me.

Why can't you come with us? They asked.

Harka, who knew me well, was silent. I said,

> *I have no reason to congratulate the King. He destroyed democracy. He took over power twice within 5 months, becoming more despotic. He betrayed us, the people. He can afford all this. Who am I to congratulate him?*

At the end of 2002, my friend Dr. Ram Prakash Yadav invited us for a welcome dinner at his home in Banesor. His wife Urmila, also a Manandhar lady, was distantly related to my wife, Sharada. After dinner the discussions between us turned to the recent political upheaval. We heatedly put forth our standpoints. His defense of the power grab by the King did not hold rational justification. I firmly believed that was an ugly and inhuman act in this day and age.

> *He did not do it good for the country.* I said.
> *This will cost him dearly in the long run. I don't think the people will buy his points, and I don't support him.*

But Ram was on his side, blinded perhaps by his gestures when Ram was in the KMTNC board. I knew he was associated with him for years through KMTNC and in the beginning as ex-officio member representing the Planning Commission's green office and later on justified as representing the Madhes community, when the slogan of 'Inclusiveness and Quota' was gaining ground.

There was no coming to a meeting point between us that evening. We had to terminate *'the evening'*, prematurely. That was it. For another few years both of us lost contact and remained *incommunicado*. Only when the political situation tipped the other side did we take initiative to say hello to each other.

The Scary Pencil

It was one of the last meetings taking place in the office of Prabhakar Rana at the Soaltee Hotel, ahead of the International Workshop on People and Protected Areas in the Hindu Kush Himalaya, May 6th to 11th, 1985.

Prince Gyanendra was chairing the meeting of the Workshop Organizing Committee. The meeting was focusing on the inauguration part of the workshop, which carried more value than the actual workshop. HM the King Birendra was inaugurating it. So the stakes were high. Nothing could be left to chance.

The seat of the Chairperson was raised a bit higher. Perhaps he could not sit at the same level with others! Or perhaps he wanted to observe the attending officials, to keep them alert. My suspicion was that it must have been the former.

Prince Gyanendra was without voice. His mouth was shut, grimacing. He conducted the meeting in a way I was not used to. I felt it was very impolite on the part of Prince Gyanendra not to utter a word. Those sitting at the table were targeted by a new pencil held between his two fingers. Every time he wanted a participant of his choice to air his view, Prince Gyanendra would aim his pencil to the person. There were no women members in the steering Committee.

With their hands in Namaskar gesture, the participants would respond bowing, '*Sirkar, Prabhu*' and were obliged to speak only pleasant words. I rejected this method and felt humiliated. I pushed my chair little away from the table to give myself an indirect view from Prince Gyanendra's viewpoint. I think he saw that I was on to his game, and I was graciously spared by his pencil. I could see the meeting would conclude without my words, as there was no need for evaluator comments.

I did not have anything better to tell him than my colleagues did, even if he had asked me. Negative comments were not forth coming, nor were they welcome, despite some constraints facing the organization of the workshop. It was necessary to say that everything was well and good. Soon I would know that all the drama was for show for a day rather than for substance.

Meeting concluded successfully; a shutter curtain opened from the meeting room. There was another room, with a table decked out with wine, whiskey, beer and snacks, the best that Soaltee could offer. All stood stiff with their glasses in their hands. A few sips of Johny Walker from their glasses would make them sway, I knew.

Prince Gyanendra had already chosen the south east corner of the room to stand alone. After a while we naturally bundled together at the northwest corner of the room, away from him, trying to keep ourselves upright after the whiskey. It looked so awkward seeing Prince Gyanendra with a glass of whiskey in his hand standing alone in the far corner, a vantage point to cast his watching eyes on us like 'Big Brother'.

Feeling uneasy, I went with my glass of beer to Prince Gyanendra. He seemed to be happy to receive me and nodded. As usual, he was tight-lipped with his lips drawn upward in the center and chin slightly pushed up, leaving the better part of his neck exposed. Yet he looked 'handsome' as per definition of our former classmate. After the initial exchange of polite gestures, I wanted to break the concocted ice in him.

What could be the best tactic I could use, other than reminding him of our picnic time? I said to him,

YRH, do you remember how we were talking while walking through the Gokarna forest, during our picnic party, almost 20 years ago?

No, not exactly!

Did he lie? He perhaps thought that would help him to be taken more seriously by commoners.

Are you still forbidden to smile by the palace? I asked.

I had not finished pronouncing the last word when he started to laugh aloud. I hadn't intended to make a joke. I just wanted to measure any change of the attitude nurtured in the palace. I felt embarrassed by his laughter. I do not know whether I was playing a fool or if he was a joker. Perhaps he wanted to tell me that he was a grown up person and was not under palace control anymore. In any case he could laugh to his heart's content at the moment.

I thought I better leave him alone. I said to him,

YRH, I had better give my colleagues the opportunity too to come over to you.

Ok, Kk.

I joined my colleagues in the opposite corner, who were mentally far from the Prince. Immediately, fellow committee members gathered around me, with heads locked and wanted to know how I could make the Prince laugh. What joke had I told him?

It seems they too had never seen him laugh or smile. It was so funny to talk about the guy so close in the other corner not farther than a few meters away. He could hear every word we uttered. I told them to go and ask the Prince themselves, a bit louder so the Prince heard it. I am sure Prince Gyanendra must have been most amused.

None of them took a step forward as to be at his side. Perhaps they were not used to him. He was left alone and lonely the whole time we were there. Perhaps he was used to it. Otherwise he too could have initiated contacts with the others.

Singing for the Palace

We were celebrating the Reunion Day, in 1966 of our Patan Degree College. All the Princes were invited, as they too were enrolled in our college. As the secretary I had the responsibility to arrange for a 'welcome song'. There were four of us, and we sang the song written by MBBShah (the pseudonym of poet King Mahendra): *Ragata sabko rato bhae, ko? dhani garib ko?* It was a forceful heart touching song. The audience applauded for a long time.

An hour or two later the secretary of Crown Prince Birendra, Chiran Thapa, slim, smart and a very tall figure for a Nepali, in Nepali dress, comes over with a tape recorder, the newest gadget available then, but not yet in Nepal, and tells us we need to sing the welcome song for Crown Prince Birendra once again. The musically melodious tune we had composed to make it inspiring and rehearsed for days. But in the library room where we sang it for the Crown Prince it did not have the inspiring atmosphere we had enjoyed in front of the large crowd of distinguished guests earlier, yet we had to sing it.

The path to the palace

That is not all. It was also the day I lost my respect for the teacher whom I held in high esteem. We were waiting for the royal guests to come over to the venue. A special venue was put up with a raised stage facing east towards the tent for the guests on the large grassy playground of the Patan High School, shared by the Patan Degree College. I was the organizer in charge; hence I had to wait outside the gate to receive the royal guests.

Prof. Narayan Prasad Shrestha was present, as the Princes were his private students too. The motorcade arrived. I could hardly see the passengers inside the black limousine with the windows rolled up. But I had to do my best to do Namaskar to the tainted glass pane of the car. An absurdity! But our professor started to kowtow from the gate, following the left side of the limo moving slowly into the high school compound and didn't stop until he was near the venue, located on the playground, east of the high school buildings.

Out came the Princes. The kowtow of our professor was worth observing. He could not have bent his back further forward and down, or he would have fallen head first. The welcome song was an apt message for the occasion: *'Ragata sabko rato bhae, ko dhani garib ko'* (all have blood red in color, what does it matter whether richer or poorer...)

In the next days' classes I raised the issue and told him how ashamed of him I was and how he had let us down! This was the guy who, upon returning from doing his MA (Engl. Lit.) at Oxford, started boosting about his sojourn in democratic UK: How much he had appreciated the royal family there, the politics for democracy and the English food. And so on. He sounded pretty much like an Indian who would take the UK as a heaven on earth, not like a normal Nepali. My reaction was ready,

Did you find democracy in Nepal, when you came back?

Many mornings he brought a few tomatoes and was telling us that he learnt this in the UK. One should eat fresh tomatoes. Did he have to go to UK to learn to eat a tomato? All this failed to impress us.

He was living then in a very small rented stable house, located on the roadside wall of Madhav Rana's house at Kopundole. He used to commute on an old Vespa to our college. Over the years his kowtow paid off and he became the Principal Private Secretary when Crown Prince Birendra became King in 1972. Soon after, he shifted to his new house at Pulchowk.

Sometimes he would invite me to see his library located at his compound gate at his Pulchok house he built while serving the palace in the late sixties The library was intended to make every visitor notice that he was 'a learned, man with a library'. Perhaps it was a new thing to NPS, yet to become a learned man. At another time he showed me a massive modern building being completed in his garden, which he was to rent it out to a World Bank official in Kathmandu. I asked him, where he got the money from. It must have cost him a fortune!

Oh, HM once graciously gave me Rs.1.25 Lakhs, just as a gift. He answered.

Then it was a fortune, in the seventies. It was just like him to think I would believe such a tale.

He was not the only one usurping power traditionally exercised by the King from behind the curtain, weakening the Monarchy, but also was making immense amounts of money. How he did it is anyone's guess. As I was always questioning him, he tried to keep me in proximity, to be safe. I was both a hated and a respected student of his at the same time.

There was an occasion when in 1988, I was given a recognition by United Nations Environmental Program (UNEP) and mentioned in the Global-500 Roll of Honor. That was the second time for that Honor to Nepal. The first was for KMTNC in 1987, but mine was the first to an individual of Nepal. I had received a telegram from Nairobi, mentioning about the citation and a Gold Pin. They were sent to the Palace directly by the UNEP.

The head of the state had to approve the award vested outside. In my case it was the King, and I do not know whether he took any notice of it. Next morning, NPS called me at ICIMOD to congratulate me. I only got the citation, delivered to ICIMOD, by the palace. The Gold Pin got stuck up in the palace somewhere, perhaps!

The Henchmen at Large

On the grassy football ground of Jawalakhel, late one afternoon, four of us sat down for a chat. PPH had just come back from his duty in the palace as a clerk. I wondered what his route to the palace administration had been! PPH's nephew, another acquaintance and I were listening to PPH telling us a strange story, for the first time ever. The reason I cannot name PPH will become clear.

It must have been well after the royal coup of 1960. Thousands of democrats had fled to India; thousands of others remained underground to keep the light burning. Politically, the situation in the country was very volatile. The coup was strongly condemned by the majority of people; democrats from the parties, people from the streets, from jails or from exiles in India; from everywhere. Only the communists seemed to be hand-in-glove with the King supporting his purges. This was to be expected as the Right and Left extremists see democrats as the dust in their eyes, when not outright enemies, and as such they needed to be removed while the extremists were marching to their dictatorial political destination.

It seemed PPH wielded far more sinister power than his position as clerk would suggest. He was not alone. He had a colleague, a certain HHP who was helping him. They both were entrusted with the common mission of eliminating the common enemies of the Palace and the communists.

The K-man was staying at his Jungle hideout in C-Jungle. His chief commander was in charge of a group of deeply brainwashed armed and uniformed 'elite troupe'.

They were entrusted with a highly secretive covert mission. The two henchmen would bait mainly the democrats who believed in freedom. They would tell them that K-man wanted to see them, that they needed an 'audition and chat' with him. Naively, believing and expecting that K-man wanted a political accommodation with the democrats, they would agree and would follow one or both of them to an unknown location in the C-Jungle. Somewhere *en route* to the promised *rendezvous*, the two accomplices would hand over the party members to the elite outfit. Their fate was sealed and they would find their heavenly abode not far from the K-man's camp in C-Jungle. Party members just vanished.

Jagatprakash Jung Shah, related to the K-man was also condemned to die. He was buried alive, and before being covered with tons of earth, he could hear the verdict in Lalmohar signed by K-man, read aloud by the high level Commissioner. The mission continued for months. PPH told us without a blink that 'there must be a mass grave out there in C-Jungle'. He would still know the place where the mass grave existed. Hundreds might have met their fate in that way. He forgot to count. He was not allowed to keep notes. At the time he was telling us of 'his adventure for the sake of the K-man'. It must have been very well organized and carried out in a planned manner.

When the commander responsible in C-Jungle operation died he made a plea to his family members from his death bed, saying he did not deserve last rites. So his, son must not mourn for 13 days as Hindu tradition required. His wife must not break glass bangles and discard the color red on her dress or on make-up, because he had committed a sin that was unpardonable in life, and even after his death.

That story was awful, and a chill ran up my spine. I changed my view of PPH immediately and became suspicious of him. I could no longer regard him as a human being. Was it just a story he was relating or part of the history he lived through afresh? This is still hunting my conscience. It would have been better not to have heard his story. It was such a bludgeon to my conscience. I hoped it was just a bad story he had concocted or dreamt of and was reliving.

I had read about the Gestapo and the midnight knocks in Germany during Hitler's time, of the excesses of the extreme right against the left. There it was the extreme right against the left; here the democrats were victimized, in the joint operation of extreme right and the left. What a difference!

I thought that no such thing could take place in the land of Buddha's Birth. At least that is what I hoped. But it seems we were not far from similar evil political hatreds and vendettas. What did the K-man get in return? He did not live to see it but his son had an awful time retaining the monarchy and within the next two decades the authority of the monarchy was shaken never to recover.

The 1990 revolution striped the monarchy of its perks, powers and prerogatives. It was the son of K-man, the C-Jungle mastermind, who was getting the chill and heat. He must have heard about the 'happenings'. Surely, that could not have eluded him. It was apparent from the moves he made after the multiparty election of 1991, that he made calculated steps to cover up the nasty history, or the story told by PPH.

King Birendra was to nominate fifteen members from the list in his pocket to the new parliament. Guess who he nominated! I was very surprised to find the two henchmen of 'C-Jungle operation' nominated for the National Assembly among others of favor.

These guys were not politicians representing any party, nor were they known in social circles for doing any job worthy of mention. They were palace 'activists'. I later heard that HHP was not even a direct employee of the palace like PPH. As members of parliament, it was thought that they would be safe from prosecution. I began to see a picture emerging. The immunity for the duo was not that valuable as against the protection of the royal image. Did the King nominate them to shut them up?

Then soon a turn of fate took place for them. As per the constitution, there was a lottery in the first hours of the assembly; one third of the members were to relinquish their role and status after two years, another third in the fourth year and another third would be after six years. The House was to get its replenishment every two years through election/nomination, to retain its status of the permanent parliament. PPH happened to be among the first third and HHP was to stay for the full term of six years.

All indications showed that the palace had done the utmost possible to protect them. It was PPH's misfortune to be out on the street to go unprotected. It simply broke link with him. Without Palace's protection and stripped of his parliamentary immunity, he started to behave strangely. Was it because he felt insecure? He started to become active in Hindu prayer groups called Satsang matters, for all to see. By seeming to be spiritual he hoped nobody would become suspicious of his past.

His nephew and I would not tell the story to others because it was too ghastly to give it further belief. He looked sick and out of contacts with friends. Soon he died. I heard he had a heart attack. I got the hint that he was telling the story of the dark history of Nepal in the recent past.

About a decade ago, some of my good old friends used to come together almost every week, in my house. It started on a very pleasant Friday. It was socially and 'professionally' refreshing. One day the entry of a person frightened me. I did not invite that person. After all what I had heard of his involvement I had either to forget him and receive him in our fold or reject his company. The others either did not have a clue of his past or did not take his past so seriously.

To receive him would have meant a morally unacceptable complicity on my part. The sad thing is that the meetings between the likeminded friends had to be stopped without having me to explain about my decision.

The cursed Royal Handshakes

Why did Prince Gyanendra shake hands with me during the wedding of his son Paras? January 25, 2000, afternoon 1530 hrs, Place Nirmal Niwas: Guests gathered in the garden under a big *Samiyana* tent. Prominent guests with name and fame were invited. In the *Samiyana*, we the people outside the periphery of royal household were to stand around crowding the limited space.

Enclosed in the Invitation Card was parking space allotment. My parking spot was to be in the police training center at Maharajganj, quite far from the groom's house. Feeling it difficult to comply, I drove a small white Vitara jeep straight to the VVIP parking lot about 50m away from Nirmal Niwas, reserved for ministers and diplomatic invitees and said to the police man there,

I cannot park inside I have to leave early, so I'd better park outside on the road (to Chundevi crossing).

Since I was dressed immaculately in Nepal dress and spoke confidently, my command to the policeman was obeyed and I even got his salute. I started walking along the footpath of Prince Dhirendra's house. Government Secretary Soorya Nath Upadhaya and Governor of Rastra Bank Dipendrapurush Dhakal had seen me leave the jeep and followed me on the footpath.

I don't know where they parked their vehicles, surely they would not get the VIP place, and they represented ministries.

How come, you parked at the entrance to VVIP parking? One of them asked me.

Look I am not invited as an ex-officio as you guys are.
My invitation was personal, so I figure I'm a VVIP for the day.
Just what, we would expect from Kk! They said.

Once inside the Nirmal Niwas, in the *Samiyana*-tent, there was a big crowd snarling and moving in waves. Some looked very proud that they were invited. I chatted with Gen. C.B Gurung, to start with,

I see you were not promoted!

He brushed this off, saying,

The present regime is choosy and selects only members of the Rana family. We are outside that circle. You know I am not a Rana.

I told him that he deserved promotion, and that it was a shame about such criteria.

I felt sad. Soon Projwal Rana the CnC joined us. I found him proud and arrogant and I had nothing to say to him. Both were in their army uniforms.

Abruptly the crowd of invitees under the *Samiyana* went into disarray. Our attention was drawn by the march of the royal entourage, approaching the tent from north east corner of the Nirmal Niwas to the left.

The royal path opened up, like the Red Sea in the Old Testament, and it lay right in front of me. All scrambled to create about a 1.2m alley separating the crowd into two halves and struggled to be in the front row just to be seen by the royals.

So I did not need to budge. Then suddenly I was being pushed backwards by two army officers. The taller one stood right in front of me, blocking my sight. Was it Gen. P. Rana?

I could hardly monitor the royal procession. With the Queen Mother leading, the King and others were following her as per their family protocol. That much I could make of through the slits of space between the officers' heads. As I was squeezed behind, I could not have felicitated the King, even if I had wanted to.

A hand reached me from the procession, over the shoulders of the two officers. It was Prince Gyanendra's. In army uniform himself, he had seen me behind the two officers; he extended his right arm and wanted that I shake his hand.

Kk!

I had to comply. I had never heard of a Royal family member ever shaking hands publicly with a fellow countryman, a commoner. They would do it to tourists, unhesitatingly. That I had witnessed in the past. At Paras' wedding, it was initially a pleasant surprise to me.

After the royals had joined the wedding procession and left Nirmal Niwas, we were allowed again to be normal, the crowd spread apart and gathered in groups with familiar ones coming together and scrambling to get to the food as it was growing late. We were surprised by what was offered to the guests in the tent. A tea party was not expected on the occasion of a royal wedding! Even in a common household it is impolite to not to treat the guests invited properly.

Most of the time, we shook hands and chatted, patted one another on the back to avoid the simple catered food.

But my shock and dismay were yet to come. Soon one of two officers, obviously not Gen. Gurung, came over and told me,

Who do you think you are, shaking hands with HH?

You saw everything, didn't you? Who extended his hand over your shoulder first? By not complying I would have disgraced a royal. How about that? Would you have liked me dishonoring the royals? You don't know me. I am living on my pride and Pasina (sweat). You have no right to complain, if you want, go to the Prince to complain.

Perhaps it was not a gesture of friendship on my part, but I knew I could not be that particular Rana's friend. I felt the Prince wanted to punish me for my confrontation with him at his palace, five years before. That he had to use an army officer to make me fall in line with the so called royal protocol was not needed. I would not follow it anyway, at any cost. What I did not tell the general was that Prince Gyanendra and I knew one another from our college days and events of 1985, the KMTNC Award in 1995 and followed by the one-to-one chat re ACAP very recently. I was simply 'Kk' to him.

The Nepali Royals in Zurich

Rain was pouring heavily when I left the train. I could not go out of the main station Haupt Bahnhof-Zurich, since I did not have an umbrella to walk over to the tram station as usual, without risking being totally drenched. The University was just 2 tram stops up the hill, over Zentral and the Leonardstrasse, or I could have taken the Funicular. I had to be in the laboratory in time to check my samples. I could not risk being late and spoiling the tests in the laboratory of the Federal Institute of Technology (Eidg.Technische Hochschule).

So for the first time in my university years I was forced to take the most expensive mode of transport in Zurich from the railway station: the taxi.

The moment I was in the taxi, on the front seat (a friend's seat), the driver started chatting. Whether want it or not it is loneliness that makes a taxi driver talkative. I have found it in other countries too. This seems to be universal behavior of the taxi drivers the world over.

He began by asking me where I was from. When I told him, he said,

Oh! Interesting; it must be very beautiful country. It is also the poorest in the world that we are aware of.

Why are you telling me this? I asked, somewhat irritated.

Aren't there many poor countries in the world? How was it in Switzerland in the past?

Calm down. There is a reason I brought it up.

What are you talking about?

Your King is here in Zurich with his family. He answered smugly.

So what? They come here sometimes. Why shouldn't they? The present King's grandfather died here in Canton's Hospital in 1955.

It may be something more than that that brings them to Zurich. You know what? There was a big commotion here, yesterday. The City of Zurich, and perhaps also the Canton of Zurich, mobilized hundreds of security personnel (I heard) in the city for their security.

This guy was really getting on my nerves.

Isn't it normal, to provide security for a guest and a head of state in this country?

Yes, but something happened!

How do you know?

Taxi drivers know everything. We communicated with each other and soon it was all over the city. Nepal's King and Queen, only the two of them, went into the Museum of Watches near the Parade Platz, Bahnhofstrasse, opposite the big banks, UBS, Credit Suisse, and Bank Verein. That was at 9 am and nobody else was allowed to follow them into the museum. Everybody thought it was a matter of an hour or two, and then they would come out for lunch. But hours went by, and they still did and did not come out. The security personnel were alarmed. Everybody feared something had happened to the royal couple, but nobody gave order to the police to storm the museum building. The situation was tense. You know when they came out? At last around 4 pm, and everybody was at ease at last.

So what's the big deal? I asked, wishing I had taken my chances in the rain.

Do you know the museum?

No, I have been here for years, but I am unaware of that museum. It must be very interesting place. It must have become more interesting since yesterday.

You know why your King and Queen went there? Surely, they are not that interested in Swiss watches.

Then what else is there?

It is put up by the banks and people say there is a special VIP room with computers, which the banks' VIP clients use.

He gestured with his hand and used his middle finger and thumb to indicate counting money.

Your king and queen went there simply to check their account. The king and queen of one of the world's poorest countries spent all day counting their money!

In the mean time I was slowly sinking on my seat. By the time I reached ETH, I felt completely humiliated by the taxi driver. Of course, he could have just been harassing me, a foreigner, as sometimes happens, elsewhere too. I just did not want to believe him. He might be telling me a tall tale, to impress me, who knows? After all he *was* a taxi driver. They entertain their customers with stories. But what if most of it was true?

Pride Prevails

Not long after that I was back home from Zurich. Taking tea in the garden one morning, I heard somebody coming jogging on the narrow road outside of our garden wall. There was a knock at my little garden gate. Mr. Narain Prasad Shrestha, my former teacher and the Principal Private Secretary to HM was there, jogging for his health.

I just wanted to check whether you were back or not, he said. I invited him in for tea.

So you were in Zurich? He asked, though he already knew.

Yes, I was but busy in my lab!

Did you know that Their Majesties were there? I was there, too!

Yes, I heard.

Why did you not come to greet HM? Or at least try to see me?

By this time I was getting a little nervous.

What did you expect from me? To come over, stand on the side walk, with a Nepali topi (cap) *and wave a national flag and expect them to recognize me? You know that is not like me. How on earth would I know when HMs would be around in the city, especially on the Bahnhofstrasse? Would anybody inform me?*

You think CH Media would cover their arrival?

Who is he to Switzerland?

In a foreign country all Nepalese are Equal. You were in Zurich. You could have found out where I was in Switzerland, through my family in Nepal. Had you just wanted you could have quickly found me or reached me by phone.

You are still too arrogant and too proud!

Thanks. Why shouldn't I be? I am the citizen of Nepal and I am proud of it. By the way, I learned of your visit through a taxi driver outside Haupt Bahnhof of Zurich, on account one particular incident that took place.

The city was talking about it for a long time. You must, surely, be aware of that incident. I better not tell you in detail of what I heard, regarding Their Majesties. I just think you guys let me down in a foreign land, that's all!

Mr. NP Srestha even asked my brother why I looked so different than him, and hinted I was just too smart. I knew it was not a compliment from him. I never called anyone, not even him, my English teacher, '*Sir*'. That just did not come to my mouth, ever. My brother was OK with, him but I was not because I seemed to know him much better, under different lights.

Men of Integrity – The Sardars

They were part of the scene and actors in helping Nepal peer out of isolation and exclusion during the fifties and the sixties. They were not only witnesses of what was happening in those crucial years, but they also played key roles in shaping development and diplomacy and international relations of Nepal. They shaped the history and intellectual thinking of our generation.

I have had contacts with both Sirdar Yadu Nath Khanal (SYNK) and Sirdar Bhim Bahadur Panday (SBBP) together at the Nayabajaar house of SBBP and individually. I noted that they had so much to share with each other and that they had much in common. Both believed in democracy. Prof. Khanal would say democracy cannot have an adjective. This is partly a response to King Mahendra's definition on democracy, adapted from Ayub Khan's Guided democracy for Pakistan.

When we look into the history being made then; Nepal was welcomed by the world community, from a nation in isolation to a member of UN, changing from a dictatorial state to a semi-democratic nation, to begin with.

But what they did not want or could not write in their books, they would tell me in response to my curiosity. I could feel that they got some relief while telling me what they wanted to share with me. I could read their faces while they spoke to me. There was a hidden wish of the persons that things be shared widely, once the situation became favorable. Things have changed in Nepal and now I can relate the things they narrated to me. Below are a few anecdotes I shall write here to in respect of these two great bureaucrats and diplomats.

Professor Sardar Yadunath Khanal: King Mahendra called him Guru, with deep respect. I came to know Sirdar Khanal through SBBP.

After the death of SBBP, SYNK and I maintained our contacts and friendship during the 1990s.

He would always try to look directly at your eyes, searching for trustworthiness in your eyes. When the eyes met he trusted you and expected the same from you. He was known for his literary contributions.

He had a distinguished career, spanning over four decades of civil service for the nation, and he was the '*diplomat par excellence* of the Himalayan Subcontinent.' Jawahar Lal Nehru of India, Zhou En Lai of the PRC, Soekarno of Indonesia, Marshall Tito of Yugoslavia and many other statesmen of his time around the world, held him in high esteem. They appreciated SYNK's contribution developing policy of Panchashila, from the Bandung conference to Non-aligned conferences.

SYNK would tell me that whenever King Mahendra went on foreign visits/jaunts, he would ask what he should bring to his Guru. The reply of SYNK was always the same,

I have everything I need, and Your Majesty must not take the trouble of bringing a gift for me.

He was upright in behavior, clear in his thinking and proud of his integrity. He was too well-known a person to many in the country and beyond for me to go into his other characteristics. One story he shared with me that raised my respect to him to a new height.

When he completed one of his last diplomatic missions as an ambassador, he decided to take home the little old VW Beetle car he had purchased. He was living a little outside of the city, at Banesor Height. Without a convenient public transportation network in the area to move around, he thought a car might be of use in Kathmandu, to go to friends, respond to invitations or most importantly to see doctors.

He consigned his belongings to Nepal by ship. The Beetle arrived at the Birgunj Customs Office. Soon afterwards, a secretary in the royal palace, called him by phone. The secretary wanted him to submit a request to HM to allow him to import the old Beetle, duty free.

How did the secretary know of his car entering Nepal? The information network the palace maintained deserves to be appreciated! SYNK reacted rather sadly and told him,

You'd better not worry about my little old car and I as usual would not request any personal favor from HM.

He brought the car with full intention of paying all the dues, such as customs duty. The Palace secretary was aghast and told SYNK that he was setting a bad precedent. This meant they would have to follow his example. They would be at a loss. SYNK told the palace secretary, who annoyed him over the phone, that what others did was their business, but he had his own standards to keep up.

One point we would come to discuss time and again was our foreign policy, relations with China and India, his personal rapport with Zhou En Lai etc. SYNK's response was highly poignant. How strong were we in foreign policy?

Accepting the reality, we need to be prepared for tough future diplomacy. At present we are self-sufficient in food most of the time. We have to manage our food production in such a way that we do not have to beg for assistance. I am convinced we can, if we want to. Food is the best asset and foundation of foreign policy.

People with knowledge, skill and industry (hard work) carry the country forwards more than material resources. I am pained when I see the state of anarchy

in education, with politicization of students and teachers going unchecked.

Could we conduct our foreign policy without relying on other's attitude? Of course I mean the South Block? I asked.
If we do not have to go around begging for food we can behave in a dignified way. We could not be pressed to take the wrong side at the UN or anywhere else. That was our strength in our foreign policy in the past. Take for example, Bangladesh, it did not have that clout, when it was surviving on food aid, or for that matter, India in the late sixties surviving on PL-470 food drops, 'Donated by the People of the Unites States of America.'

Establishment of Foreign Affairs Service: King Mahendra wanted his Guru to establish the MoFA Service. It was a difficult proposition given the situation. There were only a few intellectuals who would be eligible for Foreign Service. Policies and processes needed to be worked out to produce generations of diplomatic corps. SYNK agreed to undertake the task under one condition. King Mahendra was curious to know what that could be. SNYK made it clear to him,

I need free hand to recruit potential diplomats and foreign policy advisors. It is a challenging undertaking.
People with diplomatic credentials and diverse qualifications are required to represent Nepal, sandwiched between super sensitive nations with varying geo-political and historical backgrounds and

having perennial issues and interests also directed against us, to be resolved.

The king told him to go ahead, that he would not interfere with his work.

Not long afterwards, SYNK was handed a small handwritten chit, by King Mahendra directly. The chit had names of persons from his coterie. King Mahendra wanted to have them inducted into the 'Foreign Service'.

SYNK was surprised, reminded King Mahendra of his promise, and threatened to resign rather than chose people on this basis.

King Mahendra took back the chit and told him,

Guru, forget about it and I promise you, I will not do it again. You feel free to do what you can.

He gave Nepali diplomacy a professional touch, a combination of thought and analysis and taught a lesson that one should never be carried away by whim and *ad hoc*-ism, that diplomacy is a profession and not a privilege, especially in the precarious geo-political condition where we were, are and will be perennially.

Advisor for foreign affairs: It was after 1990 SYNK became advisor in foreign affairs to Prime Ministers. First he became advisor to Premier KP Bhattarai in the early nineties. But it was in Girija Prasad Koirala's tenure as Premier, and also Minister of Foreign Affairs, that he requested SYNK to be his foreign affairs advisor.

SYNK told the Premier to not retain foreign affairs portfolio for himself. It would be better to appoint a younger man whom he trusted who could learn under

SNYK's guidance the nitty gritty of diplomacy and learn to assert Nepal's position in business and diplomacy, particularly with the neighbors.

GP agreed, so SYNK thought it would be worthwhile to serve as foreign affairs advisor again. It was a challenging time. There were foreign dignitaries and diplomats coming and going more intensively. The world was watching Nepal paddling through the new found democratic credential. GP was bathing in new limelight.

SYNK attended his office and read the papers brought to his attention. None were of any importance. Days went by, but no call came from Premier GP. It had been different under KP Bhattarai who benefitted much from SYNK's advice. But Girija must have only needed an advisor as *decorum* to boost his own image by having SYNK as Foreign Affairs Advisor at his side.

There were immediate issues to do with India, UN and other friendly countries and organizations. Everybody was of the impression that GP was doing well in foreign policy. In fact he did not have time to indulge beyond his home focused politics. The foreign policy was at its weakest point and diplomacy was neglected institutionally which could be deduced from the rising level and frequency of foreign interference in Nepal's affairs. Not once did GP consult with his top diplomat, SYNK, on foreign policy matters. SYNK was thoroughly frustrated.

So one day SYNK had had enough, and told Girija that as he obviously did not want a foreign policy advisor, he could do without one. SNYK resigned and quit from public life for good. It was such an irony.

Prof Yadu Nath Khanal and Sirdar Bhim Bahadur Panday were good friends from their student days in Nepal and Calcutta, India. They were Yadu and Bhim to each other; in fact they were very close until Bhim's last days. 'Yadu' did not survive long after Bhim's death.

Professor Sirdar Bhim Bahadur Panday: Back in 1978, he published a book entitled '*Rastra Bhaktiko Jhalak*', mainly dealing with the history of Kaji Panday clan, the descendants of 'Kaji Ganesh Panday, the founder of the Shah Kingdom of Gorkha', SBBP's words to me.

In those days the subject of the 16th century figure Kaji Panday would have been too sensitive an issue for Durbar to overlook. When the Durbar administration made a note of his book, a close ally of HM (my former teacher NPS) called SBBP to question him on the kind and authenticity of the materials supporting his writing. I do not recollect whether he voluntarily made the manuscript available to the palace or the palace got wind of it and wanted to scrutinize it. SBBP told the secretary that he based his book '*Rastra Bhaktiko Jhalak*' on substantial historical materials, such documented on *Tamra Patra* (copper plaques), *Tad Patra* (Palm leaves), and *Bhojpatra* (Birch barks). The reaction of the man on the other end was,

I too could publish a book on the same subject, but a different version.

Sirdar retorted,

Of course history can have different versions, one truth another full of lies. Do you have materials to support

your version of the writing then? History cannot be written in whatever version that suits one. The truth is based on fact. Fact becomes history.

The reply was prompt,

Well I have heard many stories and I will write it all in a book.

Sirdar Saheb replied sarcastically,

Will that be from the Pipalko Bot (the fig tree) of New Road, the place where (your) people generate rumors? History is not written based on rumor and it is not written like a novel.

SBBP put down the receiver first, or the argument would have continued. This was sometime before 1978, and SBBP felt belittled by a small man from the Palace. That was perhaps the last time SBBP had any contact with the Palace.

According to SBBP, he had to delete and alter some paragraphs and edit the manuscript massively. The Palace wanted truth to be changed or deleted. But the problem was that no history of the Pandays could be written avoiding centuries of contributions to the nation and their collaboration with the Shah dynasty.

What was true concerning the history of Pandays had to be aligned with the history of the Shah Kings? The Pandays and the Palace shared the power and politics over four and half centuries. We cannot grasp the particular time slot of history of Nepal's unification without learning of the brave Kaji Pandays. They fought bravely to protect the nation against the colonialist British forces advancing from the south or the Chinese and Tibetans from the north. They remained instrumental in building a powerful independent great nation of Nepal.

The Palace conspired to portray the Panday clan in a bad light. But the Palace, as ever, wanted and had the power to manipulate history. It would dictate its history the way it wanted to be reflected.

As the Pandays were weakened by the decimation of their most influential members, the truth, the basis of Nepal's history too was weakened. In fact the Pandays played no small role in turning the lean and arrogant, *hathi* (stubborn), King Prithwi Narayan Shah into a symbol of unity of Nepal.

Historian Baburam Acharya was the one who could not be pressured to bend the truth. He was 'interned' for over three months, so they said, within the palace surveillance, to write history of the Shah Kings, most of it dictated. Historical materials were to be overlooked if found to be embarrassing to the Palace in contents, in doing so, the evidence of historical importance had to be omitted.

The statues of King Prithwi Narain Shah and his two Queens are the example. The life size statues constructed by Kathmandu sculptors were banished for centuries in the attics of Hanuman Dhoka palace, just because they depicted them not in conformity with the Palace's view of a 'hero'. King Prithwi Narain Shah and his two Queens looked too simple, too common; he too much of a young lean boyish looking man to be a national hero. It would have shamed the image of him projected by the Palace for centuries. The statues are displayed in the Palace Museum of Nuwakot, northwest of Kathmandu.

Prominent historian Baburam Acharya produced a book as they wanted but he took home with him the evidences of the truth. He was not able to publish the notes that were too sensitive to the palace while he was alive, but his son courageously and prudently published them posthumously in 2005 under his father's authorship, entitled: *'Let Such Not Happen Again'*. We can see in this book how much the history was manipulated. Much about the Kaji Panday can be read in this small book that gives new insight into the Panday history.

What SBBP tried through the *'Rastra Bhaktiko Jhalak'* was to dig out historical truth. While doing that he came out with matters that differed with the Durbar's version of the events in the history of the Palace and Pandays. Had SBBP published the book, he would have been prosecuted and punished for slandering the monarchy.

It was difficult for SBBP to retain the truth in his book about the Palace and maintain intellectual honesty at the same time. He seems to have compromised with the truth to a certain degree, probably under duress. Some major points that had to be left out, he communicated to me. Now that the situation has changed, I am in a position to write about what he discussed with me.

In particular, he postulated two points of history that lay in oblivion and the Palace never wanted them to come out into the open. They could have appeared in the book and challenged the historians immensely but were blocked at the last moment by the Palace courtier. Of course, such facts challenged the palace. According to SBBS's research:

> '*Prince Drabya Shah, the first of the Shah Dynasty, was about 13 years old when Ganesh Panday brought him to Gorkha in 1559 AD.*
> *Kaji Ganesh Panday was Regent for eight years before he placed*
> *Prince Drabya Shah, on the throne of Gorkha in 1559 AD*'.

> The Palace's version was much different.
> '*Drabya Shah was a strong warrior of 21 years of age at the time.*
> *He killed the Ghale King of Gorkha, single handedly.*
> *He conquered Gorkha Fort and became King of Gorkha Thakurai*'.

The story of the film 'Sima Rekha' was concocted to deceive the people. The Brahmin priest Rudra Raj Pande made his name in this film. One can now understand why the palace was unwilling to accept the truth. The Palace had always kept historical evidence hidden from the public.

Royal wrath

SBBP was a career civil servant and a renowned diplomat. He was Nepal's Ambassador to India and Germany. Way back in the 1940 he was, together with General Babar Shum Sher Rana, in the diplomatic service in London. During the Panchayat period he was the Auditor General of the Kingdom of Nepal. He had served for decades in top responsible positions, from the 1940s under the Rana Regime to the elected government of 1959 to the Partyless Panchayat period of the 1980s. He lived to feel a semblance of democracy dawning in the country in the early nineties, before he died.

While he was Auditor General, a call came from Nirmal Niwas, asking him to 'seek' audience with the Mahila Sirkar (Prince Gyanendra). He was told to come up with an explanation of the *Beruju* (report on fiscal irregularity) he had documented as a *Beruju* in the Auditor General's Report of Rs. 9.5m loan taken for Soaltee Hotel by the Prince from the Nepal Industrial Development Council.

SBBP meekly complied. He reached the 'palace of the shadow power of the Monarchy' at Maharajganj. He was ushered in at the appointed time. At the door to the living room he had to wait for the usual kind of signal, sound or gesture. He stood obediently at the door's threshold, hands folded, waiting for a response to his complementary Namaskar. At the far end of the room sat the Prince on a sofa, frozen still, puffing out smoke from his cigarettes while staring on either side and pretending to not to have noticed SBBP's presence. That was not to come. Not even a glance was cast at him, let alone a sound.

The situation was tense and awkward. The silence was unbearable. The time ticked. It seemed ages passing. SBBP's feet started to ache. As per the, so called, 'royal protocol', he could not take a seat without being told and there was none placed at the disposal of a *'non-royal'* visitor. He could not stand upright properly. For a pretty senior man at his age and with a distinguished service career, it was unfair to make him go on standing at the door. It was a disgrace to the proud man quite apart from the fact that distressing a senior citizen was unethical. SBBP looked at his watch, still standing at the door, three hours had elapsed. He lost his patience, decided to turn back from the threshold of the door and bowed the last time and said to the frozen entity,

Bida paun, Sirkar. (Excuse me your HRH, I take leave)

He was not sure whether the 'stony figure' heard his farewell words. SBBP hoped to never see him again! Feeling disgusted, he went home, sat somber for a long time before telling his life partner all about the confrontation. The moment he was sharing the experience with me, not long after the incident, at his Nayabajaar home, I could see his eyes, wet and empty. It reflected pain coming from the depth of his heart. It must have taken a lot of consequential thinking to wish to share such a profound undeserved disappointment.

While SBBP was stationed in Bonn on a diplomatic mission, the Princes were often his house guests of honor. Prince Gyanendra was one of them. Young and at similar age as his sons, SBBP thought, it would be good if they played together.

Ironically, this was the way I was treated by a man who had played with my own sons when they were children.

There was a tinge of regret, I could hear in his voice, while he said to me,

I fulfilled my duty as mandated to the Auditor General of Nepal by the law of the land, for that I was punished. I feel it was unfair!
I have always held them (the royals) in high esteem and respected Prince Gyanendra. Now see what I got as a reward?
I have worked honestly and with loyalty to the nation; from the Rana Regime to Parliamentary democracy with Koirala to the era of Panchayat hardliners.

I was impeccably upright in my service.
I never aspired to be rich. History will judge my integrity and commitment to the service of the nation.
What I earned during my career spanning five decades,
I invested in my five sons and in some social works, like the Ayurvedic Hospital and the Secondary School in Waling, Syangja.

Hearing all this I could not but hold back my tears. It made me sad and I had to suppress my inner anger.

Royal Intimidation

Bishweswor Prasad Koirala was the first elected Prime Minister of Nepal and SBBP was his trusted government secretary. BP was residing at the house which is now opposite to United World Trade Center, at Tripureswor, which later was turned into the Kantiswori School for the palace kids.

Every morning around 1100 AM, SBBP arrived at Tripureswor Roundabout in front of the white statue of '*King Tribhuwan in full regalia*', and waited a while till he could enter into the PM's compound across the road, with important files in his hand to brief the Premier and get approvals, and signatures where necessary. He would come back to Tribhuwan's statue and then go back to his office.

Promptly, an unidentified official in army uniform would be interrogating him on the road. SBBP was to brief him about the contents and decisions made by BP. SBBP had no option but to briefly tell the soldier that it was on regular administrative matters uninteresting to him. That did not happen only once. Every day the story repeated. Fortunately the soldier did not force SBBP to surrender the files to him. SBBP found out later that King Mahendra had ordered the soldier to monitor his activities. That was months before royal putsch, of 1960.

SBBP felt intimidated by King Mahendra. Like Premier Chandra Rana, King Mahendra had difficulty trusting his officers. Did King Mahendra want SBBP not to serve the Premier as government secretary? Did SBBP's integrity stand as hurdle to the King's conspiracy to manipulate the government and find ground to topple the elected government earlier than he did it?

Dipendra in Environment Activity - Uninterested

In the nineties, I got a call from Narendra Raj Panday, the Principal Secretary to HM, with whom I was familiar. He had attended several Jara Juri awards, given to environment protectors, ceremonies in the past, uninvited perhaps out of curiosity; but whose curiosity? He wanted to know whether the Crown Prince (CP) could be involved in environmental conservation programs like Jara Juri.

Could I not invite him for once? I knew such a request would not have been his brain child. I said I would do it for an appropriate event and let him know.

Then there came an opportunity. Jara Juri from many districts, from the Terai to remote Mountain areas, was being invited for participation in a workshop. The invitations had to be sent three months ahead of the day so that all got them in time to make it to Kathmandu. I told Narendra Raj Panday four days in advance that I would like the Crown Prince to participate and that he would be requested to inaugurate the workshop.

The Crown Prince was informed. He said he had body building exercise that day and wanted to know whether I could not postpone the event by several days.

I sent information back that I was utterly unable to respond to the suggestion and I could not make the Jara Juri participants wait in Kathmandu. Many would already be *en-route* to Kathmandu, and travelling was not easy in our largely a Roadless country. They could not be reached nor could they be returned home to wait.

So the Crown Prince stayed away from the Jara Juri program which made us feel comfortable. I was happy that I had kept my word. The protocol would have been too undemocratic, inhuman or even degradation of the proud people from remote areas, and that would have been hard for me to digest.

Part THREE

A Tryst with Gods

Solacing Dreams

A Tryst with Gods

The core value of Nepali Hindu Spirituality sustained over millennia is dedication to Mother Nature. All our rituals attached to our spirituality are oriented towards worshiping Nature. The mighty white Himalayan peaks or the dark boulders or deep in caves or on mountain tops, sun or moon, water or fire, wind or light, we contemplate God in the lifeless stones or on living trees, herbs and grass or in animals. In our culture no idol of Almighty can be created from man-made materials such as cement, plasters, plastics, textiles etc. We know not when the Sun of our eternal spirituality rose, nor do we believe it will ever set.

My spirituality is based on these values. What I write here may reflect my belief. I cannot say it is just a coincidence at best or my 'hallucination' at worst that I meet or see forms of Gods whose image I inherited that appear in dreams or on worldly spaces I visit. People say if you have belief and trust, God shows you its presence.

Muktinath for me alone!

In 1999, on 31st of October, on arrival at Jomosom 2740m, I left without a halt for a trip to Marpha, farther down the Thakkhola Valley. Coming back to Jomosom the next day, I felt it difficult to walk although the trail was level. On 2nd November morning, I was on my way to Muktinath. While climbing uphill from Ekle-bhatti, where the route forks uphill towards Muktinath in one direction and turns north to Kagbeni village in the other, I was experiencing the fatigue of my life.

Sapped of bodily energy and my mind full of doubts of making it to my destination, every move I was making was getting more and more strenuous.

Virtually crawling up-hill from Ekle-bhatti towards the Bhanjyang, I could hardly lift up my feet. Never in my life, during numerous treks and wanderings, had I ever felt it so difficult to walk as at this time! But I was determined to be at Muktinath Temple located at 3760m, on time. I had an inner urge to be there on that very day.

First I had to pass through Jharkot, at 3200m a highland village with about 200 households, where I could visit the Amchi, the Aurvedic doctor. Given my pace of walking it lay another 5-6 hours of walking straight uphill. I doubted if I could make it!

My chest was heavy. My heart was throbbing. I was slightly feverish too and had a bad headache, like the altitude sickness I had experienced at Dingboche in Khumbu, back in October 1967. Was it going to be my last walk? However, deep inside me I was determined to be at

Muktinath shrine that day. I hoped my end would not come before that!

After reaching Jharkot, I went to look for Soma Namge, my friend, the Amchi. At first he had difficulty recognizing me. The last time I had seen him was on 2nd of July 1995, just over four years back. This time he saw a different person from the robust one he had met in my earlier visits. Before he even held my wrist, he saw the suffering that seemed to reflect in my face.

He received me with open arms, had some good words of help for me, felt my wrist (pulse and many other movements and indications of ailments). He said,

You have heat, rising from deep inside the bones; your heartbeat is too fast. It could be something wrong with your liver. Do you drink (alcohol)?

Yes, but only occasionally, and only a little!
But not a drop have I taken over the last few weeks.

Good! How long will you stay at Jharkot?

I want to be back at Jomosom tomorrow.

You are very weak. You need special medicines and some rest. I will prepare them for you. Give me time. Please come tomorrow.

At Pratap's Lodge in Jharkot, after a cup of tea and some food I said to myself, 'I will make it to Muktinath, today and not tomorrow! I won't take time to rest.'

I was challenging my body in a cruel manner, perhaps, but I could not wait too long. I needed to be back to Jharkot before night fall. It took me an hour and a half from Jharkot, longer than on earlier visits, to walk up to the shrine. By 16:30 I was there, tired but full of hope, though I could not say what I was hoping for.

The outer gate to the inner courtyard of the shrine was wide open, so was the temple door. I could see nobody, not even the policeman in the vicinity. After I entered the courtyard, and looked into the temple through the main door, somebody called me in a soft and kind tone to come in. Was it the Pujari Ani? The inner sanctuary was relatively dark. I did not see the face of the person, asking me to come in,

Do you want Darshan?

Was it the mini-chest at the feet of the idol that the *pujari* opened for *Darshan*, for me? I had nothing to offer, had arrived empty handed but full of Muktinath in my heart. I meditated a while and immersed myself in this moment of blessing. I had the *Darshan* of Muktinath, for the first time. I felt nobody ever had such an opportunity, except me!

I was allowed to make a round of Muktinath, keeping the shrine on my right, within the inner sanctuary. The moment I came out of the temple, the door slammed shut. In earlier visits of Muktinath, I had been only up to the temple door, which remained normally closed.

It was nightfall before I reached my lodge at Jharkot, fully satisfied and empowered to face any difficulty from now on because I had *Darshan* of Muktinath! Never before from my many visits, can I recall having Muktinath to myself alone.

The next day, at 0800 I went to see Amchi Namge again. Namge, 71 years old, was meditating. So I tried to see him again at 0930. He took me to his 'teaching hospital'. There were 17 boys (I don't' remember whether there were any girl pupils) of 8-9 years of age, undergoing a 16-year Amchi training course.

The hospital building was full of fragrance of medicinal plants and minerals collected mostly in the Himalayas. They were stored in one large room. Yet, earlier he had hinted that he was not that successful looking after his own 'strange' ailments. Somehow, managing the school, his mission, gave him the energy.

Back in July 1995, he had said to me,

I need to establish a Trust Fund for the Amchi School.
I am getting old, reaching my end.
I need to produce many more Amchi before I die.
But I fear I cannot complete the Amchi course for the 17 students I have now while I am still alive.

That was so touching! He did not say, *'many more Amchi like me'*. Yet Namge was the best Amchi far and wide, I have met. It takes dedication and decades of devotion to become an Amchi like him. That also depended upon individual Amchi's efforts. But should Namge expire before the mission ended, who could take over the school?

Namge had prepared three different potions of medicines in powder form for me: one for my liver, one for me to get good sleep and one to energize my body. He had diagnosed me as, extremely weak. That said a lot. I had to be careful with my body.

The medicines were made exclusively for me from rare and thus expensive medicinal plants. To make good use of such rare medicine, I had to promise him to forego, garlic, black gram dal, chicken meat, fish, alcohol, and avoid excessive 'bodily exertions'.

While he was talking to me, a thin and emaciated European tourist entered into the room. He looked visibly ill. Namge could not understand English, but language was no barrier for his kind heart. He promised the young man he would get well again. After he got his checkup and his medicine, he asked me, how much would it cost? He had Rs. 10 note in his hand. I was just dropping an Rs.500 note in the donation box, for the service I received from Namge. The young man stared at it. Then he quickly opened his purse, pulled out an Rs.500 note and slipped it into the box.

I explained to him how much Mr. Namge would appreciate it. The school was running with donations in kind and cash. Amchi Namge was also using the donations for feeding the Amchi aspirants. He needed outside help for paying the laborers who collected and processed the herbs and minerals for the Amchi School.

I just wonder at Namge's dedication. He ran a 'teaching hospital', with prolonged courses in which a doctor-to-be grows with knowledge, exercises and experience over the span of 16 years. One wonders how Namge did it with so little means!

Yet Namge exudes confidence, trust and divine energy that you feel at his presence. You feel you will get better with his medicines and you develop trust in him.

Namge invited me to visit his brother's house, his 'family' house. I understood that Namge was a lifelong bachelor and celibate. He himself was staying alone in the teaching hospital. He had a bed in his consultation room between his medicines and a donation box, leaning on the wall towards Muktinath temple to the East. His nephew brought a wooden chest for Namge. It was full of medicines. He chipped off a piece of Neermashi (*Aconite* plant) for me and told me,

> *It is the rarest medicine. My medicine is my wealth.*
> *It is all I have, and all I want is to serve people.*

I related the effect and ability of Avijalo herbs, a folk medicine that grows in the lower warmer areas. He wanted to have the plant, intact with the roots, the next time I visited him. I invited him to visit me when he came to Kathmandu. He even promised to bring along some more medicines for me.

Seeing his current condition of health I only hoped I would see him again, if not in Kathmandu, at least here at Jharkot in my next visit to Mustang. I had difficulty saying, good bye to him this time. He looked very sick. Namge was suffering from ailments in his bowel for which he could not get treatment even in the Ayurvedic Hospital at Nardevi in Kathmandu city.

I was sad to leave him in pain with his own incurable mysterious ailment at the same time that he made me feel I would get well with his medicine. What an irony! It was a completely different trip back to Jomosom for me.

Some months later, on my next trip to Mustang, he was gone. A great Amchi had left this world, leaving behind 17 disciples. They are learning in *mukti-kchetra*, to give *mukti* (salvation) from sufferings! I pray for these servants of the sick and destitute, for their success and good health.

Baraha Avatar

In the Spring of Year 2000 AD, it was going to be my first visit to Baraha Kchetra. The time was noon. For me it was to be no more than a pleasure trip from Dharan Township to the Saptakoshi River, in East Nepal.

Baraha Kchetra is located just south of the wide gorge, on the left bank of the mighty Saptakoshi River, a few kilometers downstream from Tribeni, and the confluence of the Sunkoshi, Arun and Tamor Rivers. There were many temple buildings, most of them plastered with cement covering the stone masonry and painted white. This is the new fad of the temple 'conservation' associations all over Nepal. Perhaps unintended, out of absence of purpose, they indulge in spending donations. They turn the temples, from the serene works of art our ancestors created, where spirituality sprang from hearts, to ugly modern objects without soul. They change the very essence of temples and shrines.

I did not know which temple I was looking for. Many looked unattractive and I wondered how the deities would have felt about them. Would they reside in such *damaged abodes*? In fact I was not looking for any one particular temple. There were so many big and small shrines, some beautiful and untended that I walked by. But at one place on my right there was a temple with its door wide open. I peeped into it. Nobody was there.

I could make that this was *Baraha* temple that I had heard about, right in front of me. As I entered the temple, I saw a stone idol which seemed 'never to have been hit by chisel and hammer shots'. The form on the stone depicted typical *Baraha*, a lion's head on human body in its natural form. Nobody was around to forbid me touching the deity. The *pujari* had perhaps bathed the natural idol in the morning and was making preparations for the noontime *nitya puja* somewhere around. *Baraha* was left 'naked' for me.

Surya Binayak, the Ganesh Facing Rising Sun, 2002

At home in Bakena Batika, Jawalakhel a shrew (*chhuchundro*) would not let us fall asleep. The whole night it was moving around and making noise. Sharada and I waited until it would find its way into the small shower room by the staircase. We hastily closed the door and kept it inside. We slept well afterwards.

Next morning, to our surprise we did not find the *chhuchundro* there. We did not find a hole in the wall, or on the ceiling either, nor was the door slightly ajar which the *chhuchundro* could have used to free itself. We took it as a wonder that was beginning to unfold. Sharada said,

It is time that we visited Ganesh.

Before we saw the shrew I had told Sharada the story of Suryabinayak and me, and we were already thinking about visiting the temple soon. This was the second visit that I can remember of visiting the temple, thanks to the 'holy' shrew.

There was no trace of vermillion, flowers or any offerings in the temple. Ganesh had had a bath and the shrine was clean. It was in its naked natural form. Here too as at the Muktinath and Baraha temples, there was nobody around. It was noon. The *pujari* was preparing for the *nitya puja*, in the *pujari* house and had left the shrine unattended. Normally, there are not many devotees to throng the shrine at noon. We were an exception that day, yet the *pujari* did not hinder us from paying our homage to Ganesh.

The Ganesh idol, a relatively big piece of rock, did reflect a form of an elephant head. But the local people believed that it was not carved by man. It faced east, to the rising sun, hence the Suryabinayak, perhaps the only Ganesh to face the sunrise. All other Ganesh face south. The *pujari* came out to perform *nitya puja*. Seeing us two in the temple he let us observe the *nitya puja* of Suryabinayak, for the first time in our lives.

We could perform *puja* in our own way too, minutes after the day's *nitya puja*. We had *darshan* of Suryabinayak in his natural shape and condition and also after the *nitya puja*, covered with vermillion, garlands and ornaments of gold and silver. We found ourselves profoundly blessed. We were elated and thought we were very lucky to meet Suryabinayak, my Godfather! We thanked the *chhuchundro* for bringing us together again.

Mother had told me about her making Suryabinayak my God-father, but I cannot recollect ever visiting the temple with her. I must have been a baby when she took me there for the special ritual. How could she have made me a blessed God-son of Suryabinayak without 'dedicating me to Him? I must have been there.

I left the temples, wondering of the trysts with God in Mustang, *Baraha* and now Surya Binayak. Was it just for me?

Pawankali, the Elephant God

We just wished, Pawankali, the female elephant would come! Our youngest son, Somi was going to have his first haircutting ceremony *Chhewar* on Sunday 27th January 2008 (Magh 13, 2064). We were preparing him for the day. There would be a little *puja*, and new clothes.

That morning, we had just finished talking about taking Somi to a Ganesh Temple on *Chhewar Day*. Pawankali, the elephant from Jawalakhel Zoo nearby, made a surprise knock at our gate searching for food. How could Pawankali have known we were talking about her? It was overwhelming for Somi and for us too. When we talk of a tiger, would it too come to our gate? Understandably, Somi went into hiding. We invited Pawankali to come next

Sunday on the *Chhewar Day*. She would get a treat! Of course the *Mahout* too would get the same respect and treat.

Spirituality of my Parents and Grandmother

My father, mother and grandmother grew up and lived in the same society with the same culture and traditions in the central part of Nepal. Yet, I did not get the impression that any of them valued visiting temples.

As I reminisce, I had wondered why Father had never visited a temple to my knowledge. Did he have a grudge against temples? Did he have problems? What could it have been? Being a lonely child perhaps?

He never knew his father. He did not know how he looked. He would not remember hearing or seeing him or feeling his warm hands. Did he sometimes murmur?

Others around me saw their fathers, they had everything. Was God unjust towards me?

I felt perhaps Father could have thought deeply about it. Was he blaming God for having to live without fatherly love, and his whole childhood far from his mother's lap and motherly pats and slaps during oil massaging? To me it could be that he felt betrayed by God. He had nothing to thank God for.

Mother did not mind going to a temple with me as part of her walk. I remember visiting Dakchinkali temple at Pharping about 15km from home with her at *Chaite Dasain*. She had been there fairly regularly during festivities in the past, as part of her '*walking*', but perhaps never on Dasain. I wanted to accompany her. To my surprise she had bought a few duck eggs and carried a *puja thali* for the offerings that day, which was unusual on my mother's part.

When we reached Dakchinkali, it was crowded and people were lining up to make offerings. When our turn came to be closer to the deity we had to dodge lashing rains of blood. A butcher *pujari* had slit half the throat of a goat and pulled the head backward and was spraying the blood oozing out, to all the deities around.

I am at loss to make judgment on the guy. Must he be praised for his naivety, ignorance and missing humane thoughts, slitting mercilessly the throat of the animals that were not his enemy, nor of mankind, anywhere? Lined up by the temple, we could not be spared witnessing the gruesome act and experiencing the man's dark folly. We almost took a 'blood bath'.

Mother might have covered her mouth and nose with her *khasto* cotton shawl and kept her two piercing eyes open. I was too small to see all that was reflected on her face. I was preoccupied looking at the oozing of blood and the stony deities around the temple area enjoying the blood bath.

Mother would try again and again to obliterate my view with her shawl, but she hardly looked down at me. She too was transfixed to the blood baths that were taking place around her. I managed to pull off the *khasto* falling on my head that was intended to block at least my eyes.

I was curious but oblivious of what was happening. Though terrified and shocked, I could not stop fixing my eyes on the poor animals being slaughtered in a gruesome manner that reflected the darkest face of human beings.

After offering the eggs and doing a quick *puja* to Dakchin Kali, we left the shrine in haste, climbed up the steps and were on the Pharping road, in no time. Mother was very upset and was panting and murmuring to me,

> *This is going to be my last visit to Dakchinkali, no matter how revered she is for others.*

She was not blaming the Devi. I do not remember her going there again.

The incident kept piercing my conscience. Come every Dasain, I noticed that the Dakchinkali rituals repeated in every staunch Hindu household that literally followed the Dasain traditions. In every household there would be one guy who would have to become the 'butcher of Dakchinkali' for the day, in all naivety, ignorance and inhumane thoughts of what he would be doing, as I say, slitting mercilessly the throats of the animals that were not his enemy, nor of mankind, anywhere.

My family did not have such a tradition. We were compelled to buy a goat earlier for meat but not as part of slaughtering for *puja*. That too was stopped after the death of Grandmother, when senior guests stopped coming to us for *tika*.

Once I visited the Pashupati temple with Mother. There were people lining up to offer *puja* to Lord Pashupati Nath. The queue was long, sober and silent.

Each carried *puja* offerings on metal plates (*puja thali*) or on *tapari*, *duna bota*, made of *sal* tree leaves.

While waiting for our turn, I noticed, a few people queuing behind us and further behind saw a Marwari, jostling with his plate of offering high in his right hand. He had overtaken several devotees in the queue without hesitation. Nobody murmured a word. He was approaching us close to the temple steps. I saw that he had placed some hundred rupee notes as *bheti* on the plate.

There was a 'junior priest' *pujari* at the West door of the temple in front of the Nandi bull on duty to take *puja* offerings from the devotees lined up, signaling the Marwari to come forward. He took the offering and the money, placed some *prasads* (a flower garland and a little *chandan* paste) on the plate and returned it to the Marwari gentleman. With a wide grin, he went away, thinking perhaps he was blessed! He did his *dharma*.

We were left wondering. I never believed that there would be discrimination of this sort in the Holy Temple of Lord Pashupatinath, purely to do with greed and injustice. To myself and Mother, I said that it would perhaps be my last visit to the Shiva. But I could not hold the promise for long. I made a cultural tour with my farmer guests and friends from Sindhupalchok district.

Together with Mr. Gobind Bahadur Tondon, a doctoral candidate researching on Pashupati, we peeked into the shines and shadows of Pashupatinath Temple area. It was for me a touristic presence at the place. I had Pashupati deep in my heart but in my eyes I saw only the temples, the dirty water and the chaos between the dead and living, the smell of flesh burnt coming from cremation *ghats*, the loitering monkeys and hungry dogs and the *ganja* smoke, the sick and poor beggars. Where is the divine presence? Where is the divine justice?

A shocking revelation at Dandapakhar

Just across Kajiman Tamang's house lived poorest of the poor families of Dandapakhar. No matter what Bhim, the head of the family, did it was inadequate to feed his family of four. Two square meals a day was only a dream for him and his family.

He could not come to attend training to improve farming that I was responsible to arrange for farmers like him to try new methods. Bhim had no land of his own.

He had no time. He was working on a daily wage basis. A day in training was a loss of a day's wage, costing the day's meals for his family. When I went to see him one afternoon, he was a little sick and did not know how to earn the day's meals for his family. He was in a desperate situation. My support solved his problem that day. But his pains and poverty did not change with small gestures. He expressed his anguish with these words,

> *There is no god of the poor. God is for the rich.*
> *They can afford to offer sweets and flowers or even blood. Not us.*
> *God too is selfish!*

Temple of the Sacred Tooth Relic of Lord Buddha

It was December 1983. The train ride to Kandy, Sri Lanka, reminded me of my first hill train ride to Darjeeling in 1965, winding romantically uphill from the plains of Colombo. The lush green rice fields and terraces, coconut stands, banana trees, the farmers' huts mellowed in the landscape. Whichever direction you turned your eyes you saw green, a heaven not necessarily for a Nepali but imagine those coming from the Gulf States!

I was visiting the Temple of Gautam Buddha's left canine Tooth with my family. The white impressively large palace temple built in 16th century was located just outside the town of Kandy. The temple looked impressive and sprawling. The sacred shrine was located in the Handun Kunama of the palace. Going up a few steps and left towards the shrine, calm veiled my senses, anxious, unaware of worldly expectations and breathing deep. The queue was long and it was moving slowly towards the shrine. I had a Nepali Dhaka Topi on, and people noticed that our family came from Nepal. As we neared the entrance to the shrine, the priest gestured to us to leave the queue and come forward.

I see that you are from Nepal, the home of Lord Buddha. You have the right to have Darshan of His Tooth.

He lifted, one golden casket after another, in all seven caskets, studded with precious stones, exposed right in front of me, was the **Tooth of Lord Buddha.** My thought wandered to the time when, Buddha gave his Sermons with this Tooth somewhere in his mouth. Only words of love and peace had come out of his mouth, for the entire humanity.

I was overwhelmed by a shower of serenity. For a moment in eternity, I prayed. I do not know, how, but it seemed to dowse me with peace of mind I never experienced before. Perhaps I expected it to be so being close to Lord Buddha. I cannot describe the feeling I had then.

There were some Indian pilgrims in the queue, earlier in front of us, now it was their turn and they requested the priest to let them too have *Darshan*. I do not know why priest denied them. He only said,

Look, the gentlemen with his family came from Nepal, the Home of Lord Buddha. It is different for them.

Of course, it was different for us *Vis a Vis* others. It was a solemn reunion with our 'brother', after millennia, yet I wish the priest had permitted the pilgrims to have *Darshan* of Tooth of Lord Buddha, the Apostle of Peace as well.

Unfortunately, the tranquility of Sri Lanka was shattered a year later, and the conflict continued for a quarter of a century to end with the greatest Coup de Grace. I did not expect Buddhists could go that far.

Once, in fact, the Tooth of the Lord Buddha had come to Nepal. Way back in the early fifties, Nepal was fuming with political agitation. Peace was eluding us. We got rid of 104 years of dictatorship and family oligarchy and expected fresh air to breathe. But the turmoil was not what we expected. Someone came up with the idea, perhaps Bhiksu Amritananda Maha-Asthabir of Swayambhu Anandakuti, that the presence of the Tooth of Lord Buddha could bring us coveted peace.

I remember running over to Tundikhel in Kathmandu, leaving the school classes when I heard about the Tooth of Lord Buddha being brought in by plane from Ceylon (*Sri Lanka* now). On the grass covered ground west of the Chandra Jyoti House, there was only one sofa and on the sofa sat King Tribhuwan Bir Bikram Shah, alone, waiting for the carriage to arrive from the airport right in front of him. That was the first time I saw a King yet so close I could have shaken hands had he wanted to.

Late in the afternoon a 4 horse's drawn carriage came to a halt with fanfare, in front of King Tribhuwan. Bhikschu Amritanda Maha-asthbir, holding a pot or something, I assumed with the Tooth we were all eagerly waiting for in it, had arrived.

Many years later I saw a photograph at my uncle Subarna Jung Panday's house; the same sofa, King Tribhuwan sitting on it at Tundikhel. It must be from the day Tooth of Lord Buddha arrived on its 'home visit'. But what I did not see in the euphoria then at Tundikhel, I was able to see on the photographs:

A girl was leaning with her right elbow on the back of the Sofa, almost touching the King. No soldier, no minister, nobody was around. Just the people, the King and kids together were to enjoy the day of the historic homecoming of Lord Buddha, represented by his Tooth for

434 | Behind Her Wedding Veil

Peace in the World Over. This must have been the most peaceful Nepal ever, at least for the day that I ever witnessed. I still carry the soothing impression of the King waiting for the Tooth of Lord Buddha. The King then did not need security details at tax payers' cost as the paranoid politicians today need many times over even when they are out of power.

Solacing Dreams

My life has been full of dreams. I dreamt of events that would take place in the immediate future. Was it by accident? There are some dreams that are hanging down from the ceilings of my memory. In my spiritual mindset, gods appeared.

The Rays from my Right Palm

It must have been in 1950, I must have been not older than 7 years, at home in the red house that Father built according to his fantastic plan on a large open field. In those days there was nothing to block my view from the windows but the hills and Himal far beyond. There were only two smaller houses to the west of our house and the Jawalakhel ground beyond.

In a dream, I was standing at the window on the first floor of that house, facing west and gazing at the fields and hills beyond with my right hand raised high. I saw the hills brightly lit orange red. The light covered the hills and fields to the west as far as I could *see*. The source of the light was the beam that oozed out from the center of my right palm. I have taken this dream as a 'Divine' reward for my religious feeling and spiritual faith. I store the dream vividly in my mind even more than six and half decades after the night of the dream.

Mother continued assuring me

In 1975, as the telegram from Father reached me in Europe on 21st Feb 1975, telling me *'Mother expired...'* I was not at all in pain on receiving it. I never took it in that my mother had left me. I had had enough pain a long time ago, when she told me, then a fragile and sensitive child, numerous times,

> *I shall leave this world once you reach the age of 31.*
> *I shall not witness what you make of your life in this world, but I know you will do fine.*

That was too much to bear. I had cried then, with and without tears, for days as many times as she told me. After getting a steady supply of letters from Brother, from sisters, from niece Sushila Bhanji and friends reporting mother's condition, the telegram was not a surprise. I felt I had expected the news. It was such an awkward feeling. Now the telegram was reaching me at the crucial age of mine, that mother had convincingly mentioned. I said to myself

> *The telegram is a joke, trying to hurt me again.*

It was not necessary. I knew what was to happen, because mother had said it for ages past. For me mother had expired ages ago! From that day on I started dreaming of her, repeatedly and the dreams haunted me pleasantly. My mother would appear in her finest white *fariya* (sari-frock) and *cholo* (blouse). Standing before me she would say,

Whenever you find it difficult to cope, think of me, everything will be ok.

She was right! A few weeks after that telegram, my MSc-ETH final exam was approaching. Every day it was like climbing a vertical wall of rock. I had to concentrate mentally and physically. It was costing me a lot of energy. The exam was of utmost importance to me. Should I fail, I would have one more chance to make it or quit the professional training, to live an uncertain future.

On the day of the final exam in March 1975, a month after my mother's death, I thought of her and prayed. I was blessed! The exam seemed an uphill but an easy climb, no stress, no fear. I was full of hope. In a way I needed to make no more last minute hard preparations. What I had done regularly was sufficient to cope with difficult, contradictory and evil questions put up by the examiner provoking my confidence in answering. It did not bring me down. I passed the examinations with flying colors encouraging me and making me eligible for further studies.

Dreaming of a Fish Pond – 2001

I had designed a seating place in the shape of an old *gahiri dhara* but without water. It consisted of a stone wall, 3 stone-steps down on a stone paved seating place with one table and 3 chairs, just outside our bedroom below the wooden terrace. It was meant for the guests coming to Bakena Batika, to enjoy privacy but in the open. It was a shady, cool and cozy place for all to while-away time in the warmest of summer days.

One night towards very early morning, I was dreaming of colorful fishes swimming in the *gahiri dhara* filled with clear water. It just was magnificent to look at. I woke up. I could not wait to go to the terrace to look at the place in the dream. It was so disappointing!

But I had the urge I needed to take out the slabs and dig it. I called the gardener and asked him to start the work. He had not yet dug a pit 20cm deep, when water started to pour in from all sides. I knew that my garden had a high ground water table. Amazed, I wanted to have it deeper. By the end of the day we had a natural pond, enclosed by stone walls and stone-steps leading to it. By next day the water looked much clearer.

I thought I should go and fetch some fishes. Only goldfish were available at the nearby aquarium, at Jawalakhel. So I had a pond as dreamt of. Further improvement of the pond and redesigning was prompted and a natural water source was tapped. Water trickled from the 3m high earth wall of the Tibetan school side in the driest season. The wall was covered with plastic sheets and even a drop of water would come to a point and was collected, that was enough to give the spout a semblance of a little *dhunge dhara* (stone spout) in the dry season and it looked a pouring water spout during monsoon.

Later in 2002, we brought in 19 grass carps from Godavari. Some of them appeared golden, others with a silver shine. We also put in two varieties of lotus, including *neelkamal* (a blue lotus, the national flower of Bangladesh). They were flowering and the fishes grew fast. It soon became a pond as in my dream, a pond with fish.

The Decorated Elephant my Savior

Around 2004: I was driving. At one point of my route, there was a 90 degree bend turning to the right, past that, not far there was another bend turning to the left.

At the left bend there lay a large object. It looked like a big dark metal trunk. I was perhaps 30m away from it. Instantly, I thought it must be a bomb. I took it as a bomb planted by the Maoists to kill and maim innocent people. I was scared, almost petrified. My sixth sense told me to watch and wait even in the dream.

Then from the left bend a tusker (*matta*) appeared. A smaller *dhoee* (female) elephant followed him. The tusker seemed not to notice my presence, as I stood by the side of the jeep.

Both the elephants had their skin painted pink. Flower patterns were splashed all over their bodies, something like we do during Tihar to our cows on *Gaipuja*. The Tusker pushed the object out of the way with its left front leg. Soon both elephants disappeared towards the direction they came from. I stood there frozen and shaken. At that moment I woke up, wondering about the bomb scare and the beautiful elephants.

Sharada woke up too. I related the whole dream to her as much in detail as I could remember, minutes after the dream. Astonishingly, the background color of my mother's veil too was pink and on it embroidered were colorful flowers. The common color and designs seemed to link the dreams of elephants to my dreams of Mother assuring me.

Why did the colors and designs painted on the elephants' body match with Mother's wedding veil? In the dream I was scared and I do not remember thinking of Mother.

Sharada's natural reaction was,

Go and offer laddoo to Ganesh. Let us be careful!
It might portend an event yet to unfold.

I would soon be surprised by what was to happen the next evening.

That morning Bhrikuti (Tibetan) Primary school was felling trees obstructing their playground. When I heard of it in the morning I walked over to the school ground and cautioned the laborers chopping the trees, instructed the workers on the minimum of rules to be followed while felling big old trees. It was a difficult task and it could endanger the workers themselves.

Sharada was away with Somi visiting Hari Dai near the food go-downs at Nakhu. I was home alone, at Bakena Batika, Jawalakhel.

It was around 1700 hrs. I was about to step into the kitchen when I heard something crashing on the roof above me. I thought it was an earthquake. The crash of a large tree outside our house on the Tibetan side smashed our kitchen. I happened to be under the door to the kitchen.

I was hit hard on the right knee, by a wooden beam. Luckily the beam was not the largest one that had got stuck on the roof and did not come down to the floor. The other one slightly smaller hit me and I was in shock.

My right leg was badly hit, partially laming and bruising me badly. My body got a shower of broken pieces of wood, bricks and dust. The pain all over my body and the feeling that I was almost killed haunted me for a long time.

The biggest branch of the tree had landed on the roof of our kitchen and devastated it. The damage was substantial: a big chunk of the wall on the east side towards the Tibetan school was demolished.

Sharada came home to see the scene of devastation of the kitchen and was shocked. She thanked god that I survived. Seconds later and it would have been my end. Yet it gave me a limp, and I remained lame and was not able to walk upright for over a week.

This was another reason to visit a Ganesh temple as soon as possible. The dream with colorful patterns similar to mother's wedding veil to be found on the elephant shoving off of a box with unknown contents in the dream was ominous, yet a forewarning.

What averts what enables things we do

We needed to leave our home at Bakena Batika which had been an oasis inside for decades, but now a hell was brewing outside. The dust, the pollution and the noise were becoming unbearable. I was slowly developing chronic throat pain. I had declined to use medicine because I knew it was not a disease. I needed to go to clean air and clean water. We needed to recreate a 'Bakena Batika' without the ring road crossings outside the house.

But deep inside me was feeling uneasy. I had never sold even a piece of soil in my life. As opposed to that, I had made it possible for all of my siblings, my father and my children, to be proud owners of lands. I had to part with so much I had earned; yet selling soil was not something I had ever done.

A few months back a lady astrologer had told Sharada, my wife while 'analyzing' the soil samples from the four corners of our house and land,

> *No concrete result is foreseeable in the near future.*
> *The boy* (our youngest son Somi) *feels it difficult to part from his home.*

How accurate she was is to be noted. Many persons came and went, without a word of positive response. We reckon now that perhaps the *graha* of Somi tried to avert the process of selling our house. Only after we promised ourselves that we will perform his *Chhewar* ceremony 'at his home' first, did we get positive and serious response from a friendly family, of Sharada's acquaintance.

That prompted me to go and look for a new place. I found one in Godavari that impressed me, with a clean and green environment. In my first visit I went, *incognito*. Then on 2nd of Nov 2007, we took Somi along, to the promising site.

The owner of the land had kept some hens and a cock. The nasty cock attacked Somi from behind and brushed his cheeks with one claw hurting him a little. It shocked him and he felt the land would not be for him.

I told him if we take the land, the cock would have no chance to survive long, as the owner would eat it to celebrate the deal. A bizarre way of persuading a kid, foolishness on my part!

The house was not built properly but the location of the house and garden was unique. The regular supply of Godavari water, the fresh air and dust-free plants swaying in the cool breeze, it was just the place we were looking for. We could change it to turn it into a home for us. We must try to take it. Somi was assured.

He pinned his hope on us getting the land. The deal was sealed and over the following week we planned for his *Chhewar* ceremony to take place on 27th of January 2008 at Bakena Batika before 'abandoning' it with heavy hearts.

Centenary celebration

It was the beginning of the year 2013. Sharada and I were planning the centenary birthday celebration of Father.

The discourse centered on digging out the facts about Father, his friends and foes, in fact his whole story and history.

It was going to be difficult. But we had materials scattered in our papers, in memories and in objects we had treasured to begin with to recall his life and present it to our friends and relatives. That was to take place on his birthday.

We found we needed also to organize a *Satyanarayan* Puja that Father conducted every year on his birthday. We thought that would be a good tribute to him.

We were preparing to hold the *puja* five days after the centenary day. Then I dreamt of father. I saw him visiting us. He was standing right in front of me. He asked,

Since when have you become so spiritual and religious? I can't believe it.

He had known me in life. Of course, I was bit different from him in matters of religion and spirituality. For me religion without service was a void I could not make anything out of.

Thinking of him and paying a tribute to how he took the things we did for him as a religious and spiritual act; this was the best I could have even if it was only in dream, of him.

A Reflection

As for me I was always shy to tell about myself. But now I say one ought to write with good feelings most out of the memories, the kind of writing I am trying here. I have no reason to deny expositions on my own life. I need not try to erase or delete or suppress my feelings and happenings.

There is however a feeling of uneasiness in me. I was hesitant to even get photographed and stand in front of a mental mirror to look at my image. I had never reflected onto myself. Now I was turning to myself. It was not comfortable.

But I had to change in my thinking and behavior. The trigger to that change was the approaching centennial birthdays of my parents, Father's, in April 2013 and Mother's in February 2015. I tried to peek into the meaning and values of my clan, tribe and ancestor in relation to my parents and me. It was worthwhile. It was my turn to dedicate reflexes and moments to myself in the evening of my life. It was an opportunity to open up.